Beating the Bounds

Beating the Bounds

A Symphonic Approach to Orthodoxy
in the Anglican Communion

Sidney L. Green

WIPF & STOCK · Eugene, Oregon

BEATING THE BOUNDS
A Symphonic Approach to Orthodoxy in the Anglican Communion

Copyright © 2013 Sidney L. Green. All rights reserved. Except for brief quotations in critical publications or reviews, no part of this book may be reproduced in any manner without prior written permission from the publisher. Write: Permissions, Wipf and Stock Publishers, 199 W. 8th Ave., Suite 3, Eugene, OR 97401.

Wipf & Stock
An imprint of Wipf and Stock Publishers
199 W. 8th Ave., Suite 3
Eugene, OR 97401
www.wipfandstock.com

ISBN 13: 978-1-62032-651-0

Unless otherwise stated, Scripture quotations are taken from THE HOLY BIBLE, NEW INTERNATIONAL VERSION®, NIV® Copyright © 1973, 1978, 1984, 2011 by Biblica, Inc.™ Used by permission. All rights reserved worldwide.

Dedicated to my dearest wife, Jacqueline, with grateful thanks for her faithfulness, endless patience, and encouraging confidence in me to begin and to bring to completion this whole project.

To my three sons, Christopher, Timothy and Stephen, who have experienced, through our family life in ministry, the best and the worst that the Christian Church can be, my grateful thanks for their love.

My prayer is that the Church into which they have been baptised will yet overflow with that inclusive love and certain hope that reveals the true glory of our Lord Jesus Christ.

"To speak of orthodoxy as a truth that makes us happy is not always the first phrase that might come to mind because we have, sadly, come to think of orthodox belief as a set of obligations to sign up to, rather than a landscape to inhabit with constant amazement and delight of the discovery opened up."

—Rowan Williams, Archbishop of Canterbury, "To What End Are We Made?," in *Who Is This Man?: Christ in the Renewal of the Church*, edited by Jonathan Baker & William Davage, 11 (New York: Continuum, 2006)

"Orthodoxy or right belief is one of those subjects that need careful handling because it is often a place where bomb makers hide. Christian orthodoxy is claimed by two kinds of believers. The noisiest are those who see it as the acceptance and affirmation of propositions in creeds, texts, and doctrines. In effect, they are rationalists. For them, orthodoxy requires verbal assent to certain statements. At the extreme it is thought that, should Osama bin Laden on his deathbed accept Jesus Christ as his personal Lord and Saviour, he will go straight to heaven, while faithful and compassionate non-Christians will go to the other place no matter what. There is no doubt in my mind that a repentant terrorist can go to heaven, but the kind of orthodoxy that takes no account of the moral life but only of verbal assent is obscene. Judgment is a mystery and we leave it to God to judge between a hateful Christian and a Christlike atheist."

—Alan W. Jones, *Common Prayer on Common Ground: A Vision of Anglican Orthodoxy*, 19–20 (Harrisburg, PA: Morehouse, 2006)

Contents

Acknowledgments / xi
Foreword / xiii
Prologue / xv
Introduction: Beating the Bounds—the Rise of GAFCON / xxi

1 MOVEMENT ONE: THE CHURCH IN CONFLICT (ALLEGRO) / 1

　The Exposition
　　Principle Subject:　Orthodoxy as "Heavenly Gift"
　　　Bridge Passage:　Orthodoxy as "Dynamic"
　　　Second Subject:　Orthodoxy as the Winners' Triumph
　　　Closing Section:　Orthodoxy in the Mind of God
　The Development
　　　Elaboration:　Diversity and Deposit
　　　Modulation:　Development as Process
　　　Transformation:　Orthodoxy as Unfinished Business
　The Recapitulation
　　　Principal Subject Reworked:　Neo-Conservative Resurgence
　　　Bridge Passage Reworked:　Proto-Orthodoxy
　　　Second Subject Reworked:　Further New Testament Study
　　　Closing Section:　The Journey Continues
　　　Coda:　Heresy as "Other"
　Summary of Orthodoxy in the First Movement

2 MOVEMENT TWO: THE CHURCH THINKING
　(ADAGIO—THEME AND VARIATIONS) / 34

　Theme: Boundaries and Authority
　　　Variation One:　Fundamentalism
　　　Variation Two:　Circles, Sets, Edges, and Centres
　　　Variation Three:　The Four "Selfs"

Contents

    Variation Four: Three Illustrative Examples
      a) The Early Church with Special Reference to Donatism—Dynamism at Play
      b) The Reformation—Circles, Sets, Edges, and Centres
      c) The Emerging Church—The Fourth "Self" in Action

Summary of Orthodoxy in the Second Movement

3   MOVEMENT THREE: THE CHURCH AS ANGLICAN (MINUET AND TRIO—SCHERZO) / 96

    The Many Faces of Anglicanism (Minuet)
      First Subject: The Anglican Communion
        The Instruments of Communion
        a) The Archbishop of Canterbury
        b) The Lambeth Conference
        c) The Anglican Consultative Council
        d) The Primates Meeting
      Development: Fragmentation Past and Present
                           —The Lambeth Conferences
      Trio: Politics, Power, and Persuasion
      First Subject Re-Examined: Authority in Anglicanism
    Ecclesiology—The Key to a Distinctive Anglican Orthodoxy?
                        (Scherzo)
      First Subject: Why Ecclesiology?
      Development: The Complexity of Ecclesiology
      Second Subject: The Anglican Distinctive
        Variation One: The Place of the Thirty-Nine Articles of Religion
        Variation Two: Other Distinctive Features
        Variation Three: The Value of Comprehensiveness

Summary of Orthodoxy in the Third Movement

4 **MOVEMENT FOUR: THE CHURCH AS COMMUNITY (ALLEGRO MOLTO—PRESTO) / 182**

    Quo Vadis Anglicanum?
    Theme: The Sense of an Ending
        Variation One: The Virginia Report
        Variation Two: The Windsor Report
        Variation Three: The Anglican Covenant
        A Counter-Melody: Anticipated Eschatology

    Summary of Orthodoxy in the Fourth Movement

5 **CODA FINALE: CONCLUSIONS / 202**

    The Jazz Theology Approach
    Conclusions
        The History and Nature of Orthodoxy Itself
        The Usefulness of Heresy
        The Essential Freedom of the Postmodern Paradigm
        Fundamentalism and Legalism
        The Folly of Separation
        The Essence of Anglicanism
        Declaration of Assent
        Love Has to Be the Key

6 **CADENZA: A PERSONAL STATEMENT / 221**

Bibliography / 227
Subject/Name Index / 239

Acknowledgments

I wish to acknowledge my thanks for the support and advice so willingly given to me by the Reverend Doctor Graham Buxton, Head of Postgraduate Studies, School of Ministry, Theology and Culture and Director of the Graeme Clark Research Institute at Tabor College, Adelaide, and the Right Reverend Doctor Stephen Pickard, Assistant Bishop in the Diocese of Canberra and Goulburn and Parish Priest, St. Geroge's Anglican Church, Pearce, also an associate member of the Faculty of Theology, Oxford University, UK.

I have also been much encouraged in this project by the Reverend Doctor Phillip Tolliday, Senior Lecturer in Systematic Theology, School of Theology, Charles Sturt University, who has been unstinting in his willingness to listen me and to give me time and space to think things through with him.

I also thank Ms. Julia Walton, whose expertise in spelling, grammar, and punctuation far exceeds my own, and to whom I am grateful for her meticulous help in preparing the manuscript.

Foreword

With over 80 million members in 160 countries the Anglican Communion is remarkable in its reach and work among the peoples of the world. A map of global Anglicanism reveals variety and richness with respect to cultures, races, languages, political, social and economic life. Each church in its own place seeking to express the gospel of God in ways that creatively interact with and respect the local situation; this is part of the missional mandate of Anglicanism. This means that local autonomy is highly prized. However it is a fellowship of churches and this *koinonia* in the gospel is expressed through myriad ways and bonds of affection. These all signal a genuine interdependence and connection with churches of the Communion and with the wider ecumenical body of Christ.

What can possibly hold such a disparate and varied fellowship of national churches together? Can it be located in doctrine? Is it in common prayer or maybe connections through common concerns for the peoples of the world? The answer for Anglicans is that it is all of these and more. However this answer needs to be qualified because common belief, common prayer and common cause do not operate from on high under a tight legal framework. Anglicanism is much looser relying on the informal as much if not more than purely formal constitutional arrangements. Indeed there is no such thing as an international legal framework for Anglicanism.

All this makes for an interesting and dynamic mix for the Anglican Communion. It means that difference and division are constant companions. And in our present context with the internet and global communications we can and do misunderstand each other easily and quickly. Appeals are regularly made to standards of belief to secure orthodox Christian belief especially when there are controversial matters involved, such as questions of human sexuality. The hope is that the appeal to fixed standards of faith will settle questions of authority and boundaries for being the church. But as history shows notions of orthodoxy (and its sibling heresy) are notoriously difficult to pin down let alone achieve general agreement

Foreword

on. Moreover such attempts to delimit faith and purify the church only generate further controversy, division and sometimes schism. It has ever been thus. This does not render unimportant the exercise of authority, or the need for boundaries for faith, nor the search for forms of belief and life that give witness to the gospel of Jesus Christ. But it does raise sharply the way we approach such vital concerns and how we treat those with whom we disagree.

Sidney Green's book 'Beating the Bounds' makes an important and clarifying contribution to the above situation of the Anglican Communion today. He achieves this through a creative adaptation of the movements of a symphony to the dynamic of orthodoxy and heresy in the Church. He explores the way this dynamic has expressed itself at critical periods: the Patristic period, the Reformation and contemporary Anglicanism. The result is an illuminating insight into the nature of faith and belief for Anglicans as they seek to find their voice and song in the twenty-first century. Green's focus on ecclesiology as the 'key to a distinctive Anglican orthodoxy' is central to his approach. It is also timely given the tendency today to divorce matters of faith from the life of the Church. Christians are thoroughly ecclesial persons, bound together in the Spirit. Through our differences, disagreements, conflicts and divisions we remain 'of the Church'. How then might this fundamental reality order our quarrels, differences and divisions? Such things are more than of scholarly interest for Sidney Green who has spent a lifetime as a pastor and priest ministering in the UK and more latterly in Australia. He has written a book that draws from deep pastoral wisdom and knowledge of the issues facing the Church. Anyone who seeks a clearer understanding of the nature of orthodoxy and authority amidst the conflicts of contemporary Anglicanism will be richly rewarded by this timely book.

Stephen Pickard
Assistant Bishop, Diocese of Canberra & Goulburn,
Associate Professor of Theology, Charles Sturt University

Prologue

H. E.W. Turner, in his Bampton Lectures published in 1954, tellingly described orthodoxy in the early years of Christianity as "a symphony composed of varied elements rather than a single melodic theme."[1] The significance of his statement will be apparent later in this book—however, the use of musical metaphors for theological thought is certainly not new.

The twelfth-century mystic, theologian, abbess and preacher Hildegard von Bingen saw music as an all-inclusive prism through which could be expressed all the wonders of both heaven and earth.

"Music was, to her, the sacred technology which could best tune humanity, redirect our hearts toward heaven and put our feet back onto the wholesome pathways that will lead us to God."[2]

Życiński uses the metaphor of a God as the author of "Cosmic Symphony" to illustrate his concept of divine interaction with a world which is guided, but not coerced, by the Creator towards its final destination of beauty and goodness. God, in Życiński's vision, is at one and the same time transcendent and yet immanent, being deeply involved in the processes of the world.

"The history of the world is not then a recording played from a cosmic compact disk, but the completion of a great symphony in which man can aim at divine patterns of beauty, but can also keep his own authorial rights to cosmic dissonances and discords."[3]

A similar notion of the gift of human freedom fully embraced within the divine plan illustrated by musical metaphor is expressed by Michael Heller:

> Like in any masterly symphony, elements of chance and necessity are interwoven with each other and together span the structure of the whole. Elements of necessity determine the pattern

1. Turner, *Pattern of Christian Truth*, 9.
2. Hildegard of Bingen, *Symphony of the Harmony of Heaven*.
3. Życiński, *God and Evolution*, 164.

of possibilities and dynamical paths of becoming, but they leave enough room for chancy events to make this becoming rich and individual.... There is no opposition here. Within the all-comprising Mind of God, what we call chance and random events is well composed into the symphony of creation.[4]

This theme of divine revelation and human freedom of thought will play an important part in this book in the light of attempts by some conservatives to declare themselves as being the only true guardians of orthodoxy.

Other theologians sharing this concept of both the fixed and random or, from another view point, divine and human activity in this 'symphonic' composition include John Polkinghorne and Nicholas Beale.

> The history of the universe is not the performance of a fixed score, written by God in eternity and inexorably performed by the creatures, but it is a grand improvisation in which the Creator and the creatures cooperate in the unfolding development of the grand fugue of creation. God is not a mere spectator of this process . . . but neither are the creatures caught up willy-nilly in a process in which they have no active part to play.[5]

Hans Urs von Balthasar similarly speaks of God's revelation as the performance of a symphony. For him the Old Testament reveals a world like an orchestra tuning up before a concert in a cacophony of sound through which the piercing note of the 'A' on the oboe can be heard "as a kind of promise" recognised by the writer to the Hebrews when he reflects on Jewish history and writes, "In many and varied ways God spoke of old to our fathers by the prophets . . ."[6]

It is only at the coming of the Son, "the heir of all things," that the meaning of all these different sounds becomes clear. For Balthasar this means that, because the unity of the composition comes from God and not from human effort, ". . . the world was, is and always will be pluralist (and why not?) — and will be so increasingly."[7]

The mutual contradictions of different voices or sounds become integrated in Christ, not by suppressing differences of voice in an attempt to forcefully create unison but in the wonderful integration of sound that is the symphony.

4. Heller, *Deciphering the Mind of God*.
5. Polkinghorne and Beale, *Questions of Truth*, 15.
6. Heb 1:1.
7. Balthasar, *Truth Is Symphonic*, 9.

Prologue

If we really want to hear something intelligible, we are obliged to listen to the entire polyphony of revelation. We cannot make Christ shine through the church by destroying it or replacing it with forms of community of our own designing.[8]

How polyphony—or the hearing of differing and sometimes conflicting voices—within theological orthodoxy and other such ideas is important will be a major theme of this book.

In a previous career before becoming an Anglican priest, I trained at the Royal Military School of Music, Kneller Hall, in the United Kingdom to be a professional musician. With such a musical background, the idea of using the musical structure and form of the classical symphony as a heuristic metaphor with which to investigate and examine the theme of this book seemed obvious. It seems to me that musical vocabulary, such as words like harmony, dissonance, cacophony, themes and variations, composers' style and choice of genre, tempo and key, fit well the complex and difficult situation that now faces the Anglican Communion throughout the world.

Another value of using music as a theological tool for analysis and structure is that music has tremendous power not only to demonstrate that inner coherence that is so vital for theological argument but it also has an innate power to draw people together. It is a fact that people of differing ages, cultures, races, and creeds can listen to the same piece of music together and enjoy it, learn from it, and respond to it, albeit in different ways.

As a basis I have taken the structure of what has come to be known as the classical symphony. The symphony has a claim to be classical music's greatest creation, able to hold its head up among the great cultural genres of the West. In its early days, the symphony had to obey certain conventions. It had to be laid out in a certain number of movements, in a certain form, for a specified body of instruments. But as it grew, it changed miraculously into something like the essence of music itself. It is the form where composers put their great ideas and work them out wonderfully, using all the amazing depths of colour that the orchestra can give.

At its height, the symphony became something that for sheer substance and reach is comparable to the novel, and it cannot be an accident that the two forms began to rise to pre-eminence at the same time.

The symphony began life as a pleasant accompaniment to everyday life and pleasures in the houses of the rich and powerful. Before it became

8. Ibid.,11.

Prologue

more structured and serious it reflected such things as the hunt, the military parade, and the courtly dance. These have all left their mark on it, and their traces remained for centuries.

As understood today the classical symphony is usually divided into four movements each with very different characteristics of style, tempo, key, and structure. I have tried to use each of these stylistic movements metaphorically to introduce and describe each section of this book.

Also of interest is the fact that "... the German word for movement (of a musical work) is *Satz*, meaning 'sentence'. In the German tradition, a musical work first makes some claim or states some musical position, and then argues the case for that claim by exploring the musical consequences of the theme (or themes), or of its component musical parts, before returning to a re-statement of the initial claim (theme) at the end of the movement."[9] This seems to fit well the purpose of this book.

Even more significant, in the light of these discussions, is the Russian musicologist Mark Aranovsky's renowned classification of the movements of the typical symphony as:

Movement 1: *Homo agens*: man acting, or in conflict: (Allegro)

Movement 2: *Homo sapiens*: man thinking: (Adagio)

Movement 3: *Homo ludens*: man playing: (Minuet/Scherzo)

Movement 4: *Homo communis*: man in the community: (Allegro)[10]

I have taken the liberty of adapting this classification to form a structure for this book as follows:

Movement 1: The church in conflict: (Allegro)

Movement 2: The church thinking: (Adagio)

Movement 3: The church as Anglican: (Minuet/Scherzo)

Movement 4: The church as community: (Allegro)

This structure keeps to Aranovsky's basic description in all but the third movement. The notion of playfulness in that movement has been exchanged for that of the peculiarities of Anglicanism. The reasons for this are explained more fully in the introductions to both the Minuet and Scherzo sections of the book. The essence of playfulness is retained, even if in a somewhat muted form, as the formal dance structure of the minuet

9. "Symphonic Form."
10. Aranovsky, *Simfonichesktye Iskaniya (Symphonic Explorations)*, 27.

Prologue

examines the form and history of the Communion and the dramatic tensions between the dancing partners involved in its politics. In the scherzo that playful character is also retained as examination is made of the seemingly somewhat vague and fleeting notion of a distinctive Anglican ecclesiology.

In the end it will be seen that this formal structure, though helpful as a framework for analysis, requires something beyond itself to express the current turmoil now engaging Anglicanism. To that end the conclusions of this book are set within the framework of a modern musical form in what has now come to be known as Jazz Theology. The reasons for this will become evident.

In these turbulent times for the Anglican Communion and the church as a whole this writer hopes that this book may be used, as Hildegard prayed, as part of that "good work in the service of God."[11]

---

11. Hildegard of Bingen, *Symphony of the Harmony of Heaven*.

Introduction

Beating the Bounds—the Rise of GAFCON

THE PRECIPITATING FACTOR OR catalyst for beginning work on this book was the setting up of the Global Anglican Future Conference (GAFCON) in 2008 and its final communiqué, published as the Jerusalem Declaration, in response to the contemporary upheavals within the Anglican Communion.

I want to make it clear that this is not a book against GAFCON although it will become evident that my sympathies do not lie in that direction. Many of the participants in that event were and still are my friends. I honour and respect their point of view even though it will be evident that I do not agree with the way in which the GAFCON and its Jerusalem Declaration is being worked out within the Anglican Communion.

This book is about orthodoxy in general but more specifically about Anglican orthodoxy. Issues concerning GAFCON have become for me merely a means of entering into the issues and arguments concerning orthodoxy and enabling me to develop the dominant theme of this book.

In reality it would be difficult to write a book against GAFCON as there is so very little material produced in writing from them to argue for or against their position. What is clear is that open enquiry is not their "forté" and they seem to be reluctant to enter into the robustness of theological debate that lies at the heart of the richness of Anglicanism. There seems to be very much a "take it or leave it" attitude to their proposals.

GAFCON appears to have metaphorically resurrected an ancient custom dating back to Anglo-Saxon days but still observed in a very few mostly rural English parishes, known as "Beating the Bounds." During this ceremony the parishioners, led by the parish priest, walk the parish boundaries physically beating acknowledged boundary markers with willow wands.

Introduction

There was a two-fold purpose at work here. The first was to physically check that no one had interfered with or moved the parish boundaries. The second purpose was to make sure that every member of the parish community would know where the boundaries were so as to be able to preserve them for future generations. The whole exercise was also seen to be an act of worship and prayer during which the blessing of God was invoked upon the parish and its people.

GAFCON was, and continues to be in its incarnation as the Fellowship of Confessing Anglicans, in one sense, a form of global "Beating the Bounds" by those Anglicans who believe that the doctrinal and ethical boundary markers of Anglican orthodoxy have been violated. Doctrinally they see this as evidenced by the increasing influence of heterodox theology in certain provinces of Anglicanism, especially the Episcopal Church of the United States, which is now simply known as The Episcopal Church (TEC).

However, Phillip Tolliday[1] reminds us that to set GAFCON in context it is necessary to go back to the late 1970s. The liberalising tendencies in TEC had begun through the changes made by Prayer Book revision and the acceptance of the ordination of women in the late 70s.

Conservatives responded throughout the world by creating what became known as the Continuing Church movement, which, as more and more women were ordained within the Anglican Communion, drew its membership from all over the world. This movement followed the path of most protest movements by subdividing into yet smaller groups, with the inevitable consequent theological squabbling that so often marks such moves. It was because of these divisions that the movement did not grow or become really influential.

Despite their claims that they alone were the true Anglicans, they nevertheless decided to leave the Anglican Communion, sometimes with the suggestion that all they were doing was continuing in the tradition of the seventeenth-century Nonjurors.

These were Anglicans who felt themselves to be engaged in a fierce conflict between themselves as "conservatives" wanting to be "word keepers" and progressives who wanted to adapt the church to changing political and cultural shifts in society.

When in 1688 James II reissued the Declaration of Indulgence, it was seen by many as a first step at establishing freedom of religion in the British Isles. The Declaration granted broad religious freedom in England by

---

1. Tolliday, "Global Witness."

Introduction

suspending penal laws enforcing conformity to the Church of England and allowing persons to worship in their homes or chapels as they saw fit, and it ended the requirement of affirming religious oaths before gaining employment in government office.

By use of the royal suspending power, the King lifted the religious penal laws and granted toleration to the various Christian denominations, Catholic and Protestant, within his kingdoms. The declaration was greatly opposed by Anglicans for it did not appear to guarantee that the Anglican Church would remain the established church.

The Indulgence, as well as granting religious liberties to his subjects, also reaffirmed the King as absolute. In Scotland the Indulgence stated that subjects were to obey the King's "sovereign authority, prerogative royal and absolute power ... without reserve."[2] There was concern that the toleration rested only on the King's arbitrary will. The Anglican Church was greatly disturbed by it.[3]

There was open resistance from Anglicans. Few clergy read out the Indulgence in church.[4] William Sancroft Archbishop of Canterbury and six other bishops presented a petition to the King declaring the Indulgence illegal. James regarded this as rebellion and sedition and promptly had the seven bishops tried; however, the bishops were acquitted. Their popular support led to James fleeing England and William of Orange being invited by Parliament to be King.

However, those same bishops and over four hundred clergy felt they had sworn an oath of allegiance to James and, despite his failings, he was to them still the divinely appointed monarch. They refused to swear allegiance to William and, within two years, they and two more bishops were deprived of their livings. This was a complete capitulation of the church to the power of the state. No deprivations had been ordered by any church council.

The Nonjurors based their actions on the integrity of their oath and a clear theological conviction of the divine right of the monarch. This was a theology that had been deeply embedded in Anglican ecclesiology since the sixteenth century and was clearly found in the Elizabethan homilies.

They judged that the new demands were immoral and heretical. They simply refused to go along with it, and accepted the consequences. They

---

2. Armitage, *British Political Thought*, 95–96.
3. Harris, *Revolution*, 217.
4. Fritze and Williams, *Historical Dictionary*, 487.

upheld the authority, not of conscience, but of the demands of God upon those who lead the church.

Their integrity accepted the deprivation and, initially, they avoided setting up structures of opposition. They just disengaged themselves from what was immoral and dishonest, as they saw it.

J. W. C. Wand writes that the original Nonjurors were ". . . the very cream of the ministry at that time. . . . [Yet] it is possible that their humility disguised from the fact that in satisfying their own conscience they might still be doing harm to the church . . . isolating the men of strongest church principles and allowing them to withdraw from the church of the country [thereby] laying the whole field open for William's schemes of latitudinarian comprehension."[5]

They seemed to feel that the only choice that they had was either to compromise their convictions and ". . . stay within an errant church, or split off and become yet another small, unofficial Anglican body, unrecognised by the Anglican Communion. They unhesitatingly chose the latter."[6]

When we come to the 1990s we find Episcopalian conservatives, having learned the hard lesson that the Continuing Church movement of the 1970s led only to stagnation, realising that the path to renewal was to be found within the Anglican Church. To that end, therefore, in the late 90s, ". . . this generation of dissenters invented a new option, an untried path: involving other Anglicans, with the authority of the larger Anglican Communion, in their efforts to reform the Episcopal Church."[7]

There were two events that took place in the 1990s that caused American conservatives to make an appeal to Anglican leaders in other countries to intervene in Episcopal Church politics.

The first of these was the unsuccessful attempt by conservatives to try Bishop Righter for heresy, which raised the difficult and complex subject of what is "core doctrine" as far as Anglicanism orthodoxy is concerned. This is, of course, a matter we will come to in this study. The second was the election in 1997 of Frank Griswold, a liberal, as Presiding Bishop. American conservatives, disillusioned with the possibility of bringing about internal reform, set about encouraging African bishops to throw their weight behind conservative agendas, and what was to be, in particular, the issue of homosexuality. This they would do by ensuring that

---

5. Wand, *High Church Schism*, 12.
6. Hassett, *Anglican Communion in Crisis*, 46.
7. Ibid., 46

Introduction

the African voice would be heard effectively at the Lambeth Conference.[8] Again, this is a matter to be dealt with in detail later.

Their fears were specifically confirmed by the deviation from their ethical understanding of the scriptural prohibitions against homosexuality in the consecration of Gene Robinson, an openly gay priest living with his male partner, as the Bishop of New Hampshire in what was the Episcopal Church of the United States of America (ECUSA), together with the adoption of liturgical rites for same-sex unions in other provinces.

The introduction to the GAFCON Jerusalem Declaration claims three "undeniable facts" that underlie its promulgation. Firstly, it speaks of the "fact" that a "different gospel"[9] is being preached which it sees as contrary to the apostolic gospel. This, of course, refers to Gene Robinson's consecration and consequent approval given to an openly homosexual lifestyle for a bishop. Whether this is a fair and accurate representation of the "different gospel" Paul was talking about in Galatians is, in my opinion, very much to be doubted. Paul was clearly dealing with the heresy that said that Christian must also keep the law, including circumcision. Faith was still to be placed upon Christ, but the law also must be kept in order to be found truly righteous before God. Salvation, in this view, was no longer a matter of faith alone but required works of merit.

Important though this doctrinal issue is, it is difficult to see it as dealing with moral and ethical issues raised by the consecration of an openly homosexual bishop. Indeed, it could be argued that to try and force it to include these sorts of ethical or moral matters could almost be as heretical as attempting to unite law and gospel.

The second "fact" is the statement from the Global South provincial bodies that they are out of communion with the bishops who shared in that consecration and thus, in GAFCON's view, promote that false gospel.

The third "fact" is what they call "the manifest failure of the Communion Instruments[10] to exercise discipline in the face of overt heterodoxy."[11]

8. Tolliday, *Global Witness*.

9. "I am astonished that you are so quickly deserting the one who called you by the grace of Christ and are turning to a different gospel–which is really no gospel at all. Evidently some people are throwing you into confusion and are trying to pervert the gospel of Christ. But even if we or an angel from heaven should preach a gospel other than the one we preached to you, let him be eternally condemned!" (Gal 1:6–8).

10. The Anglican Communion is served by four "Instruments of Communion": the Archbishop of Canterbury, the Lambeth Conferences, the Primates Conference, and the Anglican Consultative Council. These will be discussed in detail in the section in Movement Three entitled, "The Many Faces of Anglicanism."

11. GAFCON, "Jerusalem Declaration."

Introduction

The fact that the notion of "overt heterodoxy" is raised forgets the fact that, as we shall see, there has always been at least a covert heterodoxy within Anglicanism. As Michael Jinkins observes, conversations on this issue alone have been the staple diet of Anglican theologians since the Reformation.

> The messiness of these conversations, the fact that they arise from a diversity of communities claiming to be Christian, challenges the most common assumptions about truth, that it is non-contradictory, that it is singular, and, therefore, that it is universal.... It is not uncommon for adherents to a particular community of faith that has enjoyed confessional hegemony over other communities to protest against the emerging diversity of voices, (which means, in fact, that the diversity is being heard whereas formerly it existed but was not accorded a public voice that could be heard by others), fearing that diversity, contradiction and heterogeneity mean the dissolution of church—and perhaps the end of civilisation as we know it![12]

Their preferred antidote to these defined evils is seen as a return to a conservative, fundamentalist view of Scripture, which is to be supported by a fresh appeal to the credal statements of the early church and, more especially, by an appeal to the Reformation teaching and confessional documents of the sixteenth and seventeenth centuries.

Hindmarsh[13] raises the question as to whether evangelicals can ever have a properly developed ecclesiology. He sees evangelical notions of unity to be rooted not in "authorised orders, forms or rites" but in "evangelical piety itself."[14] This trend was seen previously in both Wesley[15] and

---

12. Jinkins, *Church Faces Death*, 76.

13. Hindmarsh, "Evangelical Ecclesiology."

14. Ibid., 17. "This was evidenced convincingly when, in 1966 at the Evangelical Alliance meeting in London, there was a great rift between Revd. John Stott and Dr. Martyn Lloyd Jones, two major leaders of the evangelical movement in the United Kingdom at that time. Lloyd Jones challenged evangelicals 'to leave their denominations and form a national evangelical church.' This was rebuffed by Stott and a division occurred. This was to have momentous and lasting effects. Hindmarsh notes that 'The irony here, of course, is that it was a call to evangelical *unity* that proved so divisive."

15. Ibid., 32. "In conversations with non-conformist ministers 'Whitefield did not see any particular church order as the essence of the church or its ministry.... Whitefield viewed the church as essentially pneumatic."

Introduction

Whitefield[16] and has since led to the formation of what Hindmarsh sees as "a unique ecclesial consciousness."[17]

In order to facilitate an appeal to many, if not all, of these fundamentalist principles, GAFCON has inaugurated what it calls the Fellowship of Confessing Anglicans (FCA). This is a conservative group who sees itself in the forefront of a global battle against any theological position that does not follow the GAFCON party line. For the FCA the Jerusalem Declaration is not simply a restating of the fundamentals of the faith but a rule of life to set the course for the future development of what they see as "pure" Anglicanism around the world.[18]

There has been an active campaign by the FCA promoting the Jerusalem Declaration and encouraging individual Anglicans to become signed members of the FCA. They see their particular goal as the healing and revitalisation of the mission of the worldwide Anglican Communion as they wait for what they clearly feel is to be a dynamic move of the Spirit within Anglicanism in the future.[19]

The FCA declares its goals to include the evangelisation of people all over the world and the rebuttal of the "inclusivist" gospel now fed by what it calls "Western revisionist theology." It also sees its role as the provision of real support and help for disaffected Anglicans who have moved out of their churches because of "false teaching and practice" and who now need new and theologically acceptable episcopal support.[20]

---

16. Outler and Heizenrater, *John Wesley's Sermons*, 304. "Wesley himself deplored confessional politics, probably because of the religious battles he had experienced in previous years. 'I ask not therefore of him with whom I would unite in love. 'Are you of my Church?' Instead he asked one question only: 'Is thine heart right, as my heart is with thy heart?' There was clearly an early indication of a division being made between religious and ecclesiastical life."

17. Ibid., 17, 32.

18. GAFCON, "Jerusalem Declaration."

19. "We are a fellowship of Anglicans, including provinces, dioceses, churches, missionary jurisdictions, para-church organisations and individual Anglican Christians whose goal is to help reform, heal and revitalise the Anglican Communion and expand its mission to the world. The Jerusalem Declaration is the basis of our fellowship. We invite all who assent to that declaration and support the goals of the FCA to join us as we await what God will do in the Global Anglican Future" (FCA, "Welcome").

20. "To provide aid to those faithful Anglicans who have been forced to disaffiliate from their original spiritual homes by false teaching and practice. They need recognition and authentication. They need to be kept in the Anglican family. Obviously, it is the Primates' Council that is involved with this work, beginning with the situation in North America" (FCA, "Goals").

Introduction

It is also, I believe, a reflection on the tribal mentality now, sadly, intrinsic to evangelicalism within the worldwide Anglican Church.

Stuart Piggin recalls a conversation with Dr. Ian Jagelman, an Anglican minister working in the ultra-conservative evangelical diocese of Sydney, in which he speaks of an atmosphere of real fear among evangelical clergy.

> They are afraid of not being accepted by the club. They have become more concerned about their identity as evangelical Anglicans than with their identity as Christ's soldiers. To be identified with the club, one must work within certain parameters. Lines are drawn which are not to be crossed. Boundaries are set; they are not to be transgressed. This situation is the result of fear of human beings and not of God.[21]

As an Anglican priest with over forty years of wide-ranging experience of Anglican ministry and mission, I have written this book to affirm certain core Christian values. These are values that are not only core for the individual Christian life but values that should be core within a church culture. These are mutual respect regardless of age, race, gender, or social status; upholding personal responsibility; freedom of choice and the importance of voluntary involvement; and rejecting authoritarianism and manipulative pressure.

It is also important for me to affirm in this context that my tradition has always been that of a conservative evangelical. Since my days in theological college and for most of my ministry I have been a full member of the Evangelical Fellowship in the Anglican Communion (EFAC). I love the Anglican Church and its historic heritage and I weep to see it so divided and disfigured.

I have also come to know in my own experience, since emigrating from the United Kingdom to Australia in 2004, the conservative evangelical tribal mentality spoken of previously by Piggin, which emanates from the diocese of Sydney but is alive and well in the satellite churches it has spawned. It is only necessary to cross one of their self-imposed boundaries, such as support for women priests and preachers or the use of a liturgy not in their favour, or to raise a question concerning their particular interpretation of the Scriptures, and you are made immediately aware that you are no longer accepted as truly "sound."

Michael Cassidy not only denounces such attitudes but reveals dishonesty in the actions of certain of his fellow evangelicals. Rather than

---

21. Piggin, *Firestorm of the Lord*, 127.

Introduction

be direct and unambiguous about not believing everything in the Bible as old-time liberals were, Cassidy claims that modern evangelicals simply mouth platitudes about plenary inspiration and anathematise any who have a different view while, at the same time, they hypocritically undermine the inspiration of Scripture by their own exegesis. They claim that certain sections were written "for other places and for other times and use other hermeneutical devices to release from the hook of their own creation of inerrancy."[22]

John V. Taylor writes similarly about how certain Christians manipulate the Scriptures in their attempts to restrain the Holy Spirit if he is not moving in the way they feel he should: "(They) put on a sorry display of special pleading and dishonest handling of the evidence in their efforts to harness His freedom to their particular family coach."[23]

The hope is that this book will produce a new way of thinking about boundaries, especially for evangelical and other conservative Anglicans. They are caught up, at the moment, in a vitriolic and unedifying battle with, as they see it, the forces of liberalism, but seem to feel that they have no other recourse but to fight the battles of the past rather than to look to the promise of the future.

I believe that taking refuge in a biblical theology and a very constrained ecclesiology articulated in the language, thought forms, and documents of the sixteenth and seventeenth centuries is not a helpful strategy. Rather, the contemporary thinking of evangelicals and others, in their struggle to present the Christian faith in a way acceptable to men and women in this very different postmodern era, could provide a springboard towards a new *via media* for Anglicanism for the twenty-first century and beyond.

Bishop Godfrey Fryer also supports the sense of it being necessary for the church to discover a new *via media* as it seeks to fulfill its mission to the world into a new, multi-cultural setting.[24]

---

22. Cassidy, *Prophetic Word in the Crisis Context*.

23. Taylor, *Go-Between God*, 119–21.

24. Hale and Curnow, *Facing the Future*, 244. "The embrace of the 'via media' was . . . a worthy way of holding together and balancing truth, and it has served us well. In our present situation, however, we face a degree of discontent: on the one hand we are seen as being too bound to the teaching of the *Book of Common Prayer*, the Thirty Nine Articles or Religion and the Ordinal; on the other hand we have the pressing missional needs of the church to proclaim the gospel to a new generation, in ways that most effectively engage with the cultures of the diverse range of communities in this country. A vital question for our time is just how we balance tradition and mission in the expression of worship. Somehow we need a new *via media*."

Introduction

In a period of ecclesiastical history such as we are living through, this research would be expected to offer some hope to a denomination felt by many to be in decline especially in the West, and to assure weary and perplexed clergy and leaders that God has not finished yet with the church they love and serve.

A refreshed and contemporary approach to Hooker's trio of Scripture, reason and tradition, renewed for a postmodern generation, could truly breathe life into the old epithet that the Anglican Church is "still a good boat to fish from!"

To that end let the symphony begin!

1

Movement One: The Church in Conflict (Allegro)

The Exposition

IN CLASSICAL SYMPHONIC FORM the *exposition* is the place where the composer exposes the main themes that will form the structure of the movement. The symphony usually begins with the declaration of a *principal subject*, which firmly establishes the key and feel of the movement.

This is then transformed through a *bridge passage* into a second subject. This second subject is often much more lyrical and sweeter than the principal subject. It is also in a different key and gradually builds up for the next section, known as the *closing section* because it closes the exposition in the new key. In many symphonies, the composer introduces completely new material in this section.

Principal subject: Orthodoxy as "Heavenly Gift"

The classic theme or theory of orthodoxy has generally been the view that the church kept pure and untainted the teaching of Jesus and the apostles. Heresy, therefore, is seen as anything that was a departure and offshoot from that pure teaching. This view sees the rise of heresy as the prophesied "satanic" attack on the church and, consequently, an attack on Jesus Christ himself. In Hebrews 6:4 the writer describes true belief as a form of enlightenment empowered by the Holy Spirit and based on the word of God. To have such belief is a foretaste of the eschatological age to come. Such belief is seen as "the heavenly gift." To subsequently reject that gift is described in terms that make such an act the unforgivable sin. [1]

---

1. "It is impossible for those who have once been enlightened, who have tasted the

The classic theory also contrasted truth and heresy in a simplistic way, believing that the truth is one whereas heresy is multifaceted, diverse, and self-contradictory. Truth was also seen as universal, hence the epithet "catholic" could be applied, whereas heresy was seen as something that simply occurred in local areas and was really a mixture of pure Christian teaching and pagan philosophies.

Such a view inevitably locked the concept of orthodoxy in the past as a static treasure trove of truth, almost as though dropped down from heaven through the mouth of Jesus to his apostles and then, through them, to the church. This was some golden age towards which the church was bound to look as it sought to deal with the theological questions that each age raised.

Greenslade reminds us that to look back in yearning to those early days as "the undivided church" is as little justified as it is to look back at any supposed "Mediaeval Age of Faith, or a godly reformed Church." He questions what it is we rest on when we ascribe the authority we give to the early fathers. "Is it their antiquity or their catholicity? And if the latter, do we assume *a priori*, that because they lived without constricting denominations, the unhampered flow of Christian life and thought, like blood circulating freely in a healthy body, must have preserved their doctrine from error, at least from errors of distortion?"[2]

He encourages us to be realistic about the realities of personal ambition, nationalism, and, of course, plain human sinfulness that marred their fellowship with God and with each other just as it does ours. The great wealth of Christian literature and thought we have from their days was not available to them in their own day because books were scarce and travel limited. That was, of course, because ". . . many of the greatest Greek Fathers read no Latin theology, many of the greatest Latins little Greek (and) some Christian literature was sealed to both Greeks and Romans."[3]

---

heavenly gift, who have shared in the Holy Spirit, who have tasted the goodness of the word of God and the powers of the coming age, if they fall away, to be brought back to repentance, because to their loss they are crucifying the Son of God all over again and subjecting him to public disgrace" (Heb 6:4–6).

2. Greenslade, *Schism in the Early Church*, 16–17.
3. Ibid., 17.

Bridge passage: Orthodoxy as "Dynamic"

In the traditional symphonic form this passage within the first movement, often incomplete in feeling, leads into a completely new and conflicting theme.

Stephen Sykes, in his essay "Orthodoxy and Liberalism" refers his readers to the thought of Professor Daniel Hardy who, in contrast to that static view, argues for a ". . . dynamic understanding of 'orthodoxy' . . . a way of inhabiting the Christian tradition which involves hard conceptual work. . . ."[4]

For Sykes, to be orthodox is not a matter of lazily repeating the decisions and arguments of the past to meet each new critical proposal. The transformational dynamic of orthodoxy is only in evidence where theologians fully accept the contemporary task of uncovering presuppositions, analysing arguments and engaging in vigorous dialogue.

Michael Jinkins reminds us that a generation ago an ecclesiology would begin with looking at the biblical foundations and would be seen, through very rose-coloured spectacles, as a homogeneous community. Others, he says, might begin with ". . . historical/doctrinal examination of the traditions and credal formulae regarding 'Church' and they would be seen as prescriptive for the life of the contemporary church as a formula—what Origen called the 'Norm.'"

This view has been challenged as a true picture from the Bible or the early communities of faith, which should be more realistically seen as a ". . . polymorphic cloud of witnessing communities whose shape changes with the times and locales, the winds and other atmospheric necessities of pluralistic communities in different context bearing sacred traditions often at variance with other communities of faith."[5]

Jinkins reflects on the different facets of Christian theology clearly demonstrated in the life and witness of each of the Johannine, Pauline, Jerusalem, and Palestinian communities.

Second Subject: Orthodoxy as the Winners' Triumph

The first significant writing to undermine the traditional view of orthodoxy was the seminal work of Walter Bauer.[6] It was written in German in

---

4. Sykes, "'Orthodoxy' and 'Liberalism'", 76–77.
5. Jinkins, *Church Faces Death*, 4.
6. Bauer, *Orthodoxy and Heresy*.

the 1930s but, because of the restrictions that surrounded the Nazi era in Germany, it was only translated into English in the 1970s.

Bauer paints a picture of an early church where, from the very beginning, differing emphases and doctrines abound and where nothing is, as yet, set in stone.

Bauer claimed that there were so many different branches that it was impossible for them to unite and so they fragmented and were weakened. It was only the rise of the influence of the church at Rome that eventually brought some sort of order into this maelstrom of theological ideas.

Rome was the centre of what became orthodoxy and, although smaller at first, was so well organized that it was able to extend its influence into the east and establish itself as the "orthodox" form of Christianity, especially after the "conversion" of the Emperor Constantine.

This Roman dominance was due, in the most part, to its superior organisation and the fact that episcopal leadership enabled strong leadership, especially under what he called "the grand villain the Bishop of Rome." Bauer claims that orthodoxy in the West up to AD 451 was simply the Roman view. Heresy was any other view.[7]

Closing Section: Orthodoxy in the Mind of God?

Although not an essential part of the first movement of a symphony, here the composer often can introduce some completely new material.

Acknowledging his debt to Bauer, David Christie-Murray reminds us that, while it is relatively easy to define heresy as a deviation from orthodoxy, it is much more difficult to actually define orthodoxy. He goes as far as to imagine the cynic saying that "heretics are simply the minority who differ from the contemporary majority view."[8]

However, it is clear he does not fully agree with the cynics, preferring, rather, to question the possibility of finding a perfect orthodoxy, which, he says, may have to come from some sort of Platonic view that sees the true orthodoxy as existing only "in the mind of God." If that is true then heresy, he concludes, can only be held to be a "minority belief within the community of faith."[9]

---

7. Ibid., 113.
8. Christie-Murray, *History of Heresy*, 113.
9. Ibid., 46.

The Development

The *development section* of the first movement of a symphony is essentially a "free fantasia" on themes established in the exposition. This is where previous themes are elaborated, modulated, and transformed as the composer is allowed to let his imagination run wild. It is here where the drama and conflict can occur through . . .

Elaboration: Diversity and Deposit

Professor H. E. W. Turner's Bampton Lectures, "The Pattern of Christian Truth,"[10] argued that there is both diversity in the New Testament and yet also a "deposit of faith," derived from the apostolic witness and referred to in the New Testament as the "faith once for all entrusted to the saints."[11]

Turner, like Bauer, rejects the classic view of orthodoxy seeing much more fluidity in the New Testament itself, where we see a "considerable variety of theological traditions." There can be no 'single doctrinal common denominator' as different parts of the Christian world responded in different ways to the rise of theological questions and problems.

Turner was also open to the concept of development in those early days, evidenced, as he saw it, by the waxing and waning of the popularity of theologians such as Tertullian and Origen. Ideas and concepts that had been accepted as orthodox at one time were, as he put it, "superannuated in the light of later developments."[12] His conclusion was that ". . . orthodoxy in the second century must be differently interpreted in the fourth and fifth. If orthodoxy itself certainly antedated the achievement of fixed doctrinal norms, it begins to wear a different aspect after the process of doctrinal formulation had got properly under way. Even at the same period standards of orthodoxy might differ in different fields."[13]

Turner refuses to accept the more radical theories of Harnack, Werner, and Bultmann and certainly rejects Bauer's theory concerning the dominance of Roman episcopal power and its subsequent revision of ecclesiastical history. He also has little time for Newman's theory of the "Development of Christian Doctrine." Instead Turner offers an alternative

---

10. Turner, *Pattern of Christian Truth*, 9–10.
11. Jude 1:3.
12. Turner, *Pattern of Christian Truth*, 14.
13. Ibid., 16.

theory of his own. He argues for the presence of both "fixed" and "flexible" elements of Christian theology. The "fixed" he sees as:

a) *The Religious Facts Themselves.* He notes that Pliny describes Christians as "singings hymns to Christ as God" and that 2 Clement opens with the words, "Brethren, we must think of Christ as of God." He saw that Christians lived "trinitarianly long before the evolution of Nicene orthodoxy." This he finds evidenced in the baptismal formula in the name of the Trinity. Similarly, he sees eucharistic theology implicit in their "realistic experience of the Eucharist" long before such a theology was ever formally put together.

Turner makes use of the phrase *lex orandi* in describing these things but he is careful to make sure that they are not understood in too static a sense. As one of the "fixed" elements, "the religious facts themselves are capable of a variety of expressions."[14]

b) *"The Biblical Revelation."* Turner argues that the use of Old Testament "proof texts" for theological argument even before the Christian canon of Scripture was agreed, however strained and unconvincing the patristic exegesis was, shows a clear determination to "maintain at any cost the Biblical basis of Christian theology."[15]

c) *"The Creeds and the Rule of Faith,"* which, Turner said, could be seen in the ". . . stylized summaries of *credenda* which are of frequent occurrence in the first two Christian centuries to the earliest credal forms themselves."[16]

Turner calls these things "an Agreed Syllabus."[17] Finding support in J. N. D. Kelly's *Early Christian Creeds*, Turner cites Kelly's view that the notion that the Rule of Faith had been inherited from the apostles "contains more than a germ of truth." Not only was the content of that rule, in all essentials, foreshadowed by the "pattern of teaching" accepted in the apostolic church, but its characteristic lineaments and outline found their prototypes in the confessions and credal summaries contained in the New Testament documents.[18]

---

14. Ibid. 28.
15. Ibid., 29.
16. Ibid., 30.
17. Ibid., 475.
18. Kelly, *Early Christian Creed*, 29.

Turner then turns to what he calls the "flexible" elements of the Christian theology, which are really made up of differences of Christian idioms such as eschatological emphasis, different philosophical backgrounds, and the individual characteristics of different theologians. Alongside these Turner allows for variations caused by partial understanding, disagreements, and developing ideas. However, he maintains that there was, as Sykes describes his view,". . . an 'autonomy' of orthodoxy evolving from a common starting point in the biblical tradition, engaged in a running battle with heresies of various kinds, and enjoying to a greater or lesser extent cross-fertilisation from independent theological traditions."[19]

As the *lex orandi* developed from the biblical "facts" into the Rule of Faith, which was a process Turner calls "Catholic thinking," intellectual formulations slowly came into being. Thus the sources of Christian orthodoxy are Scripture, tradition, and reason, though as Sykes notes, these do not operate "independently of each other."[20] These three strands converge on one another, resisting the attempted importation of heresy but exercising ". . . a kind of Christian common sense exercised at all its levels within the Christian Church, which is merely another name for the guidance of the Holy Spirit leading the Church into all truth."[21]

However, before Anglicans begin to preen themselves at the mention of their revered Scripture, tradition, and reason, Sykes is quick to point out that Turner emphasises that ". . . (s)uch guidance is never automatic, and is consistent with the continuing presence of sin, blindness and error. To speak of 'infallibility' would be 'a misuse of categories.'"[22]

However, even Turner, despite his vehement opposition to Bauer, had to admit that in the early years of Christianity orthodoxy resembled ". . . a symphony composed of varied elements rather than a single melodic theme, or a confluence of many tributaries into a single stream rather than a river which pursues its course, to the sea without mingling with other waters."[23]

If that were the case then problems were inevitably going to emerge if the various elements in the symphony could not be kept together, and this was one factor he saw as being behind the eventual and inevitable growth of heresies.

19. Sykes, "'Orthodoxy' and 'Liberalism,'" 89.
20. Ibid., 62.
21. Turner, *Pattern of Christian Truth*, 31–35, 498.
22. Sykes, "'Orthodoxy' and 'Liberalism,'" 83.
23. Turner, *Pattern of Christian Truth*, 9.

Another factor Turner identified was "archaism," the refusal to accept that new ways of expressing God's revelation had to be developed to take account of changing ways of thinking.[24]

Despite this apparent openness to change, it is possible to criticise Turner for neglecting to focus in on the potential and actual dynamism present in the deposit. His own approach is far too simplistic, assuming a quiet sedateness and continuity within the deposit that history itself denies.

Modulation: (A Change of Key): Development as Process

Most certainly McGrath has agreed with Turner in seeing the rise of controversy over doctrine in the church as precipitating ". . . an increasing precision of definition and formulation. . . . Views that were once regarded as acceptable began to fall out of favour as the rigorous process of examination . . . began to expose their vulnerabilities and deficiencies. Ways of expressing certain doctrine that earlier generations regarded as robust began to appear inadequate under relentless examination. It was not necessarily that they were wrong; rather they were discovered to be not good enough."[25]

McGrath gives the example of how such changes are still occurring in the clear shift seen in the acceptance of the notion that God can experience suffering. The early church's view was that God is unable to suffer because that would imply change and God is immutable. The view that the Father suffered in his incarnate Son was known as "patripassianism," and was rejected as a heresy by the early church.

Today, however, the notion that "our God is a suffering God" is widely accepted. The age-old dogma that God is impassible, that is immutable and therefore incapable of suffering, is for many no longer tenable. The ancient heresy that God suffers has, in fact, become the new orthodoxy. Many renowned theologians such as Barth, Bonhoeffer, Brunner, liberation theologians generally, Küng, Moltmann, Reinhold Niebuhr, Pannenberg, Temple, and Teilhard seem to have accepted its validity.[26]

What is so significant about this shift is that it has almost happened without any great theological battles. It has almost crept up upon us silently.

24. Ibid., 132.
25. McGrath, *Heresy*, 24.
26. Ibid., 25.

Movement One: The Church in Conflict (Allegro)

Ronald Goetz sees that the ramifications of this theological change are highly significant. He sees it having an influence on almost every major Christian doctrine, such as the Trinity, the two natures of Christ, creation *ex nihilo*, and theories of the atonement. All these doctrines were originally formulated by theologians who took divine impassibility to be self-evident. Reformation Protestantism inherited the presupposition of God's impassible sovereignty.[27]

Martin Luther himself was certainly ambivalent on this issue. In his theology of the cross he affirmed the suffering of God in the death of Jesus Christ. However, in other works he seemed to backtrack on that issue as he promulgates his equally foundational doctrines of predestination and the *Deus absconditus*. When describing this concept of a God who is hidden, Luther's portrait of such a God is of "an inscrutably impassible, divine sovereignty. His views could be more severe than Calvin's."[28]

Despite the rejection or reinterpretation of much of the orthodox tradition by eighteenth- and nineteenth-century liberalism, it also kept, with a few exceptions, to the basic teaching of divine impassibility. Yet now that axiom has been discarded by many.[29]

Lest it should be thought that patripassianism was an exceptional case in terms of doctrinal development of this nature, it is also salutary to note other changes to orthodox thinking.

A second example of the way in which the church has had to change its orthodoxy under pressure is clearly seen in its reluctant acceptance of the scientific evidence of the Copernican revolution and the persecution of Galileo and his subsequent rehabilitation. This showed the power of scientific evidence to force the church to ditch the dogmas that had been held as sacred for centuries. In 1616 the propositions of Copernicus that the sun is immobile and at the centre of the universe and that the earth moves around it were judged both to be "foolish and absurd in philosophy," and the first to be "formally heretical" and the second "at least erroneous in faith" in theology. After the publication of his book, *Dialogue Concerning the Two Chief World Systems*,[30] in which he supported and proved the work of Copernicus, Galileo was called to Rome in 1633 to face the Inquisition and was accused of heresy. Under threat of torture, Galileo recanted but as he left the courtroom, he is said to have muttered, "all the same, it moves."

27. Goetz, *Suffering God*.
28. Pelikan and Lehmann, *Luther's Works*, 31:25–33.
29. Goetz, *Suffering God*, 385.
30. Galilei, *Galileo on the World Systems*.

He was sent to his home near Florence where he was to be under house arrest for the remainder of his life. In 1992, at a ceremony in Rome, before the Pontifical Academy of Sciences, Pope John Paul II officially declared that Galileo was right. The Scriptures remain but the church now has to understand them and proclaim them in a completely different way.

Another example of changes in orthodox thinking could be the way in which the church has passed through a number of seasons when different views concerning the crucial theory of the atonement have been paramount. For the first Christian millennium the dominant view of the atonement was what is now called the *ransom theory*. Especially favoured by the Eastern church around the time of Origen, it became the dominant doctrine of the atonement in the whole church after Nicaea. Supported by numerous biblical texts,[31] it was championed by Irenaeus, who saw Jesus as the one who had ransomed the redeemed by the shedding of his blood. The crucial question was, however, to whom was the ransom paid? Irenaeus believed it was paid to God while Origen saw the redemption price as being paid to Satan. In the Western church, leaders such as Augustine and Ambrose recognised the term ransom more as a metaphor for the action of Jesus in freeing his people from the bondage of the world, the flesh, and Satan. This notion of freedom in Christ is also supported by scriptural writers such as John, Peter, and Paul.[32] This theory was, in embryo, what we shall see later becomes the *Christus Victor* theory.

Anselm of Canterbury brought about a change in the eleventh century when he set forth in his book *Cur Deus Homo?* what became known as the *satisfaction theory*. In Anselm's view, Jesus, rather than paying some ransom to God or to Satan, through his death on the cross, satisfied the outstanding debt of honour that sinful men owed to God.

"This is the debt which man and angel owe to God, and no one who pays this debt commits sin; but everyone who does not pay it sins. This is justice, or uprightness of will, which makes a being just or upright in heart, that is, in will; and this is the sole and complete debt of honour which we owe to God, and which God requires of us."[33]

Man's sin had, for Anselm, created a sort of moral imbalance in creation, which a moral and righteous God could not disregard. Anselm believed, however, that the satisfaction due to God was greater than anything the totality of all created beings could ever offer, since they can only

---

31. Cf. Matt 20:28; Mark 10:45; 1 Tim 2:6; Rev 5:9.
32. Cf. John 8:32–37; Rom 8:21; Gal 3:1.
33. Anselm, *Cur Deus Homo*, 38.

do what is already required of them. It was necessary, therefore, for God to make satisfaction for himself. The problem was that, to be efficacious for the salvation of human beings, this satisfaction had to be made by a human being. Therefore only a being that was both God and man could satisfy God and give him the honour that is due to him.

This, for Anselm, meant that incarnation and atonement were inextricably linked. This was, therefore, the answer to the question raised in the title of his book *Cur deus Homo?*—"Why God Became a Man?"

Although he has been often cited as the creator of what later became known as the *penal substitutionary theory* of the atonement, Anselm himself did not major on punishment for sin but simply on the matter of God's offended honour. Protestant reformers, however, epitomised by John Calvin, reshaped and built upon Anselm's work, most especially in the context of the Roman civil law tradition. In so doing the focus was shifted from the divine offence to divine justice. This is an important difference. For Anselm, Christ obeyed where we should have obeyed; for John Calvin, he was punished where we should have been punished.

Calvin believed that God's righteousness demands that human sin be punished. The debt or price to be paid was death itself, for that was the punishment required for sin. God in his love both exacts the punishment and graciously provides the one to bear it. This particular theory of satisfaction was taken on board by both Catholics and Protestants while the Eastern Orthodox churches tended to hold on to the earlier ransom theories.

In his book *Christus Victor*, in which all these theories are examined, Gustav Aulén proposed the revival of what he deems to be the original theory of Christus Victor in the Western church. The idea was simple. The ransom was paid for the liberation from sin. Jesus' death, burial, and resurrection were not meant to buy off God or Satan but to show his victory over death, hell, and sin. In essence, Aulén proposed that *Christus Victor* could embody both ransom and satisfaction. Jesus is Saviour because he became human and defeated humanity's enemies. "The work of Christ is first and foremost a victory over the powers which hold mankind in bondage: sin, death, and the devil."[34] For Aulen the truth is that this theory of *Christus Victor* had never really disappeared from the church. It had simply been in a sort of exile in the Eastern church. Mark Galli, writing in *Christianity Today*, describes the way in which this theory is quickly overtaking the penal substitutionary theory in many of the staunchly

---

34. Aulén, *Christus Victor*, 20.

evangelical churches in America in a remarkable way.[35] This is all the more remarkable when we consider the fact that most of these churches have had the penal substitutionary theory written into their statements of faith since their creation.

In more recent days there has been another dramatic shift in atonement thinking with the rise of what is known as *reconciliation theology*. Our own world history has seen within the last century the horrors of concentration camps, the Holocaust, and the killing fields of Cambodia, suicide bombings, apartheid, and ethnic cleansings. Theologians are asking the question: What does the cross of Christ have to say to a world as unredeemed as this? A theologian such as Miroslav Volf, in his seminal work *Exclusion and Embrace*, encourages us to think beyond the totally selfish, though understandable, notion of our own individual salvation towards the salvation of the whole unredeemed world of which we are a part. In doing so we are challenged to include within the boundless borders of God's love revealed in the cross of Christ not only our own personal sense of suffering because of the power of sin in our lives but also all the victims of human sin and violence. It goes even further by taking seriously the commands of Christ obedience to which, he says, will enable us to reflect something of the perfection of the God we claim to serve.

> But I tell you: Love your enemies and pray for those who persecute you, that you may be sons of your Father in heaven. He causes his sun to rise on the evil and the good, and sends rain on the righteous and the unrighteous. If you love those who love you, what reward will you get? Are not even the tax collectors doing that? And if you greet only your brothers, what are you doing more than others? Do not even pagans do that? Be perfect, therefore, as your heavenly Father is perfect. (Matthew 5:44–48)

This means that included within the bounds of God's love are not only the victims of human sin but also the perpetrators of it. Indeed, implicit in the words of the Lord's Prayer is the sense that our own forgiveness is inextricably linked together with our own willingness and ability to forgive those who have sinned against us. "Forgive us our sins, for we also forgive everyone who sins against us." (Luke 11:4)

Volf puts it so eloquently:

> Forgiveness flounders because I exclude the enemy from the community of humans even as I exclude myself from the

35. Galli, "Problem with Christus Victor."

community of sinners. But no one can be in the presence of the God of the crucified Messiah for long without overcoming this double exclusion—without transposing the enemy from the sphere of monstrous inhumanity into the sphere of shared humanity and herself from the sphere of proud innocence into the sphere of common sinfulness. When one knows that the torturer will not eternally triumph over the victim, one is free to rediscover that person's humanity and imitate God's love for him. And when one knows that God's love is greater than all sin, one is free to see oneself in the light of God's justice and so rediscover one's own sinfulness.[36]

In light of this, it becomes incumbent on Christians to recognise that atonement means, not only that we are reconciled to God, and not only that we work at the requirement to learn to live with one another, but the far more risky and challenging step of opening ourselves to those who have traditionally always been "the enemy" and enfolding them in the same embrace with which we have been embraced by God. This view of atonement has had, and continues to have, a dramatic influence on all those Christians who are deeply involved in matters of social justice and reconciliation nationally and internationally.

Interestingly, this contemporary reshaping of atonement theology has theologians such as Ulrike Link-Wieczorek at Oldenburg suggesting that Anselm, in his original form, implies a ". . . practice of reconciliation beyond . . . theory" and sees the framework of atonement found there as the "preservation and fulfilment of a threatened creation which is suffering from the absence of reconciliation."[37]

God could be depicted as the creation's counsel and vindicator. Representative restitution through Christ could be understood as the reinstallation of those who are being victimised in the midst the sinfulness of humankind through injustice, senseless violence, or ignorance.[38]

Whether or not one can fully accept this as a view Anselm would recognise in his own teaching is open to question, nevertheless such a view has, of course, very challenging things to say to those involved in the mutually damaging internecine conflicts now raging within the Anglican Communion and that form the backdrop to this book. Indeed, there would be ample scope here for further study on the implications of reconciliation theology for relationships within the Anglican Communion. It also is a

36. Volf, *Exclusion and Embrace*, 124.
37. Link-Wieczorek, *Divine Reconciliation*, 235–36.
38. Ibid., 236.

good example of the way in which traditional orthodox teaching is being challenged and, at least for some people, being changed.

Another major orthodox dogma to go through a time of change, or better, to be going through a time of change, is that of hell and eternal punishment. Christians through the centuries have always believed (formally at least) that those who do not repent and put their faith in Christ and accept God's offer of salvation will suffer conscious, everlasting torment. The coming judgement with its implied punishments as well as rewards is a credal statement. Denial of this teaching has, until recently, been limited almost exclusively to cultic or quasi-cultic groups. Today, however, unorthodox views concerning these things are no longer limited to the fringe. Even renowned conservatives such as the late John Stott, acknowledged leader of the conservative evangelical Anglicans in the United Kingdom and around the world, espoused the notion of annihilation rather than eternal torment quite clearly.

> I also believe that the ultimate annihilation of the wicked should at least be accepted as a legitimate, biblically founded alternative to their eternal conscious torment. . . . So both the language of destruction and the imagery of fire seem to point to annihilation. . . . It would be easier to hold together the awful reality of hell and the universal reign of God if hell means destruction and the impenitent are no more. . . . I have never been able to conjure up (as some great Evangelical missionaries have) the appalling vision of the millions who are not only perishing but will inevitably perish. On the other hand, I am not and cannot be a universalist. Between these extremes I cherish the hope that the majority of the human race will be saved. And I have a solid biblical basis for this belief.[39]

Clark Pinnock, John Wenham, Philip Hughes, and Stephen Travis have all espoused the annihilationist cause within evangelicalism.[40]

It has been this search for a more loving, gentler theology that has, in the past, been the target for evangelicals to fire at within the liberal camp for being woolly and compromising. Now, it seems the two wings of the church are becoming more united on this issue. The latest manifestation of this movement away from traditional orthodoxy has been in the publication of *Love Wins* by Rob Bell, a leading American evangelical pastor.

39. Edwards and Stott, *Evangelical Essentials*, 318–27.

40. See Pinnock, "Destruction of the Finally Impenitent," 40–41; Wenham, *Goodness of God*, 27–41; Hughes, *True Image*, 398ff.; and Travis, *I Believe in the Second Coming*, 196–99.

Movement One: The Church in Conflict (Allegro)

The doctrine of endless punishment for the wicked has been taught by the church for centuries. This, however, in itself does not guarantee its correctness. Again, a new way of interpreting the Scriptures appears to be becoming accepted slowly but surely among great numbers of Christian believers. Bell, interestingly, is also inclined towards the *Christus Victor* theory of the atonement.

These historical and contemporary changes to orthodox belief show clearly the living reality of the process of ongoing development of orthodoxy that is continually at work in the church. This is something that those who maintain a more rigid and unyielding orthodoxy and claim to be the champions of true orthodoxy need to take note of. This sense of continuing movement leads directly on to the next section.

Transformation: Orthodoxy as Unfinished Business

McGrath would prefer not to use the concepts of "winners and losers" in a theological battle. He prefers to understand it "as a quest for authenticity . . . in which all options were examined and assessed."

This was, of course, both natural and necessary. It was not possible for Christianity to remain frozen in its first-century forms as it entered the second century and beyond. It was to face new intellectual challenges that would demand that it showed itself capable of engaging with both religious and intellectual alternatives to Christianity.

It could no longer be assumed that "the antiquity of a theological view was a reliable guide to its orthodoxy" as Tertullian had argued. McGrath is adamant that "mistakes were made, right from the beginning that later generations had to correct."

Indeed, it will always be true that theology, as a human attempt to understand and codify the "mysteries" of God will always prove inadequate to do justice to the realities that lie at the heart of the Christian faith. [41]

Even if appeal is made to the judgements of the fathers, such ancient authorities cannot be seen to be untouchable. Their views, revered as they are, may need to be constantly revised in the light of contemporary biblical interpretation.

This constant revision is music to postmodern ears, for whom any notion of closure is anathema. Postmodernism does not like the notion of closure. Any sense of orthodoxy can only ever be provisional. McGrath agrees with the postmodern writer Hilary Lawson, who says, "Closure can

---

41. McGrath, *Heresy*, 24–29.

be understood as the imposition of fixity upon openness." For her and McGrath theology is always to be seen as journey. We do not arrive at a destination in our intellectual voyaging but only at a "temporary resting point."[42]

McGrath agrees with her notion of a continuing journey and states clearly that "Christian orthodoxy is as much an on-going process as a fixed set of outcomes. . . . Orthodoxy is thus, in a certain sense *unfinished* in that it represents the mind of the church as to the best manner of formulation of its living faith at any given time."[43]

Nevertheless, his conservativism is evident in his clear belief that traditional orthodoxy will stand the test of constant investigation. Such remarks as these from a recognised evangelical scholar have certainly caused some conservatives to shudder.

The Recapitulation

In this section the main themes of this movement are reworked and sometimes modified.

Principal Subject Reworked: Neo-Conservative Resurgence

More recently a study by Köstenberger and Kruger, *The Heresy of Orthodoxy*, written from a clearly evangelical and conservative standpoint, has caught the rapt attention of conservatives everywhere. It is seen by them as the antidote, at last, to what they see as the "poison" of Bauer and those who have consequently accepted his book in one way or another and been responsible for what Köstenberger and Kruger call "the prevailing paradigm."[44]

Bart D. Erhman has been the most influential of these recent popularisers of Bauer, seeing it as "the most important book on the history of early Christianity to appear in the twentieth century." Linked inextricably with Bauer, Erhman's book is consequently given by Köstenberger and Kruger the epithet "The Bauer-Erhman Book."[45]

---

42. Lawson, *Closure*, 4, 527.
43. McGrath, *Heresy*, 221.
44. Köstenberger and Kruger, *Heresy of Orthodoxy*, 23.
45. Ibid., 31.

Their work is, no doubt, very thorough and very detailed but is, for the most part, a restating and updating of the original arguments against Bauer raised by Turner that we have just examined, together with the comments of a great number of older and more contemporary scholars, mostly from the evangelical and conservative wing of the church, who basically elaborate on Turner's arguments.

Bridge Passage Reworked: Postmodernism and "Proto-Orthodoxy"

McGrath argues, however, that it has been postmodernism that has done most to turn the traditional view on its head by seeing heretical ideas as the "suppressed versions of Christianity more attuned to contemporary culture as traditional orthodoxy." Heresy now needs rehabilitating in order to correct the corrupting influence of power that allowed the historical "winners" of the theological battles that raged in the early church to suppress and silence any rival theologies. Orthodoxy is given bad press today, being seen as "pedestrian and reactionary" in contrast to heresy's radicalism and innovative essence.[46]

For many, heresy is now seen as a theological victim, a set of noble ideas that have been brutally crushed and improperly suppressed by dominant orthodoxies and then presented as if they were devious, dishonest, or diabolical.

The blame for this topsy-turvy approach to orthodoxy McGrath clearly lays at the door of the postmodern emphasis on "choice as a defining characteristic of authentic human existence." Etymologically, the Greek word for heresy has strong associations with notions of choosing or choice. However, he is equally adamant that ". . . the ultimate appeal of heresy in our times lies in its challenge to authority. Religious orthodoxy is equated with claims to absolute authority, which are to be resisted and subverted in the name of freedom. (Never mind that many heresies were just as authoritative as their orthodox rivals)."[47]

For McGrath the postmodern support of this view of heresy can be compared with that of Karl Marx, for whom ideological heresy was simply the ideology of the defeated or oppressed class. What was pronounced as

---

46. McGrath, *Heresy*, 1–2.
47. Ibid., 7–8.

orthodoxy was simply the ideology of the ruling class. "Today sympathy is with the 'oppressed' and, therefore, with the heretic."[48]

The problem with that view, according to McGrath, is that the central issue has changed. The concern is no longer with what is right or wrong, or true or untrue, but who has the power to compel others to give assent to their particular way of seeing things. If that is the case, ". . . today's orthodoxy can thus easily transmute into tomorrow's heresy. All that is required is a radical change in the social relationship of the parties involved."[49]

McGrath gives an example of this when, in AD 337, Emperor Constantius turned his back on the theology of Nicaea and became a supporter of Arianism and so, in reality, that form of Christianity became the "orthodoxy" of the day. It was not until AD 381, at the Council of Constantinople, that the situation was reversed.

Similarly, the papacy in the Middle Ages used heresy as a legal or juridical tool to put down any movement that appeared to challenge the authority of the pope. It was this issue of papal authority that mattered more than any of the theological ideas that these reforming movements espoused. [50]

McGrath's view is that the formation of what is called "orthodoxy" cannot be seen just as a determined defence of long held traditional theological views but rather a process of adventure, discovery, and elaboration. In other words there has clearly been a process of development.

He is attracted to the view of Larry Hurtado,[51] who speaks of the possibility of there being a "proto-orthodoxy." By this he means that certain beliefs and practices, stage by stage and over time, were widely affirmed in Christian circles over against other views and became the root of what is now generally seen as "classical" Christian orthodoxy.

McGrath makes a clear distinction between *faith*, which he sees as a *relational* concept, and *belief*, which he sees as generally understood *cognitively* or *conceptually*.

"Faith primarily describes a relationship with God that is characterised by trust, commitment and love. . . . Beliefs represent an attempt to put into words the substance of that faith, recognising that words are often not

---

48. Ibid., 199.
49. Ibid., 200.
50. Ibid., 208.
51. Hurtado, *Lord Jesus Christ*, 494.

up to the task of representing what they describe . . . credal formulations are, in a sense, secondary to the primary act of trust and commitment."[52]

While these attempts were in process McGrath agrees that, even by the middle of the second century, most Christians appear to have been content to live with a certain degree of theological fuzziness as doctrine was developed.

What is even more interesting is that the views of a scholar so renowned on both sides of the Atlantic finds no place in Köstenberger and Kruger's book, although it was published a year before theirs.

Second Subject Reworked: Further New Testament Study

Despite that criticism, Köstenberger and Kruger do make a strong point when they argue that Bauer ignored the vital evidence from the New Testament, which he described as "both too unproductive and too much disputed to be able to serve as a point of departure."[53] It may indeed be true that "Bauer's wholesale dismissal of the primary source of our knowledge of earliest Christianity—The New Testament—is problematic . . . because it unduly eliminates from consideration the central figure in all of Christianity, Jesus, as well as the apostles he appointed."[54]

That missing evidence has, however, been fully examined by those who followed Bauer and accepted the general basis of his book. Rudolf Bultmann was greatly influenced by Bauer and praised his work highly in his *Theology of the New Testament*, which certainly did not ignore the New Testament.[55]

Also Ernst Käsemann continues the research into the text of the New Testament and fully supports Bauer's book. "The New Testament canon

52. McGrath, *Heresy*, 22.
53. Bauer, *Orthodoxy and Heresy*, xxv.
54. Köstenberger and Kruger, *Heresy of Orthodoxy*, 69.
55. Bultmann, *Theology of the New Testament*, 2:135. "The diversity of theological interests and ideas at first is great. A norm or an authoritative court of appeal for doctrine is still lacking and the proponents of directions of thought which were later rejected as heretical consider themselves completely Christian—such as Christian Gnosticism. In the beginning faith is the term which distinguishes the Christian Congregation from the Jews and the heathen, not orthodoxy (right doctrine).

W. Bauer has shown that that doctrine which in the end won out in the ancient Church as the 'right' or 'orthodox' doctrine stands at the end of a development or, rather, is the result of a conflict among various shades of doctrine, and the heresy was not, as the ecclesiastical tradition holds, an apostasy, a degeneration, but was already present at the beginning" (ibid., 137).

does not, as such, constitute the foundation of the unity of the Church. On the contrary, as such . . . it provides the basis for a multiplicity of confessions."[56]

Ephraim Radner, in his essay "Apprehending the Truth," claims that "The recent search for uniting essentials or fundamentals or 'core doctrine' testifies to the actual *lack* of community and authority by which meaningful orthodoxy might be articulated."

He claims that what he calls ". . . the thoughts of the 'primitive' or 'undivided church' . . . 'may or may not have had a lived integrity'. . . . What characterises them all, however, is that in each case such integrity is in each case *historical* . . . nothing more than a 'propositional community of the past'—and imaginary community of the present that acts as a touchstone for something not yet established."[57]

David Butler, working from an ecumenical perspective, certainly takes the same view, cataloguing all the evidences of disagreement and theological shades of opinion seen in the Acts of the Apostles and in the four Gospels. "The New Testament is regarded by many as the bastion of orthodoxy yet it contains competing theologies and enormous diversities,e.g. interpretation of Jesus, the structures of ministry of the church, ways of worship and even moral teaching."[58]

While Bauer had focussed on the expansion of the church, Eduard Schweizer also saw the need to get back to the text of the New Testament to look particularly at Jesus' conception of the church and also the diversity there even within the community of the primitive church in Jerusalem. His picture of Jesus is of one who tears down all barriers by including in his circle "tax collectors, lepers, prostitutes, the pious and the sinful, a Roman centurion and a Canaanite woman."

Schweizer, commenting on Mark 9:38–40, remarks that Jesus "would not allow the circle to be closed," and that the church must be protected from the heretical belief that adherence to a religious community, a cult, an orthodox creed, or a certain way of living is in itself enough for salvation, without the need for everyone to have that new and decisive meeting with the living God, who calls us in the words and works of Jesus.[59]

McGrath tends to blame postmodernism for this questioning of the New Testament texts. He claims that suspicion of authority has been

---

56. Käsemann, "Canon of the New Testament," 103–4.
57. Radner and Turner, *The Fate of Communion*, 64.
58. Butler, *Dying to Be One*, 4.
59. Schweizer, *Church Order in the New Testament*, 25–26.

Movement One: The Church in Conflict (Allegro)

transferred to the New Testament documents themselves, which are now seen as "official press releases from some official source, designed to conceal the truth about the origins of Christianity."[60] I feel that McGrath is overemphasising this point as, in fact, this questioning process had been *en train* centuries before the postmodern paradigm came to the fore.

Robert Morgan, in his essay "St. John's Gospel, the Incarnation and Christian Orthodoxy," takes a very different approach. He begins by agreeing with Käsemann that the New Testament is full of theological diversity,[61] and Bultmann, when he declares that "there can be no normative Christian dogmatics."[62] He therefore accepts John Hick's consequential view that if Christianity is defined as "an unchanging set of beliefs" then it has never really existed.[63]

That is not to say that he supports the general tenor of *The Myth of God Incarnate*, in fact his view is quite to the contrary. While accepting that "what counts as substantial continuity is disputed, and orthodoxy or authentic Christianity (is) therefore a contested concept," he contends that "rightly understood the *doctrine of the incarnation* provides an adequate criterion for orthodoxy."[64]

Morgan first distinguishes between what he sees as three different ways of dealing with the *mystery* of the incarnation. These are ". . . in *myth* (a narrative about God or gods); in *theology* which varies from time and place; and in *doctrine* which is more stable. Theology's disciplined reflection on Christian faith is fluid as it relates this to different believers' knowledge and experience; and *doctrine*, summarizing the church's teaching, is the sediment of many generations' life and thought."[65]

Of course, Morgan recognises that these distinctions cannot be pressed too firmly because ". . . many learn doctrine through myth and because doctrine both presupposes and requires theological activity." However, he claims that the doctrine of the incarnation is different from any other doctrine. Although it can be interpreted in unorthodox ways, ". . . when it is rightly understood, i.e. dogmatically clarified as saying that

---

60. McGrath, *Heresy*, 9.
61. Käsemann, *Unity and Multiplicity*.
62. Bultmann, *Theology of the New Testament*, 2:237.
63. Hick, *Myth of God Incarnate*, ix.
64. Morgan, "St. John's Gospel," 146–47.
65. Ibid., 147.

Jesus is truly God, truly human, it provides a material criterion of orthodoxy, excluding Ebionism and Docetism."[66]

Morgan justifies his emphasis on John's Gospel by claiming that John makes explicit what the other New Testament writers imply or presuppose: "that in knowing and relating to the crucified and risen Jesus through the Spirit we know and are in relationship with God."[67]

He argues this doctrine of the incarnation is the only one that fits the standard set by the fifth century Vincentian Canon, "What has always been believed everywhere, and by all." No theology can do that because of the wide range of theological diversity that has always existed.

Doctrines make metaphysical truth claims only when fleshed out in some theology. As the bare bones of Christian belief they indicate its general shape or form, and only enough content to exclude notorious deviations.

> Only where the identity of Christianity is at stake, as it is in one's assessment of Jesus as the saving revelation of God, are the boundaries drawn more tightly, by dogmatic definitions that which exclude some Christologies and clarify the shape of Christian belief in God, and even here the parameters are generous. Christian doctrine remains more amorphous in the areas of anthropology, soteriology, ecclesiology, and so on, but 'Brethren, we must think of Jesus Christ as of God . . . (2 Clement 1:1)[68]

After an excursus through the Gospel of John emphasising verses such as

> Then they asked him, "Where is your father?"
> "You do not know me or my Father," Jesus replied. "If you knew me, you would know my Father also." (John 8:19)

and

> Jesus answered: "Don't you know me, Philip, even after I have been among you such a long time? Anyone who has seen me has seen the Father. How can you say, 'Show us the Father'?" (John 14:9)

---

66. Ibid., 147.
67. Ibid., 148.
68. Ibid., 149.

Morgan concludes that the main emphasis in John is not the teaching of Jesus or the miracles (signs) or even the historical narrative of the gospel. Rather it is simply, but profoundly, to declare that Jesus is the revelation of God. "When people encounter Jesus they encounter God," and that in itself is a declaration of the doctrine of the incarnation.[69]

Morgan tells us that such a ". . . criterion of orthodoxy is only a rule of thumb . . . proved necessary to insist that this Jesus really was a human being and that it really is God whom we encounter in him."[70]

He sees such a doctrine as sending us back to the narratives with a means of reading them and leading us "to appropriate them imaginatively." From this will flow our various theologies, patterns of faith and worship, which, Morgan says, "some call orthodoxy." Though all these theologies and subsequent doctrines may vary, it is Morgan's contention that "The doctrine of the incarnation gives Christian soldiers a compass, pointing them onward and away from back-sliding into Christologies inadequate to their heart's relationship with their King."[71]

He believes that if we can agree on this one doctrine "along a spectrum of healthily different theologies" then Christians can claim a significant unity in orthodoxy.

Professor Daniel Hardy critiques Morgan in his own essay, "A Magnificent Complexity." He seems to find Morgan's work limiting in that it does not allow that "the existence of canon and lectionaries, ecclesial polities, ecumenical councils and liturgical norms" also have their own internal criteria for limiting the range of acceptable diversity. "Doctrine is not the only, or even the primary, means of controlling diversity." Whereas Morgan found the doctrine of the incarnation "provides a *material* criterion of orthodoxy,"[72] Hardy sees that the doctrine as providing only "a *minimal standard* of orthodoxy and in that sense it is very useful."[73] I cannot help but feel myself in agreement with Hardy and sense that his final positive comment is merely politeness towards a contributor to a Festschrift compiled to celebrate Hardy's sixty-fifth birthday. It seems to fit well the description of how to "damn with faint praise"!

For Sykes, one of the roots of the problem defining orthodoxy lies in the imprecision in general usage of both terms 'orthodoxy' and

69. Ibid., 152.
70. Ibid., 159.
71. Ibid., 159.
72. Ibid., 147.
73. Hardy, "Magnificent Complexity," 332–34.

"liberalism." They are frequently used in a polarising sense to denote mutually exclusive and antagonistic theological styles and commitments.

Os Guiness makes the observation that

> To defend conservatism well, they [Modern conservatives] must do it in a progressive way; to fight for tradition, they must use weapons that are modern. Like democrats condemned to become illiberal in the process of defending pluralism or humanitarians who become inhuman in defence of humanity, modern conservatives are caught in a double bind. . . . They will resist change to the death, but in the struggle for tradition not a single feature of their familiar world will be left unchanged.[74]

Sykes argues that such an attitude leads to a sharpening of the boundaries between themselves and those they oppose. This is made worse by the constant demand for simplistic analysis from those in the media. There is also the desire for publicity by those who would otherwise have a much more considered and differentiated analysis and who see that in order for them to be heard in the public arena such simplification and the subsequent caricaturing that occurs are the necessary price to pay.

Sykes compares the way these terms are used to the common use of the terms "Catholic" and "Protestant," where they are clearly seen as antithetical although no Protestant would accept the view that being a Protestant means they are not a member of the "catholic" church. Thus "orthodoxy" and "liberalism" are not "self-evidently antithetical." If antithetical terms are to be used then, Sykes argues, the two terms should be "orthodoxy" and "heresy." Liberalism is not, of necessity, heretical.[75]

Sykes examines the concept of "liberalism" itself. He sees its etymological root in the word "free." He makes the point that not all freedoms have to be simply freedom *from* something. Important and long developed themes in Christian theology draw equal attention to the existence of freedom *for*. In this sense "liberalism" can mean exercising a freedom from constraint.

It was first used in a negative way by Newman in his *Apologia pro Vita Sua*, where he saw it as representing the anti-dogmatic principle and its development.[76] It was, for Newman, an umbrella term for many views antagonistic to the Christian faith. Sykes describes it as marking ". . . a

---

74. Os Guiness, *The Gravedigger File*, 184 (cited in Sykes, "Orthodoxy and Liberalism" 77).

75. Sykes, "'Orthodoxy' and Liberalism,'" 77–78.

76. Newman, *Apologia pro Vita Sua*, 54.

Movement One: The Church in Conflict (Allegro)

boundary between true and false liberty of thought but it tells us nothing about where that boundary lies. It does not help us, for example, in determining how the exercise of thought may be conducted in a way consistent with revelation, which is, after all, the whole point of Christian theology. We are simply told, prescriptively, that there cannot be such a thing as liberal Christian thinking."[77]

Sykes reminds us that Newman himself was certainly not against development and change. In fact it was his "doctrine of development" that led to his secession from Anglicanism to Roman Catholicism. What is certainly true from history is that Christianity has helped the evolution of liberal thought in the secular world by emphasising the doctrine of the sacredness of the individual while, conversely and at the same time, being seen as against or, at least, anti-pathetic to worldly success and riches, which is the ultimate reward of those who individually progress.[78]

On the other hand, Christianity has always stressed the value of membership of the group or community and the allegiance required and the fulfilment of the responsibilities that follow. This is evidenced in Paul's doctrine of membership of the body of Christ: thus orthodox Christianity can be seen as having been active in the formation of both orthodox and liberal concepts within the church. It is therefore, Sykes argues, impossible for a Christian to be either totally opposed to or totally for liberalism. Rather honesty and integrity need to be applied, for example in the case of biblical criticism. As he puts it, "One cannot either embrace or reject new theories of authorship, date or historical veracity on principle. There is no alternative but to consider them one by one, and weigh the evidence upon which the various proposals rest. There is no possibility of simply resorting to theories or answers maintained in earlier generations or centuries."[79]

Raymond Brown, from his Roman Catholic perspective, agrees. "The future lies not with the rejection of the historical-critical method (which I regard as a permanent contribution to knowledge), but in a refinement of the method, so that it will answer appropriately posed questions even more accurately, and its contributions to the larger picture of biblical interpretation can be seen in better perspective."[80]

So is it now possible to define heresy with clarity? It is probably easier to define heresy than it is to define orthodoxy, which, as we have already

---

77. Sykes, "'Orthodoxy' and Liberalism," 85.
78. Ibid., 86.
79. Ibid., 87.
80. Brown, *Biblical Exegesis and Church Doctrine*, 25.

seen, has a history of being something that is rather shifting in shape and form and difficult to grasp as a whole.

McGrath says that heresy ". . . is best seen as a form of Christian belief that, more by accident than design, ultimately ends up subverting, destabilising, or even destroying the core of Christian faith."[81]

He affirms his appreciation of Charles Gore's views in his 1891 Bampton Lectures on "The Incarnation of the Son of God." Gore argues that the purpose of doctrine is to protect the central mysteries "in a new form for protective purposes, as a legal enactment protects a moral principle."[82]

He is clear that the doctrines themselves are not necessarily part of the divine revelation. They find their value and validation in so far as they are grounded themselves in that revelation and act as a safeguard for it and aid understanding of it.

In the light of that definition of doctrine, it follows that "a heresy is a doctrine that ultimately destroys, destabilizes or distorts a mystery rather than preserving it." In fact, McGrath, who at every turn tries hard not to demonise heretics, sees a heresy as an often genuine doctrinal attempt to actually defend and preserve some basic Christian truth. Initially such doctrines were thought to have accomplished that but, with the passage of time and greater understanding, these doctrines were seen to "weaken and corrupt."[83]

Heresy is not unbelief but rather ". . . a vulnerable and fragile form of Christianity that proves incapable of sustaining itself in the long term." Neither is heresy essentially ethically deviant. Many orthodox believers were guilty of moral ambivalence and failure. Heresy comes from *within* not from *without*. They share a common *doxa*—the taken-for-granted assumptions of an age or community. From an orthodox perspective the divergence creates incoherence and instability within the *doxa* as a whole.[84]

McGrath takes a special interest in Schleiermacher and his model of heresy. For Schleiermacher heresy is anything that contradicts the essential identity of Christianity. Such a contradiction could even retain the formal outward appearance of Christianity. Nevertheless, it is a deficient form of belief that preserves the *appearance* of Christianity while contradicting its *essence*.

---

81. McGrath, *Heresy*, 11.
82. Gore, *Incarnation of the Son of God*, 105–6.
83. McGrath, *Heresy*, 30–31.
84. Ibid., 82–83.

Movement One: The Church in Conflict (Allegro)

Echoing what McGrath has already said, Schleiermacher places Jesus of Nazareth at the centre of things. "Christianity is a monotheistic faith, belonging to the teleological type of religion, and is essentially distinguished from other such faiths by the fact that in it everything is related to the redemption accomplished by Jesus of Nazareth."[85]

Anything that denies the centrality of this redemption through Jesus Christ actually denies that which is the most fundamental truth that Christianity dares to proclaim and can thus only be considered as unbelief. Similarly, if the central and fundamental place Christianity gives to Jesus Christ is verbally stated but interpreted in such a way that it is implicitly denied or made of no effect, the outcome is heresy.

Schleiermacher maintains that it is possible to retain the fundamental formulas of orthodoxy, ". . . but *either* human nature will be so defined that a redemption in the strict case cannot be accomplished, *or* the redeemer will be defined in such a way that he cannot accomplish redemption."[86]

McGrath sees this as a reflection of Richard Hooker (1554–1600). "There are but four things which concur to make complete the whole state of our Lord Jesus Christ: his deity, his manhood, the conjunction of both, and the distinction of the one from the other being joined into one."[87]

Hooker says that anything that distorts these core teachings is to be rejected, e.g., Arianism by denying the divinity of Christ; Apollinarianism by "maiming and misinterpreting" his humanity; Nestorianism by "rending Christ asunder" and dividing him into two persons; and Eutychianism by "confounding what they should distinguish."

McGrath has three major criticisms of Schleiermacher's theory of heresy. Firstly, it restricts heresy to matters pertaining to person and work of Jesus Christ. This fails to deal with heresies that concerned doctrines such as the Trinity, for example Sabellianism, or those that concerned ecclesiology such as Donatism. Next, McGrath accuses him of failing to deal with the social and historical dimensions of heresy and treating it merely as an intellectual phenomenon. Thirdly, he sees a major weakness in seeking to identify heresy by its intellectual incoherence. In the case of Arianism, for example, the argument was certainly coherent and, anyway, who judges when something is incoherent?

Schleiermacher appears to believe that that heresy will, in fact, be obvious to all for what it is. McGrath, however, sees that for a movement or

---

85. Schleiermacher, *Christian Faith*, 52.
86. Ibid., 98.
87. Hooker, *Laws of Ecclesiastical Polity*, 5:54.10.

system of thought to truly be heretical it has to be judged and condemned by the church as being heretical and in contradiction to what the church has already has defined, or will go on to define, as orthodox doctrine.[88]

Closing Section: The Journey Continues

Returning to Köstenberger and Kruger's book, the most disturbing thing about it, to my mind, is that, despite their attempts to be scholarly, in the end they resort to what I can only call a faith motif. In other words, it is only possible to fully appreciate their point of view if you are able to appreciate their faith perspective about revelation. For example, writing about Paul's notion of his apostolic authority, they state that he

> ... derived his authority directly from his commissioning by the risen Jesus – as did the other apostles, the Twelve. Thus authority was not vested in an *ecclesiatical body* (as Roman Catholics hold) but in the *quality of Christological confession made possible by divine revelation* (see Matt. 16:13–19). The Bauer-Ehrman book insufficiently recognizes that at the core, power was a function of divine truth, appropriately apprehended by selected human messengers, rather than truth being a function of human power.[89]

In the same manner, when arguing for the authority of the canon against the Bauer-Ehrman book, they ultimately rest their case on faith statements.

> It assumes that there is no means that *God* has given by which his books can be identified. . . . God has not only constituted these books by his Holy Spirit but also constituted the covenant community by his Holy Spirit, allowing his books to be rightly recognized even in the midst of substantial diversity and disagreement. Ehrman's approach already assumes that the formation of the canon is a purely human event—neither the books nor the community have God working in their midst. But, again, such an anti-supernatural assumption must be demonstrated, not merely assumed.[90]

---

88. McGrath, *Heresy*, 92–97.
89. Köstenberger and Kruger, *Heresy of Orthodoxy*, 101.
90. Ibid., 155.

Thomas C. Oden may well be right that orthodoxy was certainly not the "skewed memory of winners—a matter of power," but his definition of orthodoxy as "integrated biblical teaching as interpreted in its most consensual classic period" is certainly stretching the limits of acceptance too far.[91]

I am not convinced by their arguments and, while critics have sufficiently undermined the basic tenets of Bauer's Book concerning the overarching influence of the Roman bishop, Turner's alternative view, supported as it is by Sykes, of both fixed and flexible elements within the concept of orthodoxy is attractive.

I am, in fact, convinced that there seems to have been very little consensus of opinion in the very early days and whatever consensus was achieved through later conciliar definitions was often brought about by the pressure of politics and power. This is something we will address later in this book.

Coda: Heresy as "Other"

This leads smoothly into the view of heresy espoused by Rowan Williams in his republished and updated study on Arius.[92] In an introductory chapter on "Images of a Heresy," Williams sees Arianism and, by default, other heresies as views cast as "the Other" in relation to Catholic Christianity.

Williams rebuts the demonising tendency that denounces heretics, and Arius in particular, as ". . . a kind of Antichrist' whose supposed spirituality and demeanour are nothing more than a cloak for diabolical malice, a deliberate enmity to revealed faith." [93]

Williams, in fact, presents quite a different picture of Arius. According to Williams, he was a theological conservative and biblicist who has been wrongly portrayed as a rebel. "Arius claimed with no less fervour and sincerity to speak in conformity with Scripture and Catholic practice."[94]

His real weakness was that he was from the Alexandrian school, which, both in terms of theology and political power, did not become the ascendant one in Christendom. Here Williams faintly echoes Bauer on the ever-increasing, all-embracing power of Rome. Thus Arianism was, as indeed were all contrary views, considered as the other. What they were

91. Oden, *Rebirth of Orthodoxy*, 29.
92. Williams, *Arius: Heresy and Tradition*.
93. Ibid., 1.
94. Ibid., 240.

seen as other in opposition to depended very much upon the stance and perspective of their opponents. This has been the case even up to modern times.[95]

Williams takes us through a series of scholars as examples. John Henry Newman, who, from the stand point of his Tractarian and Oxford Movement perspective, saw the otherness of Arianism in its lack of spirituality and its ". . . unintelligent adherence to the letter of the Bible combined with wooden syllogistic analyses of biblical language. . . . It is the forerunner of stolid Evangelicalism, Erastian worldliness and . . . the new style of university theology."[96]

For Harnack it was the otherness of "formalistic, moralising religion" that majored on the rational. This would include "Protestant orthodoxy and Monkish Catholicism." All this was also seen as a threat to the spiritual nature of the Christian faith.[97]

Gwatkin saw Arianism as nothing more than "irreverent philosophical speculation" that was really paganism in disguise "in its elevation of a demi-god to a central position of honour in worship." The real issue of it being other was found in its teaching about the relationship of God to the world. Here was a form of deism proclaiming a God who was distant, isolated, and despotic with no possibility of that personal relationship that is at the heart of Christian belief.

Williams warns the modern scholar against seeing heresies as part of as coherent system strictly under the control of those heresiarchs with whose names they are associated. This was the creation of their opponents and was, in today's terms, the spin that propaganda used to present them as other. On the other hand, neither should we see the "Catholic" side as uniform and fixed ". . . as if the boundaries of Catholic identity were firmly and clearly drawn in advance. . . . [T]his was not so, and, indeed, that the fact that it was not so was one of the major elements in the controversy. Of course the Christian Church had become fairly well accustomed in the second century to reflecting upon its identity and its boundaries; yet the conventions then established were not universally and unambiguously fixed."[98]

Post-Nicaea, however, the situation was changed as the church became an accepted part of the Roman Empire. Williams sees that this new

95. Ibid., 2.
96. Ibid., 5.
97. Ibid., 8.
98. Ibid., 83.

"visibility" of the church, both in its own new self-awareness and its visibility in the world, ". . . meant that the wrong sort of Christian group was regarded pretty much as the church itself had been regarded by the pagan empire, as something subversive of the sacred character of social life."[99]

Cyril of Jerusalem, in the fourth century, gave a full explanation of why he believed the church is called "Catholic."

> [The church] is called Catholic then because it extends over all the world, from one end of the earth to the other; and because it teaches universally and completely one and all the doctrines which ought to come to men's knowledge, concerning things both visible and invisible, heavenly and earthly; and because it brings into subjection to godliness the whole race of mankind, governors and governed, learned and unlearned; and because it universally treats and heals the whole class of sins, which are committed by soul or body, and possesses in itself every form of virtue which is named, both in deeds and words, and in every kind of spiritual gifts.[100]

Vincent of Lérins in the fifth century condensed that definition of catholicity into a neat and simple aphorism, defining orthodoxy as "What has been believed everywhere, always and by all," but, while irenic in sound and intention, it appears that such views were in total contrast to what was happening in the real world of their day.[101] Sadly, the result of such a reduction like this means that "all doctrines are reduced to authority and all morals to obedience."[102] Down the centuries many of our greatest minds and spirits endured the logical consequences of such a reduction: artists were enslaved, philosophers imprisoned, scientists excommunicated, and reformers burned.

---

99. Ibid., 90–91.

100. Cyril, "Catechetical Lectures," 139–40.

101. Even Vincent himself says that the consent of the ancient fathers is not to be followed in every little detail of the divine law, but only and especially as regards the Rule of Faith (Vincent of Lerins, *Commonitory*, 28.71).

102. Machle, *How Is a Heresy False?*, 229.

Summary of Orthodoxy in the First Movement

a) Despite all the best efforts of conservatives who would like to maintain the myth of a golden age of doctrinal purity in the church and a fixed orthodoxy against which heresy reared its ugly head, no such age ever existed. From Bauer, Erhman, Käsemann, Bultmann, Radner, and even Turner himself, all have argued for, or simply conceded, that there has always been what Hardy called «the transformational dynamic of orthodoxy.»[103]

b) The acceptance, even by those who have opposed Bauer, of some form of doctrinal development, such as the examples already given of the acceptance of the one-time heresy of patripassianism in much modern theology, the continually changing views on the doctrine of the atonement, the fate of unbelievers and the doctrine of universalism, is, in fact, once again a description of what has always happened as the church has come face to face with new intellectual, social, and ethical challenges.

c) Nothing, not even the teachings of the fathers, is beyond question. There can be no closure or sense of having reached a destination because the church is continually a pilgrim church, forever on a journey with unfinished business to attend to that cannot be fettered by having to resort to slavishly repeating the mantras of "themes or answers maintained in earlier generations or centuries."[104]

d) Most fascinating of all is the way in which the two concepts of orthodoxy and heresy are co-related and emergent in every time. Rowan Williams makes the point that heresy is always seen as other to orthodoxy. This otherness, however, of course depends on the stance and perspective for which the badge of "orthodox" is claimed.

e) We shall see in later chapters that the refusal by GAFCON and its supporters to accept the reality of the shifting nature of orthodoxy both in the early days of the church and in the subsequent centuries is a root fault. It is exemplified in an insistence that the Anglican Church remain rooted in the Reformation confessional statements despite the clear application of those documents to a

---

103. Sykes, "'Orthodoxy' and Liberalism," 76–77.
104. Ibid., 87.

different time, different culture, and to very different intellectual, theological, and doctrinal battles.

f) It will be at least part of the contention of this book that it is not only a conservative theology, but also a thirst for power and influence in the Anglican Communion, that drives this movement forward.

g) The ongoing development of doctrine is of the essence of Christianity and, by its very nature, entails being open to new understandings of truth rather than being closed and fixed.

h) GAFCON's claim that the form of Anglicanism it espouses is the one, true, and classical form of Anglicanism, and that any deviation from it is heresy, must be judged against Rowan Williams's contention that otherness depends on the standpoint of the protagonist.

2

Movement Two: The Church Thinking
(Adagio—Theme and Variations)

The second movement of a classical symphony is usually a slow, thoughtful movement and is often found in the form of a theme and variations. This theme and its variations are usually quite distinct from the themes in the first movement but add life, depth, breadth, and interest to the overall experience of the symphony.

In this section we examine some of the different ways in which, through the centuries, the church has tried to think through some of the practical issues that the concept of orthodoxy raises.

The Theme—Boundaries and Authority

What is really at issue in this debate about orthodoxy and heresy is the matter of boundaries, doctrinal and ethical. However, an important question has to be asked. In the very different postmodern cultural and social setting of the church today, is such a cry for a strict reapplication of Reformation thinking and theology to the Anglican Communion, as envisaged by GAFCON, a viable and justifiable aim?

Will such rigid and formal declarations of boundaries for both church and doctrine bring about the renewal and second reformation of the church as is hoped? And more importantly, will such a rigid, dogmatic, and doctrinally and ethically circumscribed church win the hearts and minds of those without Christ today and for whom the church appears nothing more than an anachronistic irrelevance?

The contrast is between the view that says, "The Bible says it. I believe it. That settles it," and the view articulated by pastor John Robinson, who in 1620 spoke these words to the Pilgrim Fathers as they prepared to leave Europe for the New World:

> I am verily persuaded the Lord has more truth yet to break forth out of his Holy Word. . . . For my part, I cannot sufficiently bewail the condition of those reformed churches which . . . will go, at present, no further than the instruments of their reformation. The Lutherans cannot be drawn to go beyond what Luther saw; whatever part of His will our God had revealed to Calvin, they will rather die than embrace it, and the Calvinists, you see, stick fast where they were left by that great man of God, who yet saw not all things. This is a misery much to be lamented.[1]

He strongly criticised those who were entrenched in their particular theological systems and interpretations of Scripture and who refused to see the points of view of others who differed from them. They failed, he said, to see the weaknesses in their own positions and the value of, at least, being open to learn something from a different perspective.

Arlene K. Nehring, the United Church of Christ feminist theologian, sees the true significance of Robinson's words as releasing God's revelation from being confined simply to Scripture or creeds or denominational statements of faith. Neither is it limited to a particular time in history. With this view she claims that God's revelation to faithful people still continues and that the Bible, far from being "sewn up and buttoned down," has still much more to teach us.[2]

McLaren takes a similar view and sees that "a freedom from the constraints of a view that is locked in an historical Reformation paradigm . . . could mark the early beginnings of a new chapter in history, the birth of an unspeakably important adventure—an exploration that could change everything."[3]

Graham Buxton, while certainly not embracing all of what McLaren and the Emerging Church have to say, nevertheless takes a very positive attitude to the opportunities the new paradigm of postmodernism offers to the church.[4] He pictures it as a traditional game of football within which somebody suddenly changed all the rules, the shape of the pitch, and the width of the goal posts. The initial result is chaos, anger, and frustration on the part of some, who vehemently plead for a return to the safety and com-

---

1. Cited in McLaren, *Church on the Other Side*, 227–28.
2. Nehring, *Yet More Light and Truth*.
3. McLaren, *Church on the Other Side*, 228.
4. Buxton, *Dancing in the Dark*, 177–78.

fort of the rules and boundaries that were once known. However, there are others who recognise that the changes, though not sought, have created new and exciting opportunities and possibilities.

Buxton proceeds to identify three possible responses by the church to the changed circumstances of our postmodern world. He uses the picture of three sailing boats "bobbing around on a stretch of water." One is securely anchored without any opportunity for movement. Another has been cut free from its anchor and is being blown away from the others into the distance. The third boat remains anchored but the rope linking the boat to the anchor is long enough to allow a limited freedom to move around and explore.[5]

The first of these three boats is seen by Buxton as representing conservative fundamentalism with its rigid, dogmatic attitude to the Bible that suffocates any possibility of responding to any creative contemporary inspiration of the Holy Spirit. There is little imagination and engagement with the world through the Word.

The second boat represents that hard postmodern approach within the church that, probably in response to the rigidity of the fundamentalists, has cast off all restraint and "abandoned the anchor altogether." This situation is seen by him as a losing sight of the essentials of the faith.

We have already seen that Buxton proposes a much more positive response to postmodernism and, for him, the third boat expresses what he calls being "experimental": "If the church is to be faithful to the gospel (attached *firmly but not rigidly* to the anchor of Christ), and if it is to be relevant to the world which is crying out for meaning and reality, then there needs to be that flexibility to manoeuvre within the area permitted by the slackness of the rope."[6]

However, if this is true, questions immediately arise, as Buxton acknowledges. What is the immutable core or centre of the gospel that cannot change—the anchor in Buxton's illustration—and how far can the circumference of acceptance extend before certain beliefs and actions become alien or contrary to that central core and therefore unacceptable, heterodox or heretical? In other words, how long is the rope between ship and anchor? Where are the boundary markers beyond which the church cannot go, and who has the power and authority to decide on these matters?

---

5. Ibid., 182–83.
6. Ibid., 183.

Movement Two: The Church Thinking

Bruce Kaye also asks the same question but sees the tension behind the question as having positive creativity. Indeed he sees diversity with interdependence as necessary within a Christian community in order for there to be any opportunity for true creativity.[7]

These are, of course, critical questions concerning the nature and exercise of authority. John Goldingay argues that there are clear differences between what he calls *extrinsic* and *intrinsic* authority. For him *extrinsic* authority is that exercised within a hierarchical institution such as the army.[8] He could well, of course, have used the example of the church at certain periods of its history and in certain contemporary settings where orders emanating from above in a fixed authority system have to be obeyed.

On the other hand, he says, *intrinsic* authority "derives its legitimacy from the contents of its statements or from its relationship with reality."[9] For Goldingay this is the sort of authority exercised by Jesus and, later, by those who claimed to speak for God through charismatic or prophetic gifts. He does, however, recognise that this type of authority runs the risk of being nothing more than, "I do my own thing." This danger is often found when individuals claim personal inspiration from God for authoritative statements about themselves or others that are difficult to question, such as, "The Lord told me . . ." or "I felt led to . . ."

It is at these times that some form of extrinsic authority becomes necessary to protect ourselves from ourselves. Goldingay finds a good example in the fact that an individual's intrinsic and personal sense of the call of God to a position of ministry within the church has to be validated by an external or extrinsic authority appointed by the church. Once appointed, ministers then take on such an extrinsic authority themselves as they are given authority to preach and teach from the Scriptures and are now validated as orthodox.

Goldingay, however, makes it clear that such an exercise of authority, in claiming to pronounce on who or what is orthodox, cannot and must not be allowed to quench the free and unfettered work and ministry of the Spirit. Although the intrinsic authority of the Spirit is evidenced whenever the Scriptures are read and taught, he cannot be confined simply to the Scriptures. He is at work within the church and speaks through its members. However, that does not mean that we should jettison the Bible.

---

7. Kaye, *Reinventing Anglicanism*, 177.
8. Goldingay, *Authority and Ministry*, 8.
9. Ibid.

On the contrary, Goldingay affirms that "here is a corpus of words which have already been recognized as inspired by God's Spirit."[10] Indeed the Spirit cannot even be confined to the institutional order. That hierarchy of form and structure requires to be complemented by the ministry of the charismatic, which can keep it on the right track.[11]

Bruce Kaye sees such an intrinsic view of authority displayed in the Anglican attitude and temperament, with its qualities of "open-endedness, porous borders, tentativeness, contingency awareness, and an authority experienced and exercised by the whole people of God."[12] Sadly, these do not appear to be the attitudes displayed by those within GAFCON and the FCA. On the contrary, their attitude demonstrates a sense of fixed borders, completed and fixed revelation, and an attitude that allows for no other interpretation of the Scriptures but their own. We will examine the matter of borders and boundaries in more detail under Variation Two.

Variation One: Fundamentalism

It is important to understand just what is meant by the epithet "fundamentalist." R. E. Webber[13] gives a contemporary definition and explanation of what it means today. He sees a threefold development from its American root in the controversy with modernism until about 1945.

It really began in 1895 when the Conference of Conservative Protestants met at Niagara Falls and issued what they called the "Five Principles" necessary for anyone to claim true Christian belief:

- the inerrancy of the Scriptures;
- the divinity of Jesus;
- the historicity of the Virgin birth;
- the substitutionary nature of the atonement; and
- the physical, corporeal return of Jesus, the Christ.

These five principles became known as "The Fundamentals".[14]

By 1910 the Conservative Protestants were publishing a magazine called *The Fundamentals* and the word *fundamentalist* had entered the

10. Ibid., 20.
11. Ibid., 23.
12. Kaye, *Reinventing Anglicanism*, 23.
13. Webber, *Younger Evangelicals*, 25–30.
14. Tickle, *Great Emergence*, 65–66.

language as a label for anyone with a clearly defined theological mindset. They also added two more principles, namely, the obligation to evangelise and the necessity of a belief in Jesus as a personal Saviour. These seven principles have now become the core doctrines of what might be called "evangelical Christianity."

As time went on such beliefs became more and more anti-intellectual, anti-ecumenical, and anti-social action and were centred on theological propositionalism and evidential apologetics.

Webber sees a reverse of these emphases from 1945 until the mid-1960s with what were known as "The New Evangelicals." This was the era of Carl Henry and the establishment of publications such as *Christianity Today*, and which also saw the emergence of new approaches to mission such as Youth for Christ, Campus Crusade, and the Billy Graham Organisation, which were more open to different traditions and deliberately ecumenical in ethos in order to facilitate evangelism on a much broader front.

From the mid-1960s until about 2000, fundamentalism became more diverse, especially concerning the matter of biblical inerrancy and a return, by some, to an appreciation of some of the more ancient traditions of the church. Nevertheless they all share a belief in the fundamentals of the authority of Scripture, the affirmation of the Trinity, the deity of Jesus, the efficacy of Jesus' death and resurrection, and the affirmation of the church as the body of Christ.

Jakobus M. Vorster, in his study on the core characteristics of religious fundamentalism,[15] agrees with Webber on those fundamentals but incisively adds a number of other factors that, for him, describe the common characteristics of Christian fundamentalism. He begins with "biblicism," which he describes as the use of the biblical texts in an over-literalistic way, often ignoring or paying scant regard to its cultural, historical, or literary background.

While biblicism reaches back to the ancient texts in order to highlight the core fundamentals of religion, Vorster adds the concept of "traditioning," describing the attempt to add further authority to these fundamentals by indicating their stand and value in the historic traditions of the faith.[16]

---

15. Vorster, *Perspectives*.

16. Ibid., 49–50. "This is the reason why some Christian fundamentalists adore the Reformation and the glorious moments where martyrs resisted the Spanish Inquisition. As was done in Geneva, they want modern society to legislate on the basis of the Ten Commandments. They single out the hymns, liturgical practices, church polity and moral codes of those times as examples for the churches today."

Vorster then notes that, having elevated certain fundamentals to absolutes and interlaced its whole ideology around these absolutes, fundamentalists promote a legalistic lifestyle often consisting of many external forms of conduct with its own symbols and social structures as means of promoting and defending their identity.[17]

Due to their common experience of fear for the loss of identity, their reactionary disposition, and their prejudice and intolerance, fundamentalists develop a strong sense of an in-group frame of mind, with a rigid homogeneous culture. Because they most often define themselves in large by what they are against, they always have a very real and easily identifiable enemy against whom they motivate and muster themselves. This battle, according to Vorster, usually requires strong, charismatic leadership that is able to motivate and encourage and willing to criticise and defend.

In its extreme form fundamentalism can condone acts of violence to promote the "sacred" cause in obedience to God. This violence can be physical, such as the attacks on abortion clinics by fundamentalist Christians in the United States, but it is more often verbal or psychological violence against those who differ from them or against those who, from within their ranks, waver in their total allegiance.

Variation Two: Circles, Sets, Edges and Centres

Hiebert's way of looking at this matter of boundaries is to make use of the mathematical concept of bounded and centred sets as illustrations of different attitudes the church can take to deciding who belongs and who does not. Hiebert gives a precise definition of what a bounded-set type of church would look like, and it looks remarkably like the vision embraced by GAFCON and the Fellowship of Confessing Anglicans. It is, of

---

17. Ibid., 51. "This rigid moralism in fundamentalism usually rotates around certain facets of human conduct. . . . Fundamentalists all tend to idealise patriarchal structures in authority and morality. Males are valued as superior according to a creational order, and women should be submissive. This point of view results in many violations of the rights of women and girl children in many societies. . . . The strict patriarchal structures also dominate families and households. Fundamentalists tend to hold strong views on the necessity of discipline and will give preferentiality to corporal punishment and other forms of authoritarian disciplinary action. . . . They regard the liberal standards of the modern world as 'westoxication.' In the application of law and order . . . fundamentalists are very adamant campaigners for capital punishment. They propose death penalties for a number of crimes."

course, also relevant as a description of all fundamentalist, conservative churches.[18]

First of all, there has to be a clear sense of being a group that believes the same things, does the same things, and thinks the same things. In other words, unity means uniformity—all Christians would think and act alike. Only those who shared the same characteristics would be allowed to join. Other churches with different membership requirements would be seen as *other* sets. A critical question would be whether they are truly Christian because, in this view, boundaries define the ultimate nature of reality.

The church would view theology as ultimate, universal, and unchanging truth and define it in general propositional statements. It would divorce theology from the historical and cultural contexts in which it is formulated.

Most of the activity of the church would be focussed on building up the church, and when it gathers for worship the emphasis would be on teaching that would support and maintain the particular identity of the church and its organisation.

These descriptors fit well with Jurgen Moltmann's own description of how much of the church works today as "Birds of a feather flocking together."[19] Moltmann sees this as a reflex-action gathering of like-minded people who feel insecure with people whose thoughts, feelings, and desires are different from their own. Such a notion of the church shows a weakness and lack of confidence that will never win the world for Christ.

Hiebert warns all those engaged in strict boundary enforcement that such an approach can produce a sort of secularism. He calls this the "worship of the group, of the corporate self."[20] In contrast, he says that the church should be accepting and open as Paul instructs in Romans 15:7: "Accept one another, then, just as Christ accepted you, in order to bring praise to God." Only in the security of our own acceptance by God are we free to accept others and released from the constant need for self-justification.

This follows Moltmann, who believes that only this attitude of acceptance can give us a new orientation and break through our limitations so that we can spring over our narrow shadows. It opens us up for others as they really are so that we gain a longing for and an interest in them. As

---

18. Hiebert, *Anthropological Reflections*, 110–16.
19. Moltmann, *Open Church*, 27–36.
20. Hiebert, *Anthropological Reflections*, 117.

a result of this we become able actually to forget ourselves and to focus on the way Christ has accepted us.[21]

Hiebert then looks at what he calls "fuzzy sets" and describes what a fuzzy set church would look like. There would still be the unchanging universal beliefs and practices needed to be adopted before anyone could be accepted as a full Christian. Others in the set might hold to some or even just a few and be considered as half-Christians. Boundaries would not be sharp and there would be a toleration of various beliefs and practices within the group even on essential matters of faith and practice. However, the aim would be to gradually teach and encourage members to accept the official teachings of the church. Again Hiebert issues a warning of danger he sees for the church in this form of "worshipping its corporate self and theological relativism."[22]

Frost and Hirsch's description of such churches is also quite negative. They regard the fuzzy set as lacking any ideological centre or boundary but being "just made up of people hanging out together. They are not sure what has brought them together or why they meet." They see this sort of group as having a very short life and probably only existing at the beginning or end of a movement.[23]

Hiebert's third form for a church is that of a "centred set." He describes the characteristics of these churches quite positively. He sees the members of a centred set as those sharing a relationship with a centre or reference point. The church as a centred set means that, as a body, it is defined by its centre, which is the person of Jesus of Christ as revealed in the Scripture. Centred on Christ in worship, obedience, and service, the church becomes a covenant community. Its characteristics are righteousness, *koinonia*, and *shalom*. Membership of this centred set is based purely on a real relationship to Christ and not on any particular knowledge base or learning, nor on behaviour. Differences in matters of race, gender, class, and theology are not reasons for exclusion.[24]

Frost and Hirsch use some interesting metaphors based on their Australian background to try and elucidate some of these concepts. They describe the foolishness of trying to fence in the land on a vast outback station in an attempt to keep the owner's livestock in and neighbour's livestock out. They compare that with the simplicity of just sinking a bore and

---

21. Moltmann, *Open Church*, 30–31.
22. Hiebert, *Anthropological Reflections*, 121–22.
23. Frost and Hirsch, *Shape of Things to Come*, 206–7.
24. Hiebert, *Anthropological Reflections*, 127–28.

creating a well that acts as a magnet to livestock who will not stray far from the living water they know is so necessary for life.

In the bounded set, it is clear who is in and who is out (fences, not wells) based on a well-defined ideological-cultural boundary. Usually this will include moral and cultural mores as well as credal definitions. However, such a set does not have much of a core definition beyond these boundaries. It is hard at the edges, soft at the centre.

On the other hand they see that in the centred-set model there is possibly a more biblically oriented way. Using the picture of the wells sunk on the outback ranch, they maintain that just as the animals are instinctively drawn to the water source, so too a community centred on Jesus will draw people from many different backgrounds and experiences to that centre. No matter how distant they are from him, they will be drawn towards him, and it is that direction of movement that is the key to belonging. Jesus must be at the centre of everything we do.[25]

In this type of set there is a very strong ideology at the centre but no boundaries. It is hard at the centre, soft at the edges. Frost and Hirsch see the centred set as the best structure for missional communities in the emerging culture.

In a centred set what counts is how each member is moving in relation to the centre (Jesus). The focus is upon the centre, and each individual is in dynamic relationship to it. Belonging, in this case, is not a matter of performing according to an agreed-upon profile; it is a matter of living and acting out of commitment to a common centre.

The focus is on the centre and on pointing people to that centre—Jesus. In this setting process is more important than definitions. The emphasis is on direction and movement. The person determines whether they are part of the centred set by their orientation to and movement toward the centre.

Centred-set thinking affirms initiatives that would otherwise not find a place in bounded-set situations because it cultivates an ethos of freedom of thought and action.

Frost and Hirsch have their own description of how they see the advantage of working within a centred-set ethos. They see that ". . . it allows for massive diversity and for a deeper underlying unity based on Jesus and filtered through our distinctive organizational value. The hard at the

---

25. Frost and Hirsch, *Shape of Things to Come*, 206–8.

center, soft at the edges paradigm allows for a wide variety of people to gather around Jesus through the church." [26]

This view of the church fits clearly the biblical theme of pilgrimage. The Christian life, both individually and corporately, is a journey toward a promised land, to a holy city, to a final destination. Any church that thinks it has stopped journeying and has arrived has opted out of God's purpose. We come from many different points of origin and all our journeys are different, but we are drawn to the common centre. This defines the set.

Like the earliest disciples of Jesus, the church is the church by virtue of his summons and its willingness to reorient its life toward him and to follow him continually, day by day and step by step. This did not, however, mean uniformity of understanding, as we shall see clearly demonstrated. Neither did it mean uniformity of vocation.

Jesus made that abundantly clear in addressing Peter in the company of other disciples after the resurrection. When Jesus foretold the difficulties and dangers awaiting Peter in his life as an apostle, he told him quite clearly that he was not to be concerned about what would happen to another disciple.[27]

Rowan Williams develops this point fully in his theological musings on the teachings of the desert fathers and mothers of the fourth and fifth centuries. He claims that the church is neither to be a community of individuals—which is not a community at all—nor is it to be a community of those enforced into uniformity. "The church is meant supremely to be a community of persons. . . . It is a place for distinctive vocations to be discovered in such a way that they are a source of mutual enrichment and delight, not threat. It is a place where real human difference is nourished."[28]

Michael Jinkins takes a similar view:

> "An ecclesiology that begins from the assumption that the church consists of individuals who have chosen to follow God, individuals who join together because they share the same faith, are similarly faithful in their behaviour, or share similar faith experiences (the tests of orthodoxy, orthopraxy, orthopathy), is built on the shifting sand of human frailty and variability."[29]

26. Ibid., 206–8.

27. "Peter turned and saw that the disciple whom Jesus loved was following them. . . . When Peter saw him, he asked, 'Lord, what about him?' Jesus answered, 'If I want him to remain alive until I return, what is that to you? You must follow me'" (John 21:20–22).

28. Williams, *Silence and Honey Cakes*, 58.

29. Jinkins, "'Gift' of the Church," 187.

This "human frailty and variability" is exactly the wonder of the existence of the church. The Divine One, who took upon himself human flesh and frailty, yet without sin, through the miracle of the incarnation, then called those who share that same human flesh and frailty with all their weaknesses and different understandings, hopes, and fears into that community of faith we know now as the early church.

For, as McGrath argues, the historical evidence suggests that both the New Testament and the early Christian writers tended to emphasise the centre of the Christian faith rather than focussing on policing its periphery. Jesus Christ was widely regarded as defining and marking the core of Christianity—"Jesus is Lord" (Rom 10:9).

Yet the focus of a Christian community does not determine its limits. Historical developments made it necessary to address the question of boundaries.[30] Of course, the major question then has to be about who defines the boundaries. How are they to be determined?

Charles Gore defined these boundaries as "Hedges around the pastureland in order to safeguard those who had found sanctuary there."[31] He saw three forms of hedge; "cultic, ethical and theological."

Cultic applies to eschewing anything to do with Jewish ritual—circumcision, food laws, etc. *Ethical* refers to certain behaviours that were seen to be beyond whatever boundary had been set and this, of course, varied from place to place and time to time. *Theological* laid emphasis on what were seen as certain essentials of the Christian faith. In all these areas "orthodoxy" was "right thinking" or "sound doctrine."

Of course, the notion of "thinking," when it comes to orthodoxy, can be seen as positively dangerous by some conservatives, especially if it leads to a development of doctrine beyond that which has been previously accepted. In the next section or variation, we see how "thinking" is taken to a different level by Paul Hiebert as he develops his theory of the necessity of "self-theologising" within the developing communities of the younger churches.

Variation Three: The Four Selfs

Of course, there is another facet to the unrest concerning the Episcopal Church and its decisions regarding the full inclusion of gay and lesbian Christians in Christian ministry. It is, after all, a new church, in Anglican

---

30. McGrath, *Heresy*, 90.
31. Gore, *Incarnation of the Son of God*, 96–97.

terms, in what became known as the New World. It has, therefore, a relatively new constitution. It could be considered by some to be in a similar category to what are considered the young churches of the Third World.

Seen in that light, the proposals of the great missionary theologians Rufus Anderson and Henry Venn, who in 1861 proposed a way for young mission churches to become independent of their founding mother churches, are relevant. They suggested that churches should be encouraged to become "self-propagating, self-supporting and self-governing."[32] This "Three Self" approach was widely adopted by most mission agencies and seen as the key to establishing viable autonomous churches. It appears that the Episcopal Church in the United States has taken these principles to heart and even gone beyond them into what Paul Hiebert calls "self-theologising."[33]

Concerning this "Fourth Self," Hiebert asks whether or not young churches have the right to read and interpret the Scriptures for themselves. His answer is unhesitatingly positive. Of course, that is exactly what they do. Today we hear of Latin American theology, Indian theology, and African theology as theologians struggle to make the gospel relevant to their cultural traditions. We even have subcultural theologies—feminist theology, eco-theology, gay and lesbian theology, etc.

Sceptics are wary, but Hiebert recognises their questioning and meets it head on, claiming that any opposition to this right to "self-theologising" is a gross form of ethnocentrism and does not encourage spiritual growth in younger churches.[34] Hiebert points out that "self-theologising" was the inevitable result of three strong forces at work in the previously colonially structured and missionary-orientated churches.[35]

As young churches mature, their leaders change from being simple tribal village pastors to college-trained theologians. These intellectually developed leaders share their country's growing nationalism and desire to break free of their past colonial history. They seek for self-rule and, within that freedom, the right to study the Scriptures for themselves. All this takes place at the same time as they become much more aware of their

32. Shenk, *Rufus Anderson and Henry Venn*.

33. Hiebert, *Anthropological Insights*, 196.

34. Ibid., 196. "If we encourage them are we not opening the door for theological pluralism and, eventually, relativism? If we oppose them, are we not guilty of the worst form of ethnocentrism and of stunting their growth? . . . This proliferation of theologies in different historical and cultural settings raises important issues about the nature of theology."

35. Hiebert, *Anthropological Reflections*, 46–47.

own cultural context, and this has a direct influence on their maturing theology.

While, of course, the American church is older than many of the younger churches of the Third World, because of its history its sense of independence from the "mother" Church of England is very strong, almost written in its DNA. The same is true of its pride in its own theological establishments and theologians and their contributions to contemporary theological thought.

It should, therefore, be of no surprise to anyone that it felt it was able to make a totally independent decision regarding the consecration of Gene Robinson despite the pleadings and protestations of the Archbishop of Canterbury and the other Anglican instruments of unity. Having said that, even such a history does not make the radical new theology it produces more easily acceptable to those of a more conservative persuasion.

Hiebert understands this dilemma instinctively. He recognises that most of us were brought up as what he calls "monotheological" and that there was basically only one way to interpret the Scriptures. Any deviations were assumed to be heretical. To find committed and sincere Christians with different interpretations challenges our own understanding and questions our certainties. It also makes us fearful of examining our own theological thinking lest we should find ourselves weakened. The end result can be a ghetto mentality as we withdraw into limited fellowship only with those of like mind.

Most importantly he reminds us that, in the end, all our theologies reflect our historical and cultural contexts and they are only a partial understanding of the wonder and greatness of God for, as Paul writes in 1 Corinthians 13:12: "Now we see but a poor reflection . . ."[36]

In many ways Hiebert reflects the ancient Celtic Christian legend of the sage who points to the moon with his finger while the idiot looks only at the finger. The church can, through its creeds and dogmas, only act as a pointer to the truth, which is in itself something far beyond our human understanding.[37]

Rowan Williams, interestingly, remarks that it is in the nature of Anglicanism to exercise caution over any formulae extra to the classic creeds. The advantage of this is that it stresses the fundamentals of the faith "in a way that allows people to 'inhabit' this tradition without too much defensive anxiety about contemporary battles." Its disadvantage is that it places

---

36. Hiebert, *Anthropological Insights*, 196–98.
37. Duncan, *Elements of Celtic Christianity*, 98.

a great deal of responsibility on theologians and teachers to explain those fundamentals in a context where external boundaries have been blurred or removed altogether.[38]

Radner makes a similar point in his essay "The Scriptural Community: Authority in Anglicanism":

> Anglicans have no constraining authority besides the "Creeds" ... Progressives believe that beyond the Creeds and the scriptural base to which they refer—variously understood— much (all?) falls into the category of *adiaphora;* this might even include the shape and duties of the three-fold ministry.[39]

He points out that radical evangelicals in, for instance, the diocese of Sydney are working in almost the exact same way as the more radical revisionists for example, with regard to their introduction (theoretically at least) of lay presidency at the Eucharist.

Allen makes what were, for his time, some striking comments about those who insist on tests for orthodoxy. He notes that the Apostle Paul did not set up any authoritative body to decide doctrinal differences and their application at a local level. There were no "*a priori* tests of orthodoxy which should be applicable for all time, under all circumstances, everywhere. He refused to allow the universal application of particular precedents."

Allen reminds those with a strict boundary mentality that they will not find such tests in the records of the apostolic church. "Negatively nothing is defined. It is very strange how difficult it is to find any clear guidance." He reminds us that Paul only once applied the rulings of the Jerusalem Council to a certain provinces such as Syria and Cilicia and Galatia but he refused to apply the council ruling in Macedonia or Achaia. Rather, he had gone to Jerusalem to defend the liberties of the other churches in the face of Jewish opposition. He did not even urge the excommunication of Galatian Christians who had submitted to the rite of circumcision, which he denounced as a falling from Christ.[40]

It seems to me that John D'Arcy May, in his address in 2001 to the New South Wales Ecumenical Council on Religious Fundamentalism, could have been speaking about GAFCON when he spoke of religious traditions that have an air of superiority and a conviction that they alone possess "the only sure road to the goal of human and cosmic fulfilment'

---

38. Williams, *Anglican Identities*, 1.
39. Radner and Turner, *Fate of Communion*, 92.
40. Allen, *Missionary Methods*, 132.

and being characterised by an *a priori* assertion of some set of tenets in defence of what is taken to be a threatened institution."[41]

Jaroslav Pelikan reminds us that the council that condemned the Hussites said that their zeal for the holiness of the church and their offence at the public sins in the church carried them to the point of violating its unity. Indeed, any schism on moral grounds, he says, is destined to go on "spawning ever new schisms, for even the new sect would not be pure enough for some, who would separate themselves yet again in their quest for a truly holy church."[42]

Indeed, he goes even further in his emphasis on the priority of unity over holiness. His interpretation of Augustine's view of the church, which was common to most of the churches, made unity the fundamental attribute of the church. The holiness of the church was clearly subordinate to this because it could never be achieved by sinful men and women but only exists "in the mind of God and in the eschatological light of eternity." Unity, however, was the condition inside the church wherein each Christian, individually and corporately "strove toward an ever greater measure of empirical holiness."[43]

Pelikan's use of Augustine here reflects the view expressed by Bishop John Jewel of Salisbury when he said, "Of a truth, unity and concord doth best become religion; yet is not unity the sure and certain mark whereby to know the Church of God."[44]

I agree with Jinkins[45] that the holiness, purity, righteousness, and unity of the church are only truly found in the person of the Lord of the Church, Jesus Christ. It is within and only through the perfections of his own nature that these qualities are in any sense possessed by those who claim to be his body, the church. To claim anything else is to ascribe to the church and to its members qualities and perfections that are beyond the possibility of sinful human beings. We may humanly desire them and, indeed, "strive" towards them, as Pelikan claims, but we know that it is only as we are in Christ that these perfections become ours. However, they are ours is beyond question, as it is for all those who truly seek to follow Christ, however falteringly and misguidedly. Surely this is the attitude with which we should engage in the *missio Dei* to which we are all called

41. Cited in McGillion, *Chosen Ones*, 109.
42. Pelikan, *Christian Tradition*, 85.
43. Ibid., 84–85.
44. Jewel, *Apology of the Church of England*, 47.
45. Jinkins, "'Gift' of the Church," 206–7.

and with which we should approach our brothers and sisters in Christ with whom we differ on matters of orthodoxy or orthopraxy.

Westerhoff has an intriguing description of Nicodemus, the teacher of Israel who comes to Jesus by night in John 3. He describes him as being "well versed in the Scriptures but blind to God's revelation."[46] If God is speaking afresh to this generation, as many believe, and if he is revealing new understandings of his truth from the Scriptures, could that charge against Nicodemus be laid at the feet of those who continue to divide the church, not simply as it has always been divided concerning interpretation and practice, but dividing it surgically by declaring those who do not share their particular interpretation and practice as being no longer within the faith and the family of God?

Hiebert, therefore, in the light of all our imperfect and limited understanding of the fullness of God, brings us back to his original question as to whether churches in other cultures have the same right as we do to interpret the scriptures in their own setting. His answer is again a resounding "Yes!" He gives the same answer to the other question that raises the possibility that they might go theologically astray. However, he is convinced that the risk must be taken or else we condemn them to "spiritual infancy and early death."[47]

Someone could well ask whether or not the reformation was all about the freedom to study the Bible and to come to conclusions independent of and different from some magisterial authority. Should that not be a salutary question to be asked of those in GAFCON and other fundamentalist conservative groupings? Of course, Luther and Calvin both eventually became known as the Magisterial Reformers, and it was difficult for their later followers to have the freedom to think beyond what their reforming heroes had taught, but it is doubtful whether that was their avowed intent.

As Hiebert points out, we cannot guarantee that the way we interpret the Scriptures and create our theologies will be accepted by those who come after us. They must come to their understanding and beliefs themselves and in their own way. "There is no way to guarantee the preservation of our theological convictions. We can write them in creeds and constitutions and can police churches and schools. But those who succeed us will come to their own convictions. Each generation in the church must come to its own living faith. Second-hand beliefs will not do."[48]

46. Westerhoff, *Tomorrow's Church*, 21.
47. Hiebert, *Anthropological Insights*, 208.
48. Ibid., 216.

Movement Two: The Church Thinking

The primary question we need to ask is: How do we react to and deal with churches or groups within our own church that come to radically different interpretations of the Scriptures from the interpretations we have traditionally known and accepted? Is the only answer to denounce out of hand the new theology, to mark out our boundary lines to separate ourselves from them as both a mark of judgement and as a statement of our superior holiness? Or is there another way, a gentler, more loving perspective that can enable us to maintain our own distinctive beliefs and theology while still continuing in fellowship with those from whom we differ and, perhaps more importantly, remain open to the possibility that the Holy Spirit might be trying to teach us something new that we need to learn?

Bruce Kaye reminds us that any hope of meaningful communication between two people who do not agree with each other's views depends entirely on the willingness of both of them to recognise that they are both fully human persons. Where that respect and recognition is absent, the temptation is always to withdraw into monochrome interest groups within which an assertive and dominant leadership and authority is most likely to develop. This process serves only to exaggerate differences and drive the group more deeply in on itself.[49]

Such a statement reflects, sadly but accurately, the condition of relationships now found within the Anglican Communion, so that open and respectful discussion between some of those who differ is now almost impossible.

As long ago as 1976, in a report on doctrine within the Church of England, Maurice Wiles wrote:

> What is important for the Christian community at large is not that it gets its beliefs absolutely clear and definite; it cannot hope to do that if they are really beliefs about God. It is rather that people within the community go on working at the intellectual problems, questioning, testing, developing, and seeking the practical application of the traditions that we have inherited from the past.[50]

Philip Turner argues that to accept such a view is to consign the Anglican Communion to being merely a debating society "rather than part of the Body of Christ commissioned to proclaim a gospel with an identifiable

---

49. Kaye, *Reinventing Anglicanism*, 92–95.
50. Doctrine Commission of the Church of England, (1976), 130.

content."[51] I am not, however, convinced by that argument. It seems to me that Stephen Sykes makes a very wise point when he writes about what he calls "The Identity of Christianity." He doubts whether there will ever be any complete agreement about the identity of Christianity. He does, however, understand that Christians will be able to coexist by containing disagreement within reasonable boundaries. In fact—and this is the key phrase he writes here—"contained diversity is, in fact, what unity amounts to."[52]

Variation Four: Three Illustrative Examples

Episcopal theologian Phyllis Tickle, in her book *The Great Emergence*, quotes American Bishop Mark Dwyer's observation that ". . . about every five hundred years the Church feels compelled to hold a giant rummage sale. And . . . we are living in and through one of those five-hundred-year sales."[53]

This notion is not new. The idea of *quinquesecularism*[54] dates back at least to the sixteenth century. During these times of shift and change, the institutionalised church throws off its chains rather like breaking out of a hard, unyielding shell so that new life and growth can occur. When that great upheaval occurs, Tickle believes that history shows that at least three things always happen.

Firstly, a new, more dynamic form of Christianity appears. Secondly, the original, dominant form of Christianity has to reassess itself and institute life-giving reforms. Tickle notes that, because of the Reformation, both the Protestant reformers and those who were the focus of their complaints ended up being better churches. This is a clear example of how the clash of contrasting ideas can be extremely creative. It is a living example of the so-called Hegelian dialectic, where thesis is challenged by antithesis with the result that a new creative synthesis is produced. This synthesis then becomes the new thesis so that, in ecclesiological terms, "*Ecclesia semper reformanda*." Thirdly, it appears that every time the accretions that

---

51. Radner and Turner, *Fate of Communion*, 126.
52. Sykes, *Identity of Christianity*, 11.
53. Tickle, *Great Emergence*, 14.
54. Cited in Sykes, *Unashamed Anglicanism*, 70. "An expression summing up Lancelot Andrewes' famous dictum: "One canon reduced to writing by God Himself; two testaments; three creeds, four general councils, *five centuries* . . . determine the boundary of our faith."

stifle life and vigour in Christianity are thrown off, the range and depth of the success of missionary work has seen a significant increase.[55]

For Tickle the last major upheaval occurred in the sixteenth century with the Protestant Reformation. An earlier cataclysm was the Great Schism of 1054, when Eastern and Western Christianity divided. An even earlier example was in the sixth and seventh centuries when Pope Gregory the Great's reforms, based on the work of St. Benedict, brought Europe into some sort of unity using the cohesive power of the monastic orders. It was these orders that actually protected and preserved Christianity even through the collapse of the power of Rome itself during the next five centuries.

Tickle sees the rise of neo-orthodox movements like the Emerging Church and their dramatic influence upon the worldwide church, not least upon the Anglican Communion, as the latest of these upheavals through which the contemporary church is passing.

Her clearly defined points of division have been, to my mind, artificially set at the five-hundred-year mark and have a different focus, majoring as they do on ecclesiastical form and structure. Nevertheless, the three periods this present study has earmarked as clearly consequential for a study of the development of orthodoxy have also been seen as significant for her. This is an interesting and unsought for confirmation. Of even more significance is her strong contention that, at every point of cataclysmic change in the history of the church, there is one question that must be central in any re-formation: "Where now is authority?"[56]

I have chosen three illustrative examples from the historical and contemporary church. I am not pretending that these are exhaustive studies but that they are simply illustrative of what has been seen earlier in this section.

The early church example of Donatism demonstrates the reality of dynamism at play in the matter of orthodoxy.

Aspects of the Reformation could be seen as a demonstration of the use of circles, sets, and edges.

The contemporary Emerging Church demonstrates the "self-theologising" of the newer church as it wrestles with its witness and life in contemporary culture. In the peculiarly Anglican setting it could be said that the history of the Lambeth Conference is the history of the emergence

---

55. Tickle, *Great Emergence*, 11.
56. Ibid., 44.

of new and younger churches within the Anglican Communion and their own wrestling with cultural changes and conflicts.

The Early Church with Special Reference to Donatism— Dynamism at Play

Each of these periods of turbulence I have chosen focuses on a different concept within the church's life.

In the early church and through the ecumenical councils the emphasis was upon how such beliefs are to be expressed in words. Unfortunately most histories of the church treat this period as one of heroes and villains when, in reality, some now branded as heretics were only seeking to help the fledgling church understand the great mysteries of the faith. We have already seen in the first movement of this "symphony" on orthodoxy that things were not even as clear-cut in the New Testament as it might be first assumed.

What immediately comes to mind is the sad history of the Donatists. The Donatists were a schismatic group in the early church of the fourth and fifth centuries, mainly in North Africa, who broke away from the mainstream church because they rejected the authority of leaders, such as bishops, who, in their opinion, had sinned. The specific problem was with Christian leaders who had compromised during a period of persecution by cooperating with the persecutors in handing over sacred books.

Greenslade makes the point that "These Puritan groups believed the church to be made up of saints and is not just stained but destroyed by the inclusion of sinners guilty of the a sin against the Holy Spirit. Their sacraments are administered by unworthy ministers and are therefore invalid and the body they belong to is no church."[57]

This heresy arose in AD 303 when the Emperor Diocletian forbade Christians under pain of death to possess books of the Holy Scriptures. Bishop Felix of Aptunga gave in to the threats of the magistrates and turned over the sacred books of the church to the Roman authorities. In the eyes of Christians, this made him a traditor, a traitor, an unholy person, a sinner, and in the eyes of the Donatists, it also made his ministrations as a bishop invalid! The issue broke wide open when Caecilian was consecrated bishop of Carthage by the same Bishop Felix. The Donatists refused to accept Bishop Caecilian because they would not accept the validity of his consecration at the "sinful" Felix's hands.

57. Greenslade, *Schism in the Early Church*, 120.

Movement Two: The Church Thinking

The Donatists were rigorists. They believed that moral sanctity was necessary to Christians, and that any sacramental ministrations of sinful bishops were invalid. Technically this view is known as *ex opere operantis* ("from the work of the one doing the working"), that is, that the validity of any ministry depends upon the worthiness and holiness of the minister conducting it. They believed that even those who communicated with those sinful bishops were contaminated, and so they came to the conclusion that they—the Donatists alone—were the only true and holy church. Their beliefs went to such an extent that they rebaptised their converts, believing their original Catholic baptism to be invalid.

The Donatists believed that everything associated with the Catholics was tainted by sin and unsuitable for Christian use. They purged any churches they took over of everything associated with Catholic worship. They melted down the silver, destroyed the Communion tables by burning them, completely washed the floors and walls, and even threw out the reserved bread and wine consecrated by Catholic clergy and gave them to the dogs. Augustine records that the bitterness was so great that the Donatist bishop at Hippo would not even let any of his flock provide food for their Catholic friends and neighbours.

The crux of the theological issue was really centred on the way in which the moral state of a minister affected the validity of his ministerial acts. The church declared Donatism a heresy in AD 411 and it was Augustine of Hippo who championed the fight against that particular heresy. He maintained, and the church accepted, that it was by virtue of the office held that the ministry of a priest or bishop was validated and not anything in their own character or person. Alister McGrath summarises Augustine's position succinctly:

> Donatus and his followers insisted that the efficacy of the church and its sacramental system was dependent upon the moral or cultic purity of its representatives. . . . For Augustine, this amounted to making salvation indirectly dependent upon holy human agents rather than the grace of Christ. . . . Christ thus plays a secondary role in either the securing or sustaining of salvation, whereas the human agent plays a primary role of crucial importance.[58]

This was necessary because, if it were not true, then nobody could ever know whether any ministerial actions were valid or not, because one could

---

58. McGrath, *Heresy*, 158.

never know whether the minister ministering to them was in a state of grace or not.

The traditional view of the universal church, therefore, had always been (and still is) *ex opere operato*, which means "from the work having been worked." This is the view that that the validity of any ministry depends upon the holiness of God and the working of his Holy Spirit—the minister being a mere instrument of God's work, so that any priest or bishop, even one in a state of mortal sin, acts validly, and the faithful are not denied the benefits of sacramental or preaching ministry because of the minister's sin. They can still be used by God.

> The Donatist approach represented a principled yet ultimately dogmatic refusal to appreciate that all of humanity—including priests and bishops—is in need of the same healing that the gospel provides. . . . the ministers . . . are to be considered as spiritual convalescents who are able to administer to others the same salves and medicines that have set them on the road to recovery but have yet to heal them fully.[59]

Gradually Donatism faded away, and disappeared entirely when the Islamic Arabs conquered western North Africa and Christianity was obliterated there.

At the Reformation, as we shall see in more detail in the next section, although some of the more extreme elements may have taken the Donatist position, the majority continued to hold that it was wrong. Article 26 of the Thirty-Nine Articles of the Church of England condemns Donatism, and actually extends the *ex opere operato* principle to ministering the Word of God as well as the sacraments.[60]

---

59. Ibid., 159.

60. Church of England, *Book of Common Prayer* (1662), The Articles of Religion, Article 26: "Although in the visible Church the evil be ever mingled with the good, and sometimes the evil have chief authority in the Ministration of the Word and Sacraments, yet forasmuch as they do not the same in their own name, but in Christ's, and do minister by his commission and authority, we may use their ministry, both in hearing the Word of God, and in receiving of the Sacraments. Neither is the effect of Christ's ordinance taken away by their wickedness, nor the grace of God's gifts diminished from such as by faith and rightly do receive the Sacraments ministered unto them; which be effectual, because of Christ's institution and promise, although they be ministered by evil men. Nevertheless, it appertaineth to the discipline of the Church, that inquiry be made of evil Ministers, and that they be accused by those that have knowledge of their offences; and finally, being found guilty, by just judgment be deposed."

Clearly the Reformers were not saying that every rebellious utterance from heretical preachers should be accepted, for they themselves were only too ready to speak out openly against such false doctrine. The article itself ends with a call for the disciplining of what it calls "evil ministers." That, however, is to be accomplished through an established, recognised disciplinary authority, and not, for example, through a self-appointed body of disenchanted primates as envisaged in the GAFCON constitution. Nevertheless, what Article 26 does show is the absolute commitment of the Reformers to maintaining unity, order, and authority within the church. They were also passing through a tumultuous period of church history. The fight against heresy was not to be fought and won by a reciprocal rebellion against established ecclesiastical authority and by attempting to "unchurch" dissident leaders.

There is a clear reference in this Article to Jesus' parable about the Wheat and the Weeds and to St. Augustine's application of this to the church in this difficult situation.[61]

Alister E. McGrath puts it more succinctly: "The ultimate grounds of sacramental efficacy lie in Christ, whose person and benefits are conveyed by the sacraments, not in the priest himself. An immoral priest can thus be permitted to celebrate the sacraments, as the grounds of their validity do not rest in him."[62]

It is difficult to see how GAFCON can both claim to uphold the Thirty-Nine Articles, including Article 26, and reconcile their affirmation with Article 13 of the Jerusalem Statement: "We reject the authority of those churches and leaders who have denied the orthodox faith in word or deed."[63]

Greenslade sees the root of this rigorism in a particular doctrinal theory, making the holiness of the church depend upon the moral purity of its members. The belief was that the good are infected by communion

---

61. Matt 13: 24–30, 36–43: "The servants asked him, 'Do you want us to go and pull them up?' 'No,' he answered, 'because while you are pulling the weeds, you may root up the wheat with them. Let both grow together until the harvest. At that time I will tell the harvesters: First collect the weeds and tie them in bundles to be burned; then gather the wheat and bring it into my barn.' . . . As the weeds are pulled up and burned in the fire, so it will be at the end of the age. The Son of Man will send out his angels, and they will weed out of his kingdom everything that causes sin and all who do evil. They will throw them into the fiery furnace, where there will be weeping and gnashing of teeth. Then the righteous will shine like the sun in the kingdom of their Father. He who has ears, let him hear."

62. McGrath, *Reformation Thought*, 176.

63. GAFCON, "Statement."

with the morally lax. It is what he calls "The theory of infection"![64] Could it be that a form of Donatism—a heresy that, curiously enough, arose and thrived (for a time) in the Church in Africa—or, at least, this "theory of infection," is still alive and well in Africa, and in the diocese of Sydney and its outposts as well as in the other places supporting GAFCON?

Despite what has been written and said by GAFCON and others, the cause of the problem is not conflict over the full acceptance of homosexuals and their relationships, or even the ordination of women, or the interpretation of Scripture, or the source of authority in the church. These are truly not that much unlike literally hundreds of such conflicts in the history of the church— indeed from its very beginning at Pentecost.

The problem arises in the present conflict when the dissidents declare as invalid the ministration of bishops whom they believe to be immoral. That is the crux of the problem—everything else involves only personal variances in the interpretations of Scripture or personal preferences and prejudices. These latter issues merely mean that some Anglicans think other Anglicans are in moral error. In other words, they are plainly sinful.

But there is nothing whatsoever new about this situation. It has existed within the Christian church ever since the beginning. What is central to the problem is the resurgence of the Donatist idea that any personal immorality invalidates bishops' ministries—that is, when some people judge some bishops to be immoral, they repudiate the ministry of those bishops.

If that did not happen today, there would be no threats of schism. If only those on either side of the argument could say to each other, as Christians have said to other Christians from the earliest days of the church, that, while they believe the other to be totally wrong in their moral judgements, it is still possible for you, as a bishop, to confirm and ordain and absolve and bless and consecrate and celebrate the Eucharist—because your validity is found in your office not and in your person.

The root of this problem seems to come from the contrast between those who look solely to Scripture for proper patterns of dealing with sinners and those who look to the church and its history for such patterns.

Scriptures such as:

> Those who sin are to be rebuked publicly, so that the others may take warning. (1 Tim 5:20)
>
> If your brother sins against you go and show him his fault, just between the two of you. If he listens to you, you have won

---

64. Greenslade, *Schism in the Early Church*, 124.

Movement Two: The Church Thinking

your brother over. But if he will not listen, take one or two others along, so that every matter may be established by the testimony of two or three witnesses. If he refuses to listen to them, tell it to the church; and if he refuses to listen even to the church, treat him as you would a pagan or a tax collector. (Matt 18:15–17)

Expel the wicked man from among you. (1 Cor 5:13)

talk about what to do with sinners in the within the congregation. However, the church has for 1700 years tempered that at least to the degree of saying that the immoral minister is not an invalid minister.

When the Inter-Anglican Theological and Doctrinal Commission met in Kuala Lumpur and issued their report in 2008, they were positive and quite confident that the ideas expressed in *The Windsor Report* would point "towards some ways to hold the Communion together at this time."[65]

While affirming the central place of scripture in the Anglican tradition, they note that "the art of living under a Scripture which is both unified and diverse is an organic part of the vocation to live together within our single yet richly variegated Communion. It is within this context that our ongoing and vital debates about the "authority" of Scripture must take place. . . . any expectation that interpretations of Scripture will ever be totally uncontested is discounted by the experience of history, if not the very character of the Bible itself."[66]

While clearly stating that ". . . for the bonds of affection in the Anglican Communion to hold together, sound doctrine, together with ethical living and the practice of Christian virtues, are both vital," it also recognises that the Communion will have to face some very difficult ethical questions about justice head on, such as ". . . in what way does the Gospel offer good news to Christians with differing sexual orientations?"[67]

What the Commission does affirm is that any discussion about a possible innovation to ethics or practice within the church cannot be undertaken independently of discussion about doctrine and belief. They always belong together.[68]

---

65. Third Inter-Anglican Theological and Doctrinal Commission, *Communion, Conflict and Hope*, 49.

66. Ibid., 34–35.

67. Ibid., 38.

68. Although what follows is critical of this Commission, and I believe the criticisms to have validity, nevertheless there is perhaps, more importantly, a new, fresh, and positive dynamic in the Commission's findings which is discussed more fully in

Beating the Bounds

It is possible, however, to argue that the Commission in making this case encourages the distinctions between dogmatic and moral theology to become blurred. Dogmatic theology—that is, the study of the dogmas and doctrines of the Church—is enshrined in the great creeds of Christendom and in the deliberations of the truly ecumenical councils. Even with the difficulties we have already noted about how settled this "core" theology of the church was—it is, nevertheless, what the church believes to be true about God and humanity and the relation between the two.

Moral theology, on the other hand, is an entirely different discipline. It is the study and teachings about the determination of the moral right and wrong of human actions. It has always been a speculative science, saying, in a sense, "action 'X' is probably wrong because . . ." But, for instance, in moral theology there are literally dozens of considerations that make an action right or wrong. These could include matters of intention, circumstances and other possible options, and so on. So, questions of moral theology need to be treated very differently from questions of dogmatic theology.

Serious theologians have always recognised that there will be valid variations in positions and attitudes to moral theology among Christians. This could be true even among and between those who hold more or less the same dogmatic theology.

And that is a serious problem now, since it is only basically two issues of moral theology around which the whole furore is raging. These are, firstly, the whole issue of whether homosexual relationships are, of themselves, in essence sinful and therefore cannot be legitimised by some form of gay marriage. The second is whether homosexual people can be admitted into the ordained ministry of the church. There is little disagreement on dogmatics concerning the theology of the creeds and ecumenical councils, the Trinity, the incarnation, the atonement, and the resurrection. These are broadly common to all, even though varying theological emphases have to be recognised here.

What is most disturbing today is that many who claim adherence to orthodox Christian tradition often seem enthusiastically to take on board the old and discredited heresy of Donatism. These protagonists make solemn unbending theological statements about issues of morality, which have always had *fuzzy* edges and have been interpreted in a variety of ways. It could be the case that we have seen the ever-learning and -reforming practical wisdom of the church replaced by an alien, rigid, literalistic, and

---

Movement Four under the heading "A Counter-Melody."

conservative view of the Bible that has almost turned what should be seen as a treasure store into something closer to an idol.

The creeds themselves were supposed to be the ultimate statements of agreement on core truths, but, in reality, they were actually a consensus reached only through often violent disagreement and, in the case of the Nicaean-Constantinople Creed, the intervention of the emperor.

The use of the non-biblical word *homoousion*—a word that had been declared heretical at the Synod of Antioch in AD 264—to describe the Trinity only "opened the door for dogmas to be promulgated which did not have the authority of scripture." This would, Christie-Murray claims, be responsible for much of the doctrinal turbulence of later centuries.[69]

Howard Thurman, in his interview with Ronald Eyre for BBC television, has an interesting take on the formation of the creeds that, in fact, history bears out. He sees a creed as

> . . . a statement of triumph over a position that was either outlawed or outvoted, even though there is nothing in the creed that tells you who lost. But if you live long enough, if the creed lives long enough, the position that lost finds its way back. In maybe fifty or a hundred years, it creeps in again as a restatement of the original idea. Those who lost have their innings, maybe fifty years, a hundred years after. . . . Religious *experience* is dynamic, fluid, effervescent, yeasty. But the mind can't handle these so it has to imprison religious experience in some way, get it bottled up. Then, when the experience quiets down, the mind draws a bead on it and extracts concepts, notions, dogmas, so that religious experience can make sense to the mind. Meanwhile religious experience goes on *experiencing*. . . . Therefore, whatever creed there is, whatever theology there is, must always be a little out of date. . . . It is not of the nature of religious experience to be stabilized.[70]

Thurman majors on the seminal influence of religious experience over the formation of dogma and he therefore sees the creeds as, of necessity, always lagging behind the dynamism of experience. Such views are similar to those we will come across in our examination of the emerging church. They again challenge the rigid, dogmatic approach taken by conservative parties such as GAFCON towards any possible development of theological understanding beyond that enshrined in the documents of the Reformation, which is the period to which we must now turn.

69. Christie-Murray, *History of Heresy*, 46–47.
70. Thurman, "Interview."

Beating the Bounds

The Reformation—Circles, Sets, Edges, and Centres

Tickle identifies the start of the Reformation not with Luther's nailing of his Ninety-Five Theses to the church door at the Castle Church in Wittenberg on October 31, 1517, but with the ungodly debacle of three contending popes that began in 1378 and was not settled until 1418. For Tickle this denigrated "the consensual illusion of unity and power presented by a unitary papacy."[71] Thus the question was raised that continually faces the church in times of change: "Where now is authority?"

The Reformation answer was "*Sola scriptura, scriptura sola*," re-emphasising the doctrine of the priesthood of all believers and the rebuttal of all notions of papal authority. However, as many now claim, it could be said only to have created ". . . a paper Pope in place of a flesh and blood one."[72] Whether that was true or not, it is certainly true that the question of authority became central yet again.

Science and technology also played their part in this turmoil. The invention of the Gutenberg printing press around 1440 enabled the distribution of the Scriptures in the vernacular in ways undreamt of before this time. It also aided the dissemination of the reformers' ideas and theology to a wider and more general audience than had previously ever engaged in such theological disputation.

To add to the turmoil, the sixteenth century produced the Copernican Revolution, which placed the earth in orbit around the sun as a minor player in the galaxy rather than, as previously taught by the church, the earth being the centre of the universe with the sun and all other planets in orbit around it.

The Catholic Church, in its dealing with Galileo, nevertheless later condemned heliocentrism as "false and contrary to Scripture,"[73] and Galileo was tried by the Inquisition and found "vehemently suspect of heresy,"[74] forced to recant, and spent the rest of his life under house arrest.

Paul Avis sees Reformation theology as being obsessed with the problem of distinguishing between the true and the false church. The problem was that, in the same way as David Christie-Murray had written of the early church struggles—that true and pure orthodoxy might only exist in a Platonic way, "in the mind of God"—now Avis claims that

---

71. Tickle, *Great Emergence*, 44.

72. Ibid., 47.

73. For much more detail see Sharratt, *Galileo*, 127–31; and McMullin, "Church's Ban on Copernicanism."

74. Galilei, *Galileo on the World Systems*, 47.

Movement Two: The Church Thinking

Luther's ideal of the perfect church, invisible and intangible as it was, did not exist in reality. Avis cites Gordon Rupp's view of Luther that he ". . . was not so much concerned with defining the circumference of the church but with proclaiming the centre."[75]

There is certainly an echo of Schweizer's observations here, and it is a theme that we saw taken up strongly by contemporary theologians of the Emerging Church. Avis reminds us how Luther himself had said that ". . . no earthly power can draw the boundaries of the Church and decide who belongs to it and who does not. . . . The Christian existence of the individual is beyond the reach of every ecclesiastical organisation."[76]

Despite his harsh treatment at the hands of the pope, Luther's view of the Roman Church was often respectful.

> We on our part confess that there is much that is Christian and good under the papacy; indeed everything that is Christian and good is to be found there and has come to us from this source. For instance, we confess that in the Papal Church there are the true Holy Scriptures, true baptism, the true sacrament of the altar, the true keys to the forgiveness of sins, the true office of the ministry, the true catechism in the form of the Lord's Prayer, the Ten Commandments and the articles of the Creed."[77]

It would be interesting to know whether or not the leaders of GAFCON and FCA would be willing to make such a statement about the Episcopal Church in the United States. Even if they refuse to acknowledge the ministry of certain bishops, they must accept that five of the six "true" characteristics of the church as outlined by Luther remain.

It was the later reformers such as Bucer, Calvin, the Puritans, and the Separatists who became far more rigid about defining the boundaries of the church, which they did by adding the note of discipline and excommunication. Avis makes it clear that soon it was ecclesiological discipline that became primary and overshadowed the Word and sacrament as marks of the church, especially in the Reformed churches on the continent and, with a vengeance, among the Anabaptists.

It was true that in the latter part of the sixteenth century a number of English Puritans came to the conviction that the Church of England would never fully reform itself, and they decided to separate from the state

---

75. Avis, *Church in the Theology of the Reformers*, 3.
76. Ibid.
77. Cited in Avis, *Church in the Theology of the Reformers*, 37.

church and organise their own congregations.[78] Known as Separatists for this reason, they would argue for what was essentially a Congregationalist form of church government.

One of their earliest leaders was Robert Browne (c. 1550–1633), who in a tract entitled "A Treatise of Reformation without Tarrying for Anie" (1582)[79] provided the clarion call of the Separatist movement. He was of the opinion that the setting up of congregations apart from the established church and its parish churches was a necessity for, he wrote that year, "... God will receive none to communion and covenant with him, which as yet are at one with the wicked."[80]

A similar tone is found in the attitude of GAFCON reported in *The Church of England Newspaper* in the United Kingdom. The Global South coalition of the Anglican Communion has anathematized the leaders of the Episcopal Church and Anglican Church of Canada as apostates who will not be saved unless they abjure and repent of their false teachings: "... the Episcopal Church, along with the Anglican Church of Canada had 'rejected the Way of the Lord as expressed in Holy Scripture.'"[81]

Also in 1582, Browne established a Separatist congregation at Norwich. Experiencing persecution, he and his Norwich congregation left England the following year for the freedom of the Netherlands. Browne conceived of the local church as a "gathered" church, that is, a company of Christians who had covenanted together to live under the rule of Christ, the Risen Lord, whose will was made known through his Word and his Spirit.

---

78. This is a similar to the view taken by the organisers of GAFCON, who claim that they have waited long enough for the Anglican Communion to reform itself, and now they must take matters into their own hands.

79. Harrison, "Treatise of Reformation."

80. Ibid. This is, of course, a similar view to that taken by the bishops who refused to attend the Lambeth Conference in 2008 because the consecrators of Gene Robinson, the homosexual bishop of New Hampshire, had been invited even though Robinson himself had not been invited.

81. Conger, *Global South Anglicans*, 2. The article goes on: "the US and Canadian Churches have continued in their defiance as they set themselves on a course that contradicts the plain teaching of the Holy Scriptures on matters so fundamental that they affect the very salvation of those involved."

These "actions violate the integrity of the Gospel, the Communion and our Christian witness to the rest of the world.... In the face of this we dare not remain silent and must respond with appropriate action,' they said, and urged Churches across the Communion to consider carefully their ties to the US and Canadian Churches.'"

Ultimately Christianity was seen simply as ". . . a matter of private conscience rather than public order, that the church is a fellowship of believers rather than an army of pressed men."[82]

When Browne returned to the British Isles he shocked many of his friends when he subsequently recanted his views, and became a member of the Church of England. But he had begun a movement that could not be held in check and that certainly has many subsequent secret followers within contemporary conservative evangelical Anglican ranks. Indeed, as British Baptist historian Barrie White has noted of the sixteenth century, "For many it was but a short step from impatient Puritanism within the established Church to convinced Separatism outside it."[83]

It seems that history may be repeating itself in the puritan ranks of Anglicanism. It is particularly interesting that those churches associated with the conservative diocese of Sydney have dropped the use of the word "congregation" and replaced it with the very Separatist-sounding word "gathering."

However, Avis believes that this Separatist ecclesiology was totally dominated by an obsession with discipline and the gospel was practically obscured by the regime under which it was preached. Tellingly, he notes that separatist ecclesiology proved to be self-defeating.[84] In their enthusiasm and even fanaticism, Avis says, they made the mistake of seeing discipline as of the "esse" (essence) of the church rather than the "ben esse" (well-being) of the church and that it is Christ himself and not merely "the Law" that reigns in the Christian community.[85]

Gensichen, in his long and detailed investigation into the "condemnations" thundered during the Reformation during the internecine controversies within Lutheranism, reminds us of what can so often happen. "The Word is no longer heard and grasped primarily as 'the living voice of the Gospel,' but in the form of doctrine it becomes something that can used to render theological judgements."[86]

Avis sees a more gentle view being taken up by the reformed Church of England. Hooper regarded the Word and God and sacraments as the marks of the true church of God. Ridley added "charity" (godly living) to

---

82. Harrison, "Treatise of Reformation."
83. White, *English Separatist Tradition*, 84.
84. Avis, *Church in the Theology of the Reformers*, 61–63.
85. Ibid., 29.
86. Gensichen, *We Condemn*, 210.

the Word of God, sacraments, and discipline. Parker's Eleven Articles of 1559 agreed, as did Bancroft and the Homilies.

Avis sees importance in the fact that, like Luther, Richard Hooker stressed that many in the past had found faith and salvation in the Roman Church. The fact that he openly held the view that a "papist" might be saved was really important at this time when Roman Catholicism was seen in England as treason as well as heresy.

Avis sees Hooker defining the visible church in a more empirical and pragmatic way than the Continental reformers and radicals had done. He reckoned that the outward expression of faith of those who claimed to be Christian had to be taken at face value for, like Queen Elizabeth herself, he did not believe that we had or, indeed, should make "windows into men's souls."[87]

McGillion also cites Hooker as an example and links his thought to that of Bruce Kaye. He understands Hooker as the one who saw the very changes taking place in the church as being part of God's plan and ordinance. Kaye himself saw this too and recognised it as a sign of God's engagement with creation and the ongoing life of the church. To Kaye that became what he called a theology that is "quintessentially Anglican."[88]

McGillion, however, notes with some sadness that what elasticity and generosity there was in Hooker is a long way removed from the hard, unforgiving position taken by conservative evangelical Anglicans on issues of gender and sexuality.[89]

Kaye stresses that Hooker sees Christ's authority as being "supreme and inward rather than external and coercive." Hooker always stresses the notion of consensus and sees that as an integral part of the pilgrimage of the Church. "It is in the context of that pilgrimage, contingency and faith that Hooker's emphasis on the grace of God in Christ becomes so critical as the touchstone for what he has to say."[90]

Butler notes that even some of the Puritans were broader and more accepting in ecclesiological thought than they are often given credit for.

---

87. Avis, *Church in the Theology of the Reformers*, 35.

88. McGillion, *Chosen Ones*, 123.

89. Ibid., 123. "He clearly seeks to address the actual historical situation of his time and to do that in a way that is properly theological. He is committed to the authority of scripture, to the early church's examples and to tradition. He is committed to the authority of the church community as a whole and therefore seeks for consensus. What is justified in one particularity does not necessarily mean it will be justifiable elsewhere or at a subsequent time or in a preceding time in the same locality."

90. Kaye, *Reinventing Anglicanism*, 129.

He cites Richard Baxter, in 1681: "I earnestly desire to see that Wall or Hedge pull'd down, that Christ's Flock among us may be one. . . . Your thorn-hedge hath enclosed but one corner of Christ's vineyard, and I have business in the rest. I will go sometime on both sides of the hedge, though by so doing I be scratcht."[91]

This same openness was also found in George Whitefield, who, in a letter to a Presbyterian minister wrote,

> What a divine sympathy and attraction is there between all those who by one spirit are made members of that mystical body, whereof JESUS CHRIST is the head! . . . Blessed be God that his love is so far shed abroad in our hearts, as to cause us to love one another, though we are a little differ as to externals: For my part, I hate to mention them. My one sole question is, Are you a Christian? . . . If so, you are my brother, my sister, and mother. . . . Yet a little while, and we shall sit down together in the kingdom of our Father.[92]

However, Whitefield's description of "a little differ as to externals" is in itself at the heart of the dispute we are examining. What to one is but a little thing is large to another. We are back to the concept of *adiaphora*! *Adiaphora* are defined as ". . . things which do not make a difference, matters regarded as non-essential, issues about which one can disagree without dividing the church."[93]

The theology of *adiaphora* has roots in divisive disputes as the second-generation Lutheran church sought to find an identity in changing political situations. Melanchthon proposed the concept to enable Lutherans to accept the Leipzig Interim, a settlement hammered out between Elector Moritz and Emperor Charles V.[94] Charles would accept Lutheran theology if Moritz could persuade the Lutherans to accept Catholic traditions of worship. This compromise was considered a possible way to reconcile the Lutherans and the Church of Rome. Melanchthon found a way of accepting ceremonial acts as matters that were not essential, or *adiaphora*. Lutheran leaders, questioning where it would end, chided Melanchthon for his weakness and asked if transubstantiation itself could be

---

91. Butler, *Dying to Be One*, 57.
92. Gilles, *Works of . . . The Revd. George Whitefield*, 1:126.
93. Lambeth Commission on Communion, *Windsor Report*, 87.
94. Cameron, *European Reformation*, 346–49.

adiaphora.[95] Those who opposed its adoption in the English church of the time, both Puritans and Catholics, echoed this fear.

For A. G. Dickens *adiaphora* was among the most attractive of all the Reformation doctrines. He argued that it enabled an escape from the demand to acquiesce to propositions, and was the mark of liberal, tolerant, reformed theology.[96] It was fundamental to the theology of Frith, who was executed in 1533, not because he denied transubstantiation and purgatory, but because he did not see them as essential to the faith.[97] The English liberal reformers, such as Starkey and Brinklow, also took such a stand.[98]

In the English Reformation *adiaphora* was used to argue for toleration and freedom, and the issues surrounding who was to judge what was essential were sidestepped. The pressure for conformity in Melanchthon's Germany and in mid-sixteenth-century England came from the civil powers.

In 1556, John Ponet, the bishop of Winchester, adopted *adiaphorism*, and while he assigned to the crown powers over "things indifferent," the essentials, he argued, were left to individual conscience.[99] Ponet argued that bishops could enforce non-essential things, such as the style of vestments worn by clergy, but not essentials, such as belief in purgatory, which was for the individual to believe or reject. It was noted that transubstantiation was regarded as non-essential, even though it is a core doctrine that divided the church.

Butler also wrestles with the problem of what the Reformation notion of *sola scriptura* actually means. If, as Jesus said in John 14:26 and 16:13, the Holy Spirit would lead the church into all truth, how is it that we see so many contradictions in what are always claimed to be his leadings and guidance in interpreting the Scriptures?

Butler compares, among many other examples, the execution of More and Fisher on the one side, with the execution of Cranmer, Ridley, and Latimer on the other side—all supposedly based on the Spirit's guidance.

Similar claims of divine guidance were made for the Thirty-Nine Articles of the Church of England in 1562 and for the Counter-Reformation decisions of the Council of Trent between 1545 and 1563, yet they are clearly contradictory.

---

95. Ibid., 363–64.
96. Dickens, *English Reformation*, 462.
97. Ibid., 116–17.
98. Dickens, *Reformation Studies*, 429–31.
99. Ibid., 430.

Tickle notes, with some distaste, the way in which even those apparently on the same side of the Catholic/Protestant divide lambasted one another in the name of truth but with little love lost between them. "Shared sensibilities and common theological affinities did not prevent their dissenting, one from another, either. Luther, in particular, was a contentious antagonist, at one point calling John Calvin a 'cow,' Bullinger a 'bull,' and proclaiming that Zwingli was from the Evil One simply because the two of them differed violently on the true nature of the host or bread at the Eucharist."[100]

This confusing state of affairs left a legacy that the church universal is still struggling with today. The problem behind this struggle is the important question: Who speaks for God? This is the heart of the constant hermeneutical debate within the ongoing life of the church. When one interpretation or claimed revelation is put alongside a conflicting view, how can we know which one is "of the Spirit" and which one is not?

Sensus plenior is a term that means, literally, "fuller sense" or "deeper meaning." The term is used to refer to those passages that, at their most obvious level, speak of one person or event, but which also have a deeper meaning hinted at through that specific event in question. In other words, *sensus plenior* is the term that acknowledges that some historical persons and events in the Old Testament are really "types," and that the passages treating of those persons and events speak not just of themselves alone, but also of the "anti-types" (i.e., the fulfilments of the types) that they foreshadow.

A good example of a case in which the principle of *sensus plenior* must be applied is Moses' striking the rock in the wilderness, so that water flowed out to nourish the people. This passage relates a very real historical event, and its most basic level of meaning refers simply to a physical rock that flowed with physical water; but this event was also a type of how Christ, the rock of our salvation, was struck with the rod of divine justice, and henceforth there flowed from his wounded body the forgiveness and spiritual life that we need. In other words, there is a *sensus plenior* or deeper meaning to this event than just the real, historical occurrence.

In 1 Corinthians 10:4, Paul gives express instruction for us to see a *sensus plenior* in this passage; and a little later, he says that all the things recorded in the Old Testament were written as for our instruction (1 Cor 10:11). Some have seen this as giving warrant to see a *sensus plenior* in all the Scriptures. This is, however, a dangerous precedent that would open

---

100. Tickle, *Great Emergence*, 57.

the door for anybody to claim authority for any fanciful interpretation offered.

This is exactly the dilemma created for many by those who wish to interpret the biblical texts concerning such issues as the role of women in the church or homosexuality or any other situation where new claims are made about fresh and different interpretations from the traditional and historical views. To examine that approach we must look now to the contemporary church, where many are valiantly wrestling theologically with the issues raised by today's culture and, most especially, with the paradigm shift of postmodernism.

The Emerging Church

Looking at the contemporary scene, Peter Toon opens his discussion on doctrinal development with yet another reminder that different interpretations of ancient texts have always been in the church. Christians of later centuries and even today do not interpret the clauses of the early creeds in the same way as those who initially wrote them or used them. It is clear that there were many differences of interpretations in the Western church before the sixteenth century. It was, however, the cataclysmic upheaval of the Reformation that made rival confessions of faith a permanent feature of Christendom.[101]

While all these rival confessions still govern the understanding of doctrine in our major denominations and each claims to summarise or expound accurately biblical teaching, Toon notes that they were each composed "by particular men in specific circumstances"[102] and must, therefore, be seen and understood from within their historical, religious, cultural and political contexts. Toon then raises the questions of the relationship between doctrine and teaching formulated in one language and its development as it is expressed later in a different language and cultural setting.

James Barr[103] takes this idea even further describing how selective the evangelical appeal to orthodoxy can be. He accuses evangelicals of positively highlighting those elements that accord with evangelical thinking while ignoring much of early orthodox faith and practice that would today be quite alien to modern evangelical faith and practice. Ancient

---

101. Toon, *Development of Doctrine*, 2.
102. Ibid., 3.
103. Barr, *Beyond Fundamentalism*, 178.

orthodoxy looked and felt very different from what passes as evangelical orthodoxy today.

Barr points out that the same is true of the attachment shown by evangelicals to the theology of the Reformation. There is again a partial and selective representation of Reformation theology. This, he says, is because evangelicalism has developed out from the Reformation rather than having simply reproduced it. In fact the Reformation movement was very different from modern evangelicalism, which really has its roots in the evangelical revivals of the eighteenth and nineteenth centuries and "the influence of post-Reformation developments of Protestant orthodoxy on the one hand and pietism on the other."[104]

Toon also traces the history of the understanding of how doctrine "develops." He leads us through the responses to Newman in both the nineteenth and twentieth century of Mozley, Rainy, Hodge, and Harnack. He seems persuaded by James Orr's view that the only criterion with which it is possible to judge any development of doctrine is "the unerring verdict of history," or, in Toon's words, "The history of dogma was the judgement of dogma."[105]

However, Toon is, in my opinion, too soft regarding the judgment of history, when Orr says that the clock of history never goes back. "It never returns upon itself to take up as part of its creed what it has formally, and with full consciousness, rejected at some bygone stage."[106]

This statement flies in the face of contemporary history when we consider the adoption now, in many mainline churches, of changes that were previously unthinkable, such as the ordination of women, the marriage of divorcees, and, in the United States, the consecration to the episcopate of an openly homosexual priest. These are not only ethical issues but have deep theological and doctrinal significance and have, therefore, caused deep divisions within the body of Christ.

Nevertheless Toon realises that the theological questions being asked today are often very different from those asked in the sixteenth or seventeenth centuries. He senses that there is a need for more contemporary confessions of faith. What is needed today, Toon emphasises, is not "... more 'Luthers' to stand against the world and then go their own separate Lutheran, Calvinist, or Methodist ways. We need people who, seeing

---

104. Ibid., 151.
105. Toon, *Development of Doctrine*, 45–46.
106. Ibid., 58.

the divisions, also see the possibility of deeper and more practical unity in Christ."[107]

Not everyone agrees with that point of view, however. McGillion records an interview with John Woodhouse, the principal of Moore College, Sydney, in which he seems to imply that he would be quite happy to see the Anglican Church split in the same way as the Reformation split the medieval church. He sees what he calls the artificial unity of the Anglican Communion as being a hindrance to the gospel because it inhibits freedom of conscience and free speech.[108] McGillion interprets his words as seeing such splits providing new energy and innovation within the Anglican Church.

Anderson, in recognising the huge changes that have occurred in the world in which the contemporary church is called to its mission, goes much further than either Toon or Woodhouse by claiming the need for an emergent theology for emerging churches. For him such a theology must emerge "more out of the future than out of the past."[109] It is the mission agenda that is now central rather than ecclesiology.

While GAFCON and its supporters would happily agree to that definition of the agenda, their understanding of what that means in practice would be very different.

Anderson compares notions of time and history (*chronos* and *kairos*) with the ideas of *movements* and *moments*. The Fellowship of Confessing Anglicans, in the first sentence of its statement of its goals, declares, "The language of GAFCON declares that it was a movement, not a moment,"[110] and in doing so agrees with Anderson when he describes movements such as the traditional churches as being rooted in a high degree of continuity with the past. He gives the example of the church in Jerusalem, which, even after the dynamite of Pentecost, managed to absorb the event into continuity with the tradition of the Twelve.

---

107. Ibid., 82.

108. McGillion, *Chosen Ones*, 124. From an interview with John Woodhouse: "Everybody thinks that if only we were united that will progress the gospel. . . . But a false, superficial unity inhibits freedom of conscience, it inhibits freedom of speech and I think it inhibits the freedom of the gospel. . . . Institutional unity is of very, very little value. I mean, it's false. Whatever unity there is in the Anglican community today, what is it? It's just a unity that is pretending that we don't disagree, or not talking about our disagreements. It's an agreement not to discuss certain things. Well, what value is that?"

109. Anderson, *Emergent Theology*, 15.

110. FCA, "Goals."

While Anderson's view that Jerusalem contributed nothing to the emerging church in terms of plants or support is certainly too sweeping, there is no doubt that the mission and ministry of Paul and his apostolic team was largely independent of practical support from Jerusalem. Indeed, the Scriptures record that, in reality, any practical support went the other way as Paul encouraged the Gentile churches to collect money to help their fellow Christians in Jerusalem.[111]

Moments, in contrast to movements, have a high degree of discontinuity with anything that has gone before. His prime example of this is Paul's experience of the risen Christ and his subsequent theology of revelation claimed to be as authoritative as that of the apostles. Anderson claims that this was revolutionary because the Spirit was opening up new dimensions of truth as a basis for theological reflection on what has already been revealed. There was theological continuity with Christ in the context of a critical discontinuity with religious forms and traditions. This evident tension between Word and Spirit is only resolved as the Spirit is recognised as "the Spirit of Christ."[112]

Anderson calls his revolution the "eschatological preference," which, he says, ". . . refers to the work of Christ that comes out of the future into the present by the Holy Spirit. In defending his own apostolic authority Paul cannot appeal to historical precedence as did the others at Jerusalem. His call to be an apostle comes from the risen Lord Jesus, not the historical Jesus."[113]

He also refers to the ordination of women, marriage of divorcees, and the possible acceptance of homosexuals into the church and ministry as examples of this. He stresses the revolutionary nature of the command to "love your neighbour as yourself" (Rom 13:9) and this leads him to believe that "The law of love accepts diversity but does not make diversity a moral virtue. Rather, all that divides and differentiates us finds its unity and wholeness in our common humanity. It is this form of humanity that has been assumed by God in Christ and, for Paul, became the human form of emerging churches."[114]

---

111. "Now about the collection for God's people: Do what I told the Galatian churches to do. On the first day of every week, each one of you should set aside a sum of money in keeping with his income, saving it up, so that when I come no collections will have to be made. Then, when I arrive, I will give letters of introduction to the men you approve and send them with your gift to Jerusalem" (1 Cor 16:1).

112. Anderson, *Emergent Theology*, 26–29.

113. Ibid., 126–27.

114. Ibid., 154.

Dr. Lewis Smedes, a theologian in the Christian Reformed Church and a former ethics professor at Fuller Theological Seminary, recounts the turning point in his own church when the reality of this truth hit home. Since the 1940s the Synod had decreed that divorced and remarried people were not eligible to share in the Lord's Supper on scriptural grounds.[115] Speaking of the place of remarried divorcees in his own church, he criticises the hypocrisy that allowed them to worship, give their money, and enjoy the church life and be well liked by all, ". . . but banishment from the Supper signed and sealed the church's judgment that they were banished from the circle of grace and the fellowship of Christ."[116]

Smedes tells how the church came to see that, in the light of the hurt and pain that people who loved the Lord and supported the church were suffering, surely Jesus would not have meant the church to be so cruel and hypocritical. Instead, Smedes is suggesting that a way of interpreting Jesus' words is to see him as simply placing before us God's ideal for marriage but being well aware of human frailty and our inability to maintain that ideal in practice: ". . . but once it factored human reality into its reading of the Lord's words, it was bound to ask: Could Jesus have actually meant the church to cast away people who were committed to him, on grounds that they were committed to each other too?"[117]

We can only live in fellowship with God and with one another as we each recognise our need for His grace and forgiveness. He then asks the all important question of his own church. "Was the church's embrace of people who were once divorced and are now living faithfully in second marriages a precedent for embracing homosexual people who live faithfully in covenanted partnerships?"[118]

A similar argument is put forward by James Jones, bishop of Liverpool, in his presidential address to the Liverpool Diocesan Synod in March 2010. His entry into the debate is very significant because he has always been seen by conservative evangelicals, in England at least, as one of the episcopal bastions of Anglican orthodoxy and a campaigner against the rising tide of liberalism.[119]

---

115. "Anyone who divorces his wife and marries another woman commits adultery against her. And if she divorces her husband and marries another man, she commits adultery" (Mark 10:11–12).

116. Smedes, "Like the Wideness of the Sea?"

117. Ibid.

118. Ibid.

119. The diocese of Liverpool itself has always been seen as declaring clearly for conservative evangelicalism since its famed evangelical founding bishop, John Charles

Movement Two: The Church Thinking

Jones argues that the church has had to wrestle with conflicting ethical views in many circumstances. His primary example is pacifism. He compares the arguments for the theory of just war with the Anglican Articles, which claim the right for the magistrate to call men to carry arms, contrasting that with the long-held teachings in church history, particularly in the period from the early church to the conversion of Constantine, when pacifism held sway.

He notes that throughout the two World Wars the church had been involved in passionate and often fierce debates when conscientious objectors were subjected to inhuman and hostile treatment, which they faced with great courage and moral determination. The church now looks back at those times with a quite different perspective. "The fact that conscripts and pacifists divided along one moral line does not detract from our admiration now nor deflect us from acknowledging now the moral courage of both. . . . In other words, we can now stand on either side of the moral argument and still be in fellowship despite disagreeing on this the most fundamental ethical issue, the sixth of the Ten Commandments."[120]

Jones sees this as a template for the way in the Anglican Communion in the future will treat the matter of homosexuality.

> Just as the church over the last 2000 years has come to allow a variety of ethical conviction about the taking of life and the application of the sixth Commandment so I believe that in this period it is also moving towards allowing a variety of ethical conviction about people of the same gender loving each other fully. . . . I believe the day is coming when Christians who equally profoundly disagree about the consonancy of same gender love with the discipleship of Christ will in spite of their disagreement drink openly from the same cup of salvation.[121]

Jones recognises that such a stance is difficult and will require much of God's grace to hold people together. He asks what seem to be disarmingly simple questions about what he sees is at stake here.

> If on this subject of sexuality the traditionalists are ultimately right and those who advocate the acceptance of stable and faithful gay relationships are wrong what will their sin be? That in a

---

Ryle, set its pattern in his long tenure from 1880 to 1900. Liverpool was, in fact, the diocese where I was ordained and served my first curacy.

120. Jones, "Presidential Address," 2.
121. Ibid., 3.

> world of such little love two people sought to express a love that no other relationship could offer them?
>
> And if those advocating the acceptance of gay relationship are right and the traditionalists are wrong what will their sin be? That in a church that has forever wrestled with interpreting and applying Scripture they missed the principle in the application of the literal text?
>
> Do these two thoughts not of themselves enlarge the arena in which to do our ethical exploration?[122]

Mark Batterson could be echoing these sentiments and developing them. "The last reformation was a reformation of creeds. The next reformation will be a reformation of deeds. The last reformation was symbolized by one central figure. The next reformation will be led by millions of reformers living compassionately, creatively, and courageously for the cause of Christ. It will be marked by broken hearts and sanctified imaginations. And the driving force will be the love of God." [123]

He speaks of this love being compassionate, curious, and energetic; a primal truth to be rediscovered and needing to be applied radically in the life of the church. "So what does our generation need to rediscover? What primal truth needs to be re-imagined? What is our reformation? Simply put, we've got to be great at the Great Commandment. Anything less isn't good enough. Or I should say, great enough."[124]

Even Peter Jensen, the ultra-conservative Archbishop of Sydney, has made some surprising reference to changing interpretations and new understandings of Scripture in his presidential address to the Sydney Diocesan Synod in 2001.

> But orthodoxy is not an intellectual isolation ward. In the first place it acknowledges the immense debt we owe to the Christians who have gone before us. It learns to interpret the Bible in the light of the reading of the Bible down the centuries. In particular it learns from the early centuries of the church's reading of scripture, and it learns from the Reformation of the sixteenth century as well as genuine advances of the more recent historical approach. And orthodox evangelicalism is also prepared to learn from contemporary thought. It recognises that current experience will always force us to ask new questions of the Bible

---

122. Ibid., 6–7.
123. Batterson, *Primal*, 4.
124. Ibid., 10–11.

and to discover truths of God's revelation which may have been neglected or not understood.[125]

Even earlier than that, in 1996, while he was still at Moore College, he wrote:

> It is useless to believe that our attitude to the Bible can remain completely unchanged. We no longer think about the world in the way that our ancestors did. We cannot believe, for example, that the sun goes around the earth. In addition, the study of history has shown us many things about the world of the Bible that have a bearing on the way we understand it. In various ways we are better off than our predecessors. If we wish to maintain a strong belief in the inspiration of the Bible we must take these things into account.[126]

Similarly, James Packer, a hero to many in GAFCON because, at great personal cost, he resigned from the Anglican Church of Canada because of its liberal teaching and blessing of same-sex unions, has also noted, in an unusual and remarkably powerful way, that a slavish adherence to Reformation and, in particular, Puritan teaching is a danger to be avoided.

> We can parrot their language and ape their manners, and imagine thereby we place ourselves in the true Puritan tradition. But the Puritans would impress on us that that is precisely what we fail to do if we act so. They sought to apply the eternal truths of Scripture to the particular circumstances of their own day—moral, social, political, ecclesiastical, and so forth. . . . To content ourselves with aping the Puritans would amount to beating a mental retreat out of the twentieth century, where God has set us to live, into the seventeenth, where he has not. This is unspiritual as it is unrealistic. The Holy Spirit is pre-eminently a realist and he has been given to teach Christians how to live to God in the situation in which they are, not that in which some other saints once were. We quench the Spirit by allowing ourselves to live in the past.[127]

Stephen Sykes makes the point that the church, because of its human frailty and sinful nature, must always consider the possibility that it might be wrong. "If we are open to His truth, God will not deny us His grace,

---

125. Jensen, "Presidential Address."
126. Jensen, *Doctrine 1*, 63.
127. Packer, *Quest for Godliness*, 233–34.

especially not at His Eucharist. I am prepared for my Church to be in error until such time as God vouchsafes it a new vision."[128]

In a clear reference to John Robinson's Puritan sermon to the Pilgrim Fathers, Archbishop Keith Rayner seemed to want to ask new questions of the traditional Anglican view on homosexuality when speaking to the Australian Anglican General Synod in 1988: "May it be that God is calling us to review the tradition [on homosexuality] to see whether further light is to be shed on it?"[129]

It was clear at that time, however, that Jensen was not prepared to go that far despite his later claims that he was open to the possibility of new revelation being received from God's Word. McGillion records that they rebuked Rayner and distanced themselves from any such suggestion. McGillion describes that response as "ideology masquerading as theology."[130]

Another ultra-conservative, Thomas Oden, recognises the diversity of God's working as he sees that the Holy Spirit is acting today through "antinomies, historical development, signs of contradiction and paradox,"[131] though it is unlikely that he could countenance the more radical suggestions of acceptance Anderson and Smedes see as possibilities.

From his clearly Protestant Reformed standpoint, he finds himself able to accept the differences between Catholic and Protestant, high and low church, etc., only because he can claim that they find common faith, ". . . by affirming together that the texts upon which classic Christianity are grounded are intrinsically and obviously ecumenical, undeniably catholic in the cultural range. . . . All believers can claim the Fathers and the Creeds."[132]

Anderson, however, using a turn of phrase that is remarkably powerful despite its obvious hyperbole, believes that such a backward look to an ecclesiological emphasis is counterproductive, believing as he does that Emerging Church communities truly live in a way that is totally different from anything that has gone before. "What marks emerging churches as different is that they let go of what the church has been in order to become what the church will be."[133]

---

128. Sykes, *Unashamed Anglicanism*, 139.
129. Cited in McGillion, *Chosen Ones*, 122.
130. Ibid., 122–23.
131. Oden, *Rebirth of Orthodoxy*, 63.
132. Ibid., 64.
133. Anderson, *Emergent Theology*, 199.

Everything is made subject to that overarching priority of the *missio Dei*. With this emphasis, the old confessional and ecclesiological struggles of the past, while I am sure Anderson does not wish to totally negate them, are made subservient to the primary call to mission and evangelism in the postmodern world. However, he is under no illusions that to live in this way is both risky and difficult. It certainly is not the easy option. "A venerable history is far more compelling than a vulnerable future. A historical Christ (even though wrapped in tradition) is more predictable than a Christ emerging out of the future in the breath of the Spirit."[134]

Thus, for Anderson, clearly defined boundaries are not needed where there is a real presence of Jesus at the centre. It is only when Jesus is not visible at the centre that boundary lines tend to be enforced. What results then is that those people whose spiritual identity is not yet fully formed become excluded. Consequently emerging churches will often be a little messy around the edges just as the early church was. Anderson, however, assures us "Christ can handle that!"[135]

What Anderson does not deal with here, however, is the crucial question of how the Jesus he wishes to be at the centre is to be defined. Who is the Jesus he is speaking about? That definition requires at least some boundaries and constraints or else the centre may become as messy as the edges.

Len Hjalmarson has an interesting view on this matter.

> "Remember, it isn't the church of God that has a mission in the world; it's the God of Mission who has a Church in the world.
>
> If our lives as God's people are to be lived out in full view of the world, we need to take conscious, deliberate steps to be sure this is happening. This is why God is breaking down our definitions and resetting the boundaries. . . .
>
> Water gives life, but water, the same as words, is shaped by its context. Water takes on the form of the container. The church had one kind of form in the modern world; it needs a new form in the new culture. We need new wineskins."[136]

Helmut Thielicke's maxim puts the same point tersely. "The gospel must be constantly forwarded to a new address, because the recipient is repeatedly changing place of residence."[137]

---

134. Ibid., 200–201.
135. Ibid., 209.
136. Hjalmarson, *New Way of Thinking bout Church*.
137. Thielicke, *How Modern Should Theology Be?*, 10.

Graham Buxton certainly shares this view. "It *is* a new world out there, and we need both to understand it and respond appropriately to the challenges presented by the postmodern world—in which—whether we like it or not—we now live."[138]

This reflects, in a strange way, the words of James Packer we read in an earlier chapter, when he described his belief that a true following of the Puritan tradition is best served by living in the present rather than hanging on to the past.

Brian McLaren recognises that there are two dangers in this approach. These are what he calls "hostile exclusion" and "naïve inclusion." He argues that there has to be a third way which he calls "purposeful inclusion." This gentler, more loving way, as he sees it, has within it a kingdom paradox. "To be truly inclusive, the kingdom must exclude exclusive people, to be truly reconciling, the kingdom must not reconcile with those who refuse reconciliation, to achieve its purpose of gathering people, it must not gather those who scatter. The kingdom of God has a purpose and that purpose isn't everyone's cup of tea."[139] What McLaren makes clear is that this form of exclusion is really a form a self-exclusion by those who refuse the clear call to radical discipleship and reconciliation.[140]

Of course, the real danger lies in the mistake people make in thinking that the Emerging Church is something defined and concrete like one of the traditional denominations. It is not. To try and define it is like trying to grasp hold of smoke. That is why Dr. Katharine Sarah Moody of Lancaster University in England prefers to speak of the Emerging Church as a "milieu":

> I speak of a milieu for several reasons: to signal the global and local diversity amongst emerging churches which refuses their depiction as a closed movement; to sketch the emerging church characteristics which may overlap other manifestations of Christianity; and to hold an ear to the milieu itself, in which hostility towards restrictive classification resounds. Without either conclusively demarcating the limits of its boundaries or exhaustively itemizing its contents, there are identifiable literatures, organizations, and networks within the milieu, with which

---

138. Buxton, *Dancing in the Dark*, 178.

139. McLaren, *Church on the Other Side*, 169.

140. McLaren quotes Luke 14:33 and 9:62 as examples of Jesus' call to those who would enter the kingdom to be sure that they count the cost of doing so. Some will not be prepared to do that and will, instead, turn to violence against the kingdom and those who proclaim it. Only a change of heart will enable them to be included.

individuals and communities have multiple relationships—as well as particular ideologies that these structures maintain. These ideological commitments include: global contextualization in contemporary culture, organizational experimentation, radicalization of Christian theology, engagement with postmodern theory, an "ancient-future" (re)discovery of Christian tradition, and social and political activism.[141]

Rodney Clapp emphasises that any reappropriation of the Christian tradition cannot be simply some form of rote imitation or copy of how the tradition was in the distant past. It must be a re-appropriation. That means it must be contextualised in the light of the challenge of postmodernity.[142]

In 1912 Roland Allen, an Anglican priest and Missionary in both China and East Africa, wrote in a remarkably similar vein. His book, published again in 1962, contains insights that would gladden the hearts of many of the Emerging Church leaders. He notes that theological questions are not settled once and for all but reappear in each different ages and countries in different forms. Answers need to be given that are relevant to the contemporary context in which the questions are asked. He particularly criticises the practice of engaging in legislative battles in order to try and promote unity of doctrine. This, he says, only promotes further schism.[143]

A similar approach taken by Nehring, who asserts that we can never believe that we have read, heard, and understood everything that God is calling His church to be and to do.[144]

Buxton puts it another way. "Our perspective shifts from a narrow focus on the present to a healthier incorporation into the continuing flow of God's gracious work in history. We actually participate in *Heilsgeschichte*, God's saving history!"[145]

I am also intrigued by Brian McLaren's view of this matter. He seems convinced that definite statements about God are simply outdated. He

---

141. Moody, *New Kind of Christian*, 1.

142. Clapp, *Border Crossings*.

143. Allen, *Missionary Methods*, 133 "Nothing is more dangerous than to substitute judgment by precedent for judgement by conviction, and nothing is easier. To appeal to Jerusalem, to Trent, or Lambeth or Westminster, is easy, but it is disastrous. It makes for an appearance of unity: real unity it destroys. Definitions and precedents have created more schisms than they have healed. . . . If it is a true doctrine that 'every man must bear his own burden', it is equally true that every age must produce its own definitions and every church its own precedents."

144. Nehring, *Yet More Light and Truth*.

145. Buxton, *Dancing in the Dark*, 48.

dismisses them as of the "old world" of modernity where it was believed that the mysteries of faith could in some way be encapsulated into documents and kept forever. "Mysteries, however, can not be captured so precisely. Freeze-dried coffee, butterflies on pins, and frogs in formaldehyde all lose something in our attempts at capturing defining, preserving, and rendering them less jumpy, flighty, or fluid. In the new world, we will understand this a little better."[146]

McLaren concludes that orthodoxy does not demand that *we* hold all the right beliefs; it does, however, demand that right beliefs exist, even if only the being we call "God" knows them. Orthodoxy is redefined away from ". . . 'what *we* think' as opposed to 'what *they* think' and towards 'what God knows,' some of which we believe a little, some of which they believe a little, and about which we all have a whole lot to learn."[147]

Witham, in his booklet "The Church at Risk," is quite clear about this dilemma. He contrasts "fluidity" and "rigidity." "Fluidity," he claims, accepts the possibility of ambiguity and room for debate even when a firm stand is being taken on an issue. "Rigidity," on the other hand, takes a position of certainty, especially concerning the Bible, and does not allow for any other possible interpretations.[148]

In fact, Witham is only reflecting what Martin Luther said in one of his sermons: "It is the nature of faith that it presumes on the grace of God. . . . *Faith does not require information, knowledge or certainty, (emphasis added)* but a free surrender and a joyful bet on his unfelt, untried, and unknown goodness."[149]

Witham sees reconciliation not just as a theological doctrine concerning personal salvation but a practical necessity among the redeemed community. It is so important that he sees the necessity of Christians going out of their way to go to those they differ from and to try and be reconciled. He sees this action as a reflection of Christ taking the initiative in the reconciliation of sinful man to God. It will, he says, involve "learning the dialect of our fellow Christians" from whom we differ. In many ways he was a forerunner of the Reconciliation Theology considered in the discussion of theories of the atonement.

He recognises that "Debate, for many, is not 'high priority,'" nevertheless he urges such face to face talking even though he readily admits that

---

146. McLaren, *Church on the Other Side*, 89.
147. McLaren, *Generous Orthodoxy*, 32.
148. Witham, *Church at Risk*, 49.
149. Luther, Sermon 25 (1522), cited in Pelikan, *Christian Tradition*, 165.

there are risks involved. Most difficult of all is the possibility that "when we begin to converse with those who are different, we may be persuaded that we need to change our views."[150]

Of course, there are those for whom the very notion of respectful and reasonable conversation with those of differing opinions is anathema. MacArthur, though not an Anglican, expresses in his comments about the Emerging Church what many within GAFCON would voice about the leadership of The Episcopal Church in the United States.

> We are not to allow such false teachers to remain unmolested inside the church, calling themselves Christians, spreading their evil doctrines. We don't need to be hesitant about engaging them in conflict or refuting their lying words; especially for the sake of those they are seducing. We don't need to waste a lot of angst wondering if we are alienating them—because they have already deliberately rejected the truth, and they have already been ordained to condemnation.[151]

He saves most of his vitriol for high profile writers within the emergent stream such as Brian McLaren who he accuses of being apostate. "Their apostasy eventually poisons all their doctrine. They twist and pervert and reinvent teachings of Christ. They adjust the gospel to suit their own tastes. When you get to core of where they are, they simply want to be kings of their own domain."[152]

It is of course true that Emergent theology, as a protest against both conservatism and liberalism, has produced some extremes. Nevertheless the subjects of its protest are certainly valid and would be supported by many mission-minded Christians still within the traditional churches.

Jim Belcher seeks to describe the main tenets of the Emerging Church in his native USA. He begins with the Emerging Church claim that traditional churches are still very much in captivity to Enlightenment rationalism. This, they feel, keeps the church of today from being prophetic and counter cultural.[153]

An argument against that view, which Belcher fails to pursue, is the phenomenology of the Orthodox Church, especially in Russia, where there was no Enlightenment and yet a traditional, culturally empathetic

---

150. Witham, *Church at Risk*, 49–51.
151. MacArthur, *Truth War*, 132.
152. Ibid., 143.
153. Belcher, *Deep Church*, 40–42.

church has continued and is growing in its most conservative form without the so-called restraints of the Enlightenment.

The Emerging Church criticises the traditional churches as having too narrow a view of salvation. They claim that priority is given to the Pauline Epistles over against Jesus' teaching in the Gospels, and thus salvation is seen as simply forgiveness of sin and entry into heaven rather than the fullness of kingdom life that is for living in the present and in the world.

Rejecting the use of doctrine as a gatekeeper, they espouse the concept of belonging before believing. They believe the boundaries that many of the traditional churches set up to keep people in and others out have emasculated the mission of the church. They stress the primary importance of community in evangelism.

The Emerging Church stresses the importance of worship that is relevant and contextualised. Too often traditional churches make little effort to communicate with the present culture and seem to have a mind-set that is completely alienated from the world. This, they say, makes them incapable of reaching contemporary culture for God. A consequence of this is that traditional preaching is often ineffective being too cerebral and knowledge based. Better learning is through shared experience within the community, which has the power to change people.

The Emerging Church sees traditional ecclesiology as being more concerned with form and structure than true mission. It is more concerned with the survival of the institution and the protection of its assets than actually being the people of God in the world. This has led to a form of tribalism in which the desire for power is at its heart. This again creates a negative attitude to the world and makes the church known more for what it stands against than for what it is actually for.

One of the most interesting things to me is the fact that many of these protests enumerated by Belcher could be aimed at GAFCON, the Anglican movement of protest. John V. Taylor accuses the Church of institutionalising Christ and attempting to legislate for the Holy Spirit. However, he notes that the Book of Acts shows clearly that "The Holy Spirit does not appear to have read the rubrics! He will not and cannot be bound. . . . We cannot command the wind. And when the Spirit disobeys our canons we should avoid the absurd sin of rigidity."[154]

Similarly, Daniel O'Leary, writing from a Roman Catholic perspective in *The Tablet*, notes that when organisations become fearful and insecure the first casualties are imagination, courage and freedom of expression

---

154. Taylor, *Go-Between God*, 119.

and action. Instead reactionary instincts produce "uniforms, rigid rites and rubrics," although we know in our hearts that the Holy Spirit will not be controlled.[155]

I am struck by the picture given by Westerhoff, who, taking the old picture of the church as a ship, sees much of the traditional church having been deliberately run aground and settling for an easy island life rather than setting off courageously, full of faith, on the adventure God has called His pilgrim people to.

> That wouldn't be too bad, if subsequently we had not forgotten our seafaring days and come to believe that the Bible, once our book on shipbuilding and navigation, to become a book on meaningful island life. . . . Is the church, the community of faith which claims Christ as Lord, helping us to build a ship and set sail with courage or is it only providing us with a drug to help us live painlessly on an island beset with human woes? I am not sure I like the answer I hear. But I do know one thing. It was not always this way. The church, once inspired by God's Word, was a seafaring people.
>
> What not only need a new crew, we need a new ship. . . . How do we go about building this new ship?[156]

Westerhoff, with prophetic insight ahead of his time, saw our greatest need now being a new and radical vision of what the contemporary church should be if it was truly grounded in the Scriptures. In particular he saw that the history of the church teaches that there is a great need for differing emphases reflected in the different groupings of liberal, conservative, evangelical, and radicals within the church to see in one another facets of truth that are the gift of God to his people.

> We have categorized too many persons and missed the truth in alternative understandings. We have insisted on either/ors rather than both/ands. In doing so the Christian church has been cruelly ruptured. We have pitted liberals and conservatives, evangelicals and radicals against each other. The church of Jesus Christ requires all four. . . . The Biblical faith does not know the exclusivistic categories by which the church has divided her people. . . . It requires us to live harmoniously in the presence of the Lord of history.[157]

---

155. O'Leary, *Defining Moments*, 12.
156. Westerhoff, *Tomorrow's Church*, 15–17.
157. Ibid., 25–26.

Kathryn A. Tanner has explored this very concept of theological creativity in her book *Theories of Culture: A New Agenda for Theology*. In her chapter on "Diversity and Creativity in Theological Judgement" she asks why it is that Christians are not comfortable with diversity. She suggests answers such as their concern for the witness of the church or even our standing before God. Therefore, she says, they feel that they must always seek for consensus in argument. She questions whether this sort of consensus is always as necessary as is supposed. Could it not be, she argues, that there are certain benefits and advantages to be gained from failing to reach agreement?

Because theological creativity inevitably leads to change it is often put under severe restraint by more conservative Christians. Whether and how strongly this happens depends, she says, upon whether there is a "modern" or a "postmodern" view of culture. A modern view sees differences as failure or "improper socialisation." However, she argues, rules on theological study cannot be rigidly prescriptive. There must be a flexibility that allows free and unhindered investigation, otherwise it is not true and honest theology. Uniformity then becomes an impossible dream. Different views on how to live the Christian life cannot either be legislated into existence or even seen to be a bad thing. They are, as Tanner says, "the product of equally sincere, uncorrupted and fully capable efforts to live a Christian life."[158]

In fact, she argues strongly that Christian culture does not demand uniformity in practice. "The same facts of human existence might prompt, it seems, a valid diversity of opinion about how to make Christian sense of them. . . . Christian discipleship is an essentially contested notion."[159]

It is not possible, she argues, to push this away by attributing every differing view to corrupting outside influences or by de-Christianising those who differ. In a post-modern approach to Christian culture conflict may arise through the simple efforts of all parties to be faithful Christians. "Conflict is inherent in the kind of culture Christianity is."[160] It cannot be hidden or pushed under the carpet or demonised.

Greenslade makes a similar point in the light of all the political and organisational posturing that goes on in the name of holiness. "Blue-prints will not heal schisms; they must be faced as concrete historical entities in which dogmatic and constitutional issues are tangled up with the

---

158. Ibid., 158.
159. Ibid., 159.
160. Ibid.

historical memories and a host of personal feelings which need delicate consideration and tactful handling."[161]

Tanner makes much of the differences between a modern and a postmodern worldview in dealing with the matter of theological creativity. A modern view, she claims, makes a number of questionable assumptions. Firstly it tends to restrict the whole activity of theological creativity to simply adjusting to the surrounding non-Christian culture. It is seen to have little relevance internally for the church. Secondly, it creates clear and rigid rules for the handling of what she calls the "given materials" that are used on the clear assumption that they are definite and internally consistent in order that uniformity might be produced. It also, thirdly, makes the assumption that all Christians are "passively uniform."

Postmodernism disputes these assumptions. It recognises what it sees as the variety, vagueness and differing versions of "given materials" available. They are not taken to be as internally consistent and as definite as supposed.

Christian culture is not a passive one. Every Christian, in some sense or another, must make their own theological judgements about how to live their Christian life. They either take responsibility themselves or acquiesce in some else's judgement.

In the modern paradigm, parties with particularly fixed views police the church by allowing the use of the materials in a particular way only. Postmodernism gives much more leeway. In this situation a theologian may interpret in a way that could well sit uneasily with the practices of a particular time and place. In this paradigm everything is contestable.

When it comes to the demands of tradition, Tanner argues that this is nothing more than a particular selection from materials that could have been so designated. Traditions are simply the choices of a particular party. She argues that "we are free to ask whether that particular organisation of material makes sense today about how Christians think and what they do." She elaborates:

> The freedom of Christian discipleship to follow God's Word where it leads is blocked by any human claim that refuses to allow itself to be criticised or altered in the course of the ongoing argument about true discipleship that Christianity is. Binding the freedom of theological interpretation to a human authority in that way actually threatens to interrupt the obedience of Christians to the Word.[162]

161. Greenslade, *Schism in the Early Church*, 57.
162. Tanner, *Theories of Culture*, 160–63.

Even where agreement has been reached, the fact remains that such an agreement remains vulnerable to the same processes that produced it. A minority opinion could well come in and disrupt an achieved consensus.

After all, not all agreements are as widespread as stated by the participants. There could certainly be power play here. The most powerful players could well have kept out opposing views or material. Why should the future not amend things as indeed happened to the early churches' stance on communism as a way of life?

The truth is that the existence of internal strains always holds the potential for change (like tensions in tectonic plates bring earthquakes). They are never totally "under control" but are just held in place by sanctions by human authorities and by penalties against deviance.

It could be theoretically possible, Tanner argues, to think of rewriting the Scriptures and removing all the errors, contradictions, and different versions that cause so many problems and divisions, but this would never be possible. Whoever could be trusted to undertake the task and who would agree to such a proposal?

She sees the enforcing of uniformity of belief and action as only serving to magnify the very dangers of factionalism and division that make Christian diversity so troublesome. "The insistence that there is only one right way of being a Christian is even more likely to rupture Christian fellowship, to make a mockery of the virtue of the love and peace of Christ, than the existing diversity of practice for which it is the supposed remedy."[163]

It has already been noted that statements like the Apostles' Creed are understood differently by different groups. As Tanner observes, "The common affirmation of a verbally identical formula provides no evidence in that case of common understanding."[164]

The above may be stating the obvious but it has important ramifications when we come in a later chapter to deal in more detail with the notion of a formal, written covenant for Anglicans to which all are asked to agree.

Tanner's conclusion is clear. "Conflict is best contained not by trying to ignore it or smooth things over. Instead, its existence must be honestly recognised if its possible harmful effects on Christian fellowship are to be averted."[165]

163. Ibid., 172.
164. Ibid., 173.
165. Ibid., 174.

She also maintains that conflict also has a good effect within the Christian community. "Human judgement is fallible and the opportunity for correction by others who disagree is a valuable thing. . . . Diversity reminds us that Christians cannot control the movements of the God they hope to serve. It keeps them more open to the Word by keeping them from taking their own view of things for granted. This strengthens the bonds of Christian fellowship as they seek to make something good out of the conflict."[166]

Paul Avis makes a similar point, although I doubt he would agree with Tanner completely.

> The deleterious effects of unrestrained conflict are obvious. It reduces collaboration between various components or sub-groups of the organisation. It leaves the defeated damaged and unfit for productive work. It wastefully diverts energy from work to warfare. It polarises conflicting groups or individuals in a way that may take years to overcome. On the other hand, conflict gives vitality to an institution. It allows internal interest groups to pursue their aims, which may be for the overall benefit of the system. It opens up the system to its environment as fresh energies are drawn in to replace those consumed in internal conflicts. It clarifies the true interests of the organisation, corrects imbalances and stimulates reform and renewal.[167]

Another way that theologians look at the notion of diversity in unity is through the doctrine of the Trinity and there has been a significant growth in theological work in this area.

Bruce Kaye recognises that this growing emphasis on the doctrine of the Trinity is very helpful. It is something that is both a foundational doctrine of Anglicanism and central to the Anglican liturgical calendar as envisaged by Cranmer, with its long period of Sundays after Trinity Sunday in the Church Year in the Book of Common Prayer—that, of course, despite the unfortunate change in contemporary calendars to remembering Sundays after Pentecost. He encourages attention to the work of Barth and Jürgen Moltmann in this area seeing this Trinitarian emphasis helpful in overcoming the political nuances of the Reformation documents and pointing to «the life of faith in God's world and thus is about God's character in relational terms.»[168]

---

166. Ibid., 175.
167. Avis, *Authority, Leadership and Conflict*, 120.
168. Kaye, *Reinventing Anglicanism*, 125, 131.

Kerry Dearborn reminds us that, sadly, many evangelicals have a distorted view of the Trinity that can be caricatured as belief in "The Father, the Son and the Holy Scriptures." Over emphasis on the centrality of the Word can lead to a negation of the contemporary ministry of the Holy Spirit, as though he has nothing more to say or to do now that the canon of scripture has been closed. "Weakened understandings of the nature of the Trinity and the nature of God's presence by the Spirit impoverish our ecclesiology and our sense of the sacramental nature of the Church and all of life."[169]

Miroslav Volf emphasises that the way we think about the nature of God "will decisively shape, not only ecclesiology but the entirety of Christian thought."[170]

Kaye sees the current Trinitarian emphasis as a rediscovery of a truth that the Cappadocian Fathers had discovered and which seems to have been, in some sense, long lost. They saw the creative power of the relationship of the three persons of the Trinity and developed the notion of *perichoresis*. This vision of the "divine dance" and "mutual interchange" becomes a rich picture of the church as a community of interdependent people.

Kaye describes this community in the light of both the Reformation doctrines of faith and the Trinitarian concept of mutual interchange. Christians are caught up into the very life of God through the gospel, which it is the mission of the church to express in life and proclaim in word. The church's primary experience of forgiveness because of its failure and sin should lead it to be also a community of patience. This is a patience that should be extended to all within the church community as we recognise our mutual frailty as human beings. "It is first and foremost an interdependent community of diversity."[171]

Dearborn speaks about the way this Trinitarian sense of community should enable us to relate with others with confidence. "If our own identity is firmly anchored to our Triune God, then we can approach others humbly and with respect, expecting to learn from them. Much of this would depend on our willingness to view those with whom we differ in a sacramental way as bearers of Christ's presence."[172]

---

169. Dearborn, *Recovering a Trinitarian and Sacramental Ecclesiology*, 40.
170. Volf, *After Our Likeness*, 191.
171. Kaye, *Reinventing Anglicanism*, 177.
172. Dearborn, *Recovering a Trinitarian and Sacramental Ecclesiology*, 68–69.

Movement Two: The Church Thinking

However, Volf takes care to state that, as he sees it, the relational aspect of the Trinity can only apply between individuals and not to ecclesiastical corporate bodies. Only those who are indwelt by the Spirit can know the mutuality of relationship. An ecclesiastical community has no "spirit" or life of its own apart from each of its members' individual relationship with the triune God. For Volf, then, there can be no perichoretic relationships of unity between churches or denominations but only between the individual members of those communities. It is at this personal level that matters of unity will be eventually concluded and not at provincial or denominational levels.[173] If this view is accepted then any notion of a unity brought into being through confessional means is brought under question.

Angelo Maffeis, in his essay "Current theological Discussion on the Unity of the Church," has another point of view. He sees the differences between confessional groups as actual expressions of what he calls "universal unity."

> The way in which the universal unity between confessionally separate churches is manifested is created through dialogue understood as a process of continuous exchange between subjects who must maintain their differences. So the dialogue is not aimed at consensus which eliminates diversity; it cannot be regarded as an imperfect realization of communion but represents the very form of church unity. [174]

Taking this view, Maffeis aligns himself with Oscar Cullman,[175] who sees the differences in each of the confessional traditions as evidence of the gifts of the Spirit which always contribute to unity. It is "a unity through difference." "The different charisms aroused by the Spirit remain each with its own physiognomy, and there is no attempt to unify them or assimilate them to one another."[176]

In the same book of essays Hans Dieter Betz, in speaking of the present disunity of the church, takes up the phrase "a church in fragments." He sees the possibility of two meanings to this phrase. Negatively, he compares the notion of fragments to the pieces of a broken jar which might, after much slow and painstaking work, be able to be put back together again carefully and in order to reproduce the original. On what he clearly

---

173. Volf, *After Our Likeness*, 203.
174. Ruggieri and Tomka, *Church in Fragments*, 26–27.
175. See Cullman, *Einheit durch Vielfalt*.
176. Ruggieri and Tomka, *Church in Fragments*, 26.

sees as a more positive note, he says the fragments can be viewed as the pieces used by a mosaic maker. Each piece has equal value and potential in the eyes of the mosaic maker.

> Applied to the church, this would then mean that any particular case is one of many possibilities which has taken the form which we now know from the historical fragments. We have to accept it as it is, as 'a church in fragments'. In principle, in other circumstances, it could have been different but that is no objection to the fact that it has now become what it now is. Thus it is of its nature to be fragmentary, but because it is so, it need not necessarily be either defective or inferior.[177]

Martin Jinkins expressed the same idea just as clearly and with equal force.

> What if the perfection of the church is its human existence and not something beyond the actuality of this existence? What if its roughness and raggedness, its lack of smoothness and seamlessness, is the shape of its peculiar wholeness? What if, indeed, its limitations, its utter need for God, its spiritual bankruptcy are the infallible signs of its perfection? What if, then, the miracle of truth is that God makes the Word of God vulnerable as human speech, that it is this act itself that is truth(and not something spoken about this act)? And so, what if the contradictory, unseemly, disorderly and frequently indecent din and cacophony of diverse communities of faith, speaking of and about God and speaking to and against and past one another, is the sign of the truth of who God is and what church is? What if?[178]

---

177. Ibid., 36.
178. Jinkins, "'Gift' of the Church," 76.

Movement Two: The Church Thinking

Summary of Orthodoxy in the Second Movement

a) This traditionally slow movement finds the church thinking aloud and deliberately about the matter of boundaries and authority as they are relevant to this whole matter of orthodoxy. In doing so it is allowing itself the freedom to reconsider previously held positions and being willing and open to learn from different perspectives.

b) Although such freedom is disparaged by those of a more conservative and fundamentalist viewpoint, we have seen how scholars of quite different outlooks and backgrounds have been seen to be willing to grasp the new and exciting opportunities offered to the church to re-examine or re-articulate views and accepted norms concerning orthodoxy in the context of their own contemporary thought and culture. This is especially true within the postmodern paradigm within which the church now exists.

c) Variation One examined the concept of *fundamentalism*, especially in the writing of Jakobus Vorster. Its defining characteristics are biblicism, legalism, and a rigid homogeneous culture that identifies itself most readily by standing against a well-defined enemy.

d) Variation Two took this further by using the theories of Paul Hiebert in contrasting *bounded* and *centred* sets as pictures of the church as a community. The bounded set fits the fundamentalist perspective with its emphasis on strict, enforceable boundaries that have the effect of putting people in or out of the group according to the perceived soundness of their doctrine and purity of their ethics. Hiebert sees also what he calls *fuzzy* sets where boundaries are not as sharp but members of the set are only considered full members when they accept the official teaching of the church. The aim of such a set is clearly to reach the bounded-set status, which is seen as the ideal.

In contrast, the centred set is more concerned with attitude and direction or movement. With Jesus at the centre what matters most is the direction in which people are moving vis-à-vis Jesus. In such a set different positions or understanding of doctrine or behavioural issues will be varied. These differences are not reasons to exclude anyone from the set. What matters is a living relationship with Jesus. Such a set encourages an ethos of freedom of thought and action.

Rowan Williams makes the point that the church is neither to be a community of individuals, which is not a community at all, nor is it to be a community of those enforced into uniformity. McGrath agrees that the New Testament and the early church tended to emphasise the centre of the Christian faith rather than the matters around the periphery. Its central creed was simply "Jesus is Lord!"

e) Variation Three majored on the "Fourth Self" or "self-theologising." Hiebert recognised that as colonial churches found independence and new churches were founded, it was inevitable that they would claim the right to study the Scriptures for themselves in the light of their own context and in that this would influence their developing and maturing theology. Hiebert saw that the traditional "monotheological" view that there was only one way to interpret the Scriptures could not be sustained. He also saw that differing interpretations challenged and raised questions about our own theology. This can result in a withdrawal into theological ghettoes. In the end all our theologies are the product of our historical and cultural contexts and can only be a partial understanding of the greatness of God.

From the New Testament to Augustine, from John Jewel of Salisbury to modern theologians such as Pelikan, it is clear that unity is the fundamental attribute of the church with holiness clearly held as subordinate to this. Hiebert reminds us that we cannot guarantee that those who come after us will interpret the scriptures in exactly the same way as we do. They must come to their own understanding and beliefs in their own way. What is essential is love and respect and a readiness to listen to others open to the possibility that the Holy Spirit might be trying to teach us something new that we ought to learn. In the end, as Stephen Sykes says, unity is nothing more than contained diversity.

f) Variation Four took three examples from church history to illustrate what we have already noted and which Phyllis Tickle sees as times of rearrangement and upheaval leading to new and more vital forms of Christian orthodoxy.

The Donatist heresy in the fourth and fifth centuries was an argument about discipline and rigour. Sinfulness, which is true of every human being, does not invalidate authorised ministry. God, in his grace, uses sinful people to fulfil his holy will. Perceived ethical failures are not grounds for refusal to accept ministry or to deny eucharistic hospitality.

Reformation theology became obsessed with distinguishing the true church from the false church and, in doing so, left behind the more gentle approaches taken even by Luther. The boundary markers of discipline and excommunication were certainly enforced by the later reformers and led, in turn, to the Separatist movements of the sixteenth century. The Church of England had a more generous and open approach under the guidance of Richard Hooker, who saw authority as "supreme and inward rather than external and coercive," and this has always been a hallmark of Anglicanism.

The Emerging Church reminds us that there have always been different interpretations of the ancient texts within the church and these have led to different ways of life. Each of these interpretations must be understood from within its own historical, religious, cultural, and political context. Emerging Church leaders stress that theology today needs to emerge from the future rather than from the past. It is the risen Lord Jesus through the power of the Spirit who calls the church rather than the historical Jesus. There has to be a letting go of what the church has been in order to become what the church will be. Orthodoxy is then redefined away from the fixed boundaries of propositional certainty to the more fuzzy boundaries that acknowledge that we have so much more to learn. A particular form of doctrine can no longer be used as the gatekeeper. Diversity is not to be seen as a failure but rather as something that enriches and revitalises the community. The Trinitarian concept of perichoresis, first found within the church fathers but now reinvigorated among contemporary figures such as Jurgen Moltmann, Miroslav Volf, and John Zizioulas among others, has much to teach us about the dynamism of unity in diversity.

3

Movement Three: The Church as Anglican

(Minuet and Trio—Scherzo)

THE THIRD MOVEMENT OF a symphony traditionally takes the form a dance. In the classical period this was usually a *minuet*. Originally this was a social dance for two people in which the dancing couple exchanged curtsies and bows in a very formal manner. It is in triple metre and usually played at a moderate tempo, which was slow, soft, ceremonious, and graceful, reminding us of stately kings and courtiers and courtroom balls. This may well be a suitable theme for this section on Anglicanism with much of its beginnings rooted, as they were, in the courts of kings and queens with all the political manoeuvring that entailed.

The minuet form was often ternary with the structure A-B-A where A was the main subject and B was a different form, usually called the *trio*, which relied on instrumentation for just three instruments. In later years the term *trio* was applied to this section even when a more complex instrumentation was used. There was then a return to the main subject with musical glances back to the trio subject and possibly some newer material. We will use this minuet structure to examine the historic roots of the structure of the Anglican Communion.

The Many Faces of Anglicanism (Minuet)

First Subject: The Anglican Communion

The Anglican Communion is the family of nearly eighty million Christians throughout the world who accept the title Anglican or, in some cases,

Episcopalian. In one sense "Anglican" is the family or generic name and "Episcopalian" is the name used in specific countries and denotes the particular ministerial structure of the Church under the authority of bishops exercising their episcopal oversight.

It is made up of thirty-eight provinces, which generally coincide with the geographical boundaries of particular countries. In some instances a province might include more than one country. Each province has as its head a primate. In many countries these are archbishops. In the United States the constitution of the Episcopal Church has not allowed anyone to hold the title of archbishop since its inception because of the egalitarian nature of the society set up by the founding fathers of the nation after the War of Independence. Instead, the primate of the Episcopal Church is called the "presiding bishop." There are, therefore, thirty-eight primates in the Anglican Communion. Each province is divided into dioceses with a diocesan bishop at its head. Diocesan bishops may have assistant or suffragan bishops to help them in their task. In some dioceses the diocese itself is divided into areas and the assistant or suffragan bishops are given responsibility, under the authority of the diocesan bishop, to exercise episcopal and pastoral authority in their own areas.

Stephen Pickard and Paul Avis reminds us that, contrary to popular belief among Anglicans,

> . . . (i)n an episcopally-ordered polity, such as that of the Anglican Communion, the fundamental unit of the universal Church is the diocese. . . . Of course, a diocese is made up of those parishes or congregations that fall within its geographical bounds, but those parishes or congregations are not independent of the diocese in which they are placed, but depend for their vital ministry of word, sacrament and pastoral care on what the bishop provides or permits and are under the oversight and jurisdiction of the bishop. So, although for most Anglicans the parish is closer to home and more immediate in their experience than the diocese, the parish is not the fundamental unit of the Church."[1]

The Anglican Communion as a formal entity has only existed for less than one hundred and fifty years. It really began as a gathering of the leaders of Anglican churches that were seen as outposts in the British Empire of the Church of England. It represented the missionary work of the Church of England.

---

1. Avis and Pickard, *Instruments of Communion*, 1.6.

Beating the Bounds

The Lambeth Conference of Anglican Bishops first met in 1867 but it was not until its meeting in 1930 that it issued a quasi-authoritative definition of what constitutes the Anglican Communion. It described the Anglican Communion as a fellowship of dioceses and provinces in national churches in communion with the Archbishop of Canterbury and maintaining "the catholic and apostolic faith" as found in the Book of Common Prayer, but expressed in a way that is appropriate to the culture, experience, and history of those churches. Such a fellowship is not bound together by any central legislative authority but "by mutual loyalty sustained by the common council of the bishops in conference."[2]

Each province is, therefore, fully self-governing and any collective decisions can only be made by consensus. There are thirty-eight autonomous provinces, each with its own laws and governing bodies called synods or conventions. Although the Anglican Communion is worldwide it is not a worldwide church in the same way, for example, as the Roman Catholic Church, governed from Rome with an authoritative world leader in the person of the pope.

Douglas describes it in this way:

> Anglicanism is not monolithic globalised extension of English, or any other monocultural form of Christianity. Rather Anglicanism is the ongoing incarnational expression of the good

---

2. Lambeth Conference 1930, Resolution 49, "Anglican Communion" (all quotations of Lambeth resolutions are taken from the Lambeth Conference Resolutions Archive, online at http://www.lambethconference.org/resolutions/index.cfm). The resolution in full:

"The Conference approves the following statement of nature and status of the Anglican Communion, as that term is used in its Resolutions: The Anglican Communion is a fellowship, within the one Holy Catholic and Apostolic Church, of those duly constituted dioceses, provinces or regional Churches in communion with the See of Canterbury, which have the following characteristics in common:
  a) they uphold and propagate the Catholic and Apostolic faith and order as they are generally set forth in the Book of Common Prayer as authorised in their several Churches;
  b) they are particular or national Churches, and, as such, promote within each of their territories a national expression of Christian faith, life and worship; and
  c) they are bound together not by a central legislative and executive authority, but by mutual loyalty sustained through the common counsel of the bishops in conference.

The Conference makes this statement praying for and eagerly awaiting the time when the Churches of the present Anglican Communion will enter into communion with other parts of the Catholic Church not definable as Anglican in the above sense, as a step towards the ultimate reunion of all Christendom in one visibly united fellowship."

Movement Three: The Church as Anglican

news of Jesus Christ in an endless variety of particular cultural and social contexts that are bound together in a global family of churches through a shared history and service to God's mission. Put another way, Anglicanism is the embrace and celebration of apostolic catholicity within vernacular moments.[3]

The Instruments of Communion

The Anglican Communion relies on what it calls the four "Instruments of Communion" or "Instruments of Unity" to hold together these thirty-eight autonomous provinces with their approximately eight hundred bishops in what are called "the bonds of affection." They are: the Archbishop of Canterbury, the Lambeth Conference of Anglican Bishops, the Primates' Meeting, and the Anglican Consultative Council.

The musical setting within which this book is set resonates well with the concept of "instrument." An instrument of itself, without the life and vigour of a musician to take hold of it and use it, is lifeless. Of course, there have been in existence for some time now instruments that are automatons. They function mechanically relying totally on the input imprinted upon them through recording mechanisms, whether that be the spiked cylinders in musical boxes or pianola rolls of times past, or the electronic chips of today. However, the semblance of life they demonstrate is a mere shadow of the reality of life, having neither the capacity nor the will to engage with the environment within which they exist and the audience whom they are meant to serve. They are dead and lifeless. What is missing is that sense of "communion" or relationship that is so necessary between the musician and instrument and the instrument and the audience.

Avis and Pickard quote Michael Polanyi, who says of the living relationship between instruments and their users, "We pour ourselves into them and assimilate them as part of our own existence. We accept them existentially by dwelling in them."[4] This requires a "purposive effort," "commitment," and "a manner of disposing ourselves."[5] They then go on to make their own comment: "The external object becomes an instrument or tool when it is assimilated into the operation of the user. A merger takes place and the instrument becomes an extension of the body."[6]

3. Douglas and Zahl, *Understanding the Windsor Report*, 103.
4. Cited in Avis and Pickard, *Instruments of Communion*, 6.2.5.
5. Ibid., 60–61.
6. Ibid., 6.2.5.

Beating the Bounds

With these thoughts on instruments in mind let us now go on to examine the Instruments of Communion in the Anglican Communion.

a) The Archbishop of Canterbury is seen as the first Instrument of Communion. He is the symbolic focus of the whole Communion. "The litmus-test of membership of the Anglican Communion is to be in communion with the See of Canterbury. Of course, this cannot be the only condition for membership of the Communion. A common faith and order; a shared tradition of liturgy, theology and spirituality; and participation in the [other] instruments of the Communion are also involved. But it is the ultimate criterion."[7]

The Archbishop of Canterbury is not, however, a pope. He has no legal authority outside of his own diocese of Canterbury. His primacy within the Anglican Communion is one of honour in the light of the office's history of over 1,500 years. It is, however, a position with responsibility but without any real legal power. Any authority he carries can be only moral and spiritual. He has the influence of his office and his persona but can exercise his legal authority only in the diocese of Canterbury.

b) The Lambeth Conference is the second Instrument of Communion. This is a gathering in London of over eight hundred bishops from around the world who meet to study, pray, and discuss together the pressing issues of the day. It meets every ten years and invitations to attend the Conference are sent personally from the Archbishop of Canterbury.

Like all the Instruments of Communion it has no actual legal authority but it does have considerable spiritual, moral, and pastoral authority. It is, after all, the coming together of the most representative ministers of the Anglican Communion. Within its membership there are representatives from all the other Instruments of Communion.

Its resolutions have only the force of utterance and are an indicator of the mood of the Conference at that particular time. Each independent province has the right to make its own decision whether or not to take any notice of what is resolved or stated at Lambeth.

---

7. Avis, *Identity of Anglicanism*, 62.

Movement Three: The Church as Anglican

c) The Anglican Consultative Council is the third Instrument of Communion. This is the one elected body within the international structure of the Anglican Communion and the only one to include lay people. It meets every two or three years and it discusses reports and papers that have been prepared for it. Nevertheless it, like the other Instruments of Communion, has no legal authority to enforce its decisions. It is, as it name implies, only consultative. It may offer policies but they can be totally ignored by the provinces if they so desire. It has only the force of moral utterance.

d) The Primates' Meeting is the fourth Instrument of Communion. This is a gathering of all the thirty-eight primates from around the world. They meet usually around every eighteen months or so under the chairmanship of the Archbishop of Canterbury. He is, however, only "the first among equals." They may discuss many things and come to decisions about what ought to happen but they have no legal authority to enforce any of those decisions upon the whole Communion. Their only authority is that bestowed on them by their own province and only carries any weight in that province. In reaction to this lack of real authority and inability of the primates to restrain recalcitrant provinces, GAFCON has now instituted its own Primates' Council, to which it has given far more authority and disciplinary powers. This is, however, as has already been noted, alien to traditional Anglican ecclesiology.

Avis and Pickard stress the foolishness of any attempt to try and jettison the Instruments of Communion just because they have failed to live up to the expectations of many who want to see them as some sort of "puncture repair kit" that can bring a quick fix to the deep and complex problems. "The wound needing healing can't be fixed with a patch. Healing and repair can only come through deep listening and forbearance. The Instruments are in fact persons in relation seeking Divine wisdom through common counsel. Unfortunately they have been depersonalised and subject to significant ecclesiastical jostling and power play."[8]

Instead they see the Instruments as gifts from ". . . the Holy God to the church for the nurturing of the bond it has in Christ. On this account the 'Instruments' arise from the working of the Spirit among the faithful in the world."[9] Seeing them in this way endows them with an almost

---

8. Avis and Pickard, *Instruments of Communion*, 6.4.7.
9. Ibid., 6.4.3.

sacramental character as signs of God's continuing active presence and work in the world. With this perspective the Instruments "are uniquely placed to intentionally and prophetically recall the Communion to its true purpose in God's kingdom."[10]

Nevertheless, it is clear that the Anglican Communion is a worldwide body without a centralised authority and held together by nothing more than the reliance on consensus and the spiritual adhesive of "the bonds of affection."

The lack of any overarching governing body or individual has, until recently, meant that the general ethos of the Anglican Communion has been to act on the premise that "what touches all is decided by all." It was, therefore, a cataclysmic event in Anglican terms when the Episcopal Church in the United States, through its General Convention, approved the consecration of Gene Robinson, an openly gay and partnered priest, as the bishop of New Hampshire because something that "touched all" had not been "decided by all." It was a unilateral decision that was seen as a total reversal from what had been the theological practice and history of the worldwide Anglican Communion. This action has provoked a crisis within the Communion.

In order to set this present crisis in context it is important to note that this is not the first major crisis to strike at the heart of the Anglican Communion. History can teach us much about how the Communion has previously dealt with dissent, heresy, and threatened schism.

Development: Fragmentation Past and Present— The Lambeth Conferences

In this section a particularly detailed look is taken at the proceedings of the Lambeth Conference since its inception. A close examination of many of the resolutions passed at each Conference reveals clearly how, with the passage of time and with the benefit of experience, ideas about what is and what is not acceptable orthodoxy or orthopraxy ebb and flow within the Anglican Communion.

From its earliest days the Anglican Communion, through the Lambeth Conference, has wrestled with the placing of the boundaries of orthodoxy and orthopraxis. Most especially I want to emphasise the depth of the changes in theological outlook and practice concerning human gender and sexuality and diversity and unity within the Anglican Communion.

10. Ibid., 6.5.1.

The first Lambeth Conference was called in 1867. The first time only 76 bishops attended out of the 144 who were invited. Many of those absent, including the Archbishop of York, questioned whether this was really a good idea. Might they be creating some novel group with an authority not known before? What might the consequences of such an action be?

The Archbishop of Canterbury was certainly unsure about it. Archbishop Longley was reported as saying clearly, "It should be distinctly understood . . . that at this meeting no declaration of faith shall be made, and no decision come to which shall affect generally the interests of the Church, but that we shall meet together for brotherly counsel and encouragement. . . . I should refuse to convene any assembly which pretended to enact any canons, or affected to make any decisions binding on the Church."[11]

Nevertheless, many senior figures refused to come, including the second most authoritative figure in England, the Archbishop of York. Such was the feeling of novelty and strangeness that the dean of Westminster refused to allow Westminster Abbey be used for the final worship, citing as one of his reasons "the presence of prelates not belonging to our Church."[12]

Archbishop Longley made certain stipulations clear in his invitation. They were sent only to those who were "avowedly in communion with our Church," assuring them that

> . . . such a meeting would not be competent to make declarations or lay down definitions on points of doctrine. But united worship and common counsels would, he hoped, "tend to maintain the unity of the faith. . . . It has never been contemplated that we should assume the functions of a general synod of all the churches in full communion with the Church of England, and take upon ourselves to enact canons that should be binding upon those here represented. We merely propose to discuss matters of practical interest, and pronounce what we deem expedient in resolutions which may serve as safe guides to future action."[13]

Nevertheless, it was not long before the bishops at Lambeth were asked to consider a problem faced by one of their number. The Archbishop of Cape Town raised the difficulty he faced because one of his bishops, John William Colenso, had created a controversy by publishing his liberal views on the historicity and authorship of the Pentateuch.

11. Cited in Webber, *Brief History of the Lambeth Conference*, 2.
12. Ibid.
13. Ibid.

The Archbishop of Cape Town had deposed him and replaced him with a new, more conservative bishop. Colenso, however, had refused to step down. The Archbishop of Cape Town wanted Lambeth to back him.

The great majority of the bishops at Lambeth supported Cape Town but the Archbishop of Canterbury's previously stated views about the role of this Conference meant that the matter was referred to a committee and subsequently died as far as Lambeth was concerned.[14]

This could almost sound contemporary. What actually happened here was that the bishops at Lambeth were not willing to support the deposition of what they would describe as a liberal bishop who, in their opinion, was serving his community successfully and with local support. They could not condone the installation of a rival bishop to serve in that same community. At that time the issue was the right of the African church to freedom from foreign interference; today it is North American churches that claim to be asking for the same freedom.

Colenso also upset many by his willingness to accept polygamists for baptism. He questioned whether the immorality of polygamy could be resolved by what he called the "immorality of divorce." Colenso agreed that the practice of polygamy was unacceptable in the long term, but for the sake of mission he felt it better to bring the polygamists into the Church than either to repel them or to force them to choose one wife and leave the other wives and children without support.

Here again, something that many of the bishops at Lambeth first opposed was a view that became acceptable by a resolution at the Lambeth Conference of 1988.[15]

---

14. Lambeth Conference 1867, Resolution 6: "That, in the judgement of the bishops now assembled, the whole Anglican Communion is deeply injured by the present condition of the Church in Natal; and that a committee be now appointed at this general meeting to report on the best mode by which the Church may be delivered from the continuance of this scandal, and the true faith maintained. That such report be forwarded to His Grace the Lord Archbishop of Canterbury, with the request that he will be pleased to transmit the same to all the bishops of the Anglican Communion, and to ask for their judgement thereupon."

15. Lambeth Conference 1988, Resolution 26, "Church and Polygamy": "This Conference upholds monogamy as God's plan, and as the ideal relationship of love between husband and wife; nevertheless recommends that a polygamist who responds to the Gospel and wishes to join the Anglican Church may be baptized and confirmed with his believing wives and children on the following conditions:
   (1) that the polygamist shall promise not to marry again as long as any of his wives at the time of his conversion are alive;
   (2) that the receiving of such a polygamist has the consent of the local Anglican community;

Movement Three: The Church as Anglican

The second Lambeth Conference of 1878 was very cautious about getting involved in disputes. The Archbishop of Canterbury, Archibald Campbell Tait, made things clear.

> There is no intention whatever on the part of anybody to gather together the Bishops of the Anglican Church for the sake of defining any matter of doctrine. Our doctrines are contained in our formularies, and our formularies are interpreted by the proper judicial authorities, and there is no intention whatever at any such gathering that questions of doctrine should be submitted for interpretation in any future Lambeth Conference any more than they were at the previous Lambeth Conference.[16]

At the third Lambeth Conference of 1888, for the first time, open disagreement became visible.[17] Even though previous Conferences had determined not to be involved in "defining any matter of doctrine," it was this Conference that accepted the principles known now as the "Chicago-Lambeth Quadrilateral"[18] as a sufficient basis for Christian unity.

Remarkably for its time, the conference suggested that the Thirty-Nine Articles could well be amended in some particulars.[19] This certainly

---

(3) that such a polygamist shall not be compelled to put away any of his wives, on account of the social deprivation they would suffer;

(4) and recommends that provinces where the Churches face problems of polygamy are encouraged to share information of their pastoral approach to Christians who become polygamists so that the most appropriate way of disciplining and pastoring them can be found, and that the ACC be requested to facilitate the sharing of that information."

16. Webber, *Brief History of the Lambeth Conference*, 3.

17. Resolutions on not admitting polygamists to baptism had from 20 to 40 percent of the bishops in opposition. Lambeth Conference 1888.

18. Lambeth Conference 1888, Resolution 11:

"That, in the opinion of this Conference, the following articles supply a basis on which approach may be by God's blessing made towards home reunion:
  a. The Holy Scriptures of the Old and New Testaments, as 'containing all things necessary to salvation,' and as being the rule and ultimate standard of faith.
  b. The Apostles' Creed, as the baptismal symbol; and the Nicene Creed, as the sufficient statement of the Christian faith.
  c. The two sacraments ordained by Christ himself – Baptism and the Supper of the Lord—ministered with unfailing use of Christ's words of institution, and of the elements ordained by him.
  d. The historic episcopate, locally adapted in the methods of its administration to the varying needs of the nations and peoples called of God into the unity of his Church."

19. Lambeth Conference 1888, Resolution 19: "That, as regards newly constituted Churches, especially in non-Christian lands, it should be a condition of the

stretched the constraints that had cautiously been placed upon the Conference at its conception and earlier meetings.

The fourth Lambeth Conference of 1897 emphasized that what is called today 'contextualisation' should be encouraged.[20]

The 1908 Conference, the first in the twentieth century, is significant because of its emphasis on human sexuality and relationships. It seemed to those present that at this time the institution of marriage and its sanctity were under threat. The bishops challenged what they called all "right-thinking and clean-living men and women" to defend the institution.[21]

Divorce was still out of the question except for cases of adultery and fornication. There was a close vote concerning the possibility of remarriage in church of those who had been divorced, even if they had been the so-called innocent party. The refusal to give permission was carried by eighty-seven to eighty-four votes, although they did concede that that the innocent party, if remarried in a civil ceremony, might be readmitted to communion. Birth control and abortion were condemned as well. It also condemned the practice of artificial birth control.[22]

---

recognition of them as in complete intercommunion with us, and especially of their receiving from us episcopal succession, that we should first receive from them satisfactory evidence that they hold substantially the same doctrine as our own, and that their clergy subscribe articles in accordance with the express statements of our own standards of doctrine and worship; but that they should not necessarily be bound to accept in their entirety the Thirty-Nine Articles of Religion."

20. Lambeth Conference 1897, Resolution 19: "That it is important that, so far as possible, the Church should be adapted to local circumstances, and the people brought to feel in all ways that no burdens in the way of foreign customs are laid upon them, and nothing is required of them but what is of the essence of the faith, and belongs to the due order of the Catholic Church."

21. Lambeth Conference 1908, Resolution 37: "The growing prevalence of disregard of the sanctity of marriage calls for the active and determined co-operation of all right-thinking and clean-living men and women, in all ranks of life, in defence of the family life and the social order, which rest upon the sanctity of the marriage tie."

22. Lambeth Conference 1908, Resolution 39: "This Conference reaffirms the Resolution of the Conference of 1888 as follows:
   (a) That, inasmuch as our Lord's words expressly forbid divorce, except in the case of fornication or adultery, the Christian Church cannot recognise divorce in any other than the excepted case, or give any sanction to the marriage of any person who has been divorced contrary to this law, during the life of the other party.
   (b) That under no circumstances ought the guilty party, in the case of a divorce for fornication or adultery, to be regarded, during the lifetime of the innocent party, as a fit recipient of the blessing of the Church on marriage.
   (c) That, recognising the fact that there always has been a difference of opinion in the Church on the question whether our Lord meant to forbid marriage

Movement Three: The Church as Anglican

This 1908 Lambeth Conference also agreed that the "ministry of the laity requires to be more widely recognised." It was ironic, however, that when they thought about the creation of a consultative council, which had, in fact, been mooted at the previous Conference, they decided that the composition of such a council should be of eighteen bishops elected by the different provinces.[23]

Delayed by the horrors of the First World War, the next Lambeth Conference did not convene until 1920. By that time, and because of all the world had been through, views on many subjects had been forced to change.

It was this Conference that decided that women should be admitted to all councils in the church in which laymen served. This was, for its time, revolutionary and, surprisingly, it took the Episcopal Church in the United States another fifty years before it agreed to women deputies attending its General Convention. The USA was remarkably slow on gender equality in those days compared to its haste on gender and matters of sexuality today.[24]

On other matters of gender, however, the bishops at Lambeth were much more hesitant. The use of contraception was still seen as a "grave danger—physical, moral and religious," and the distribution of physical

---

to the innocent party in a divorce for adultery, the Conference recommends that the clergy should not be instructed to refuse the sacraments or other privileges of the Church to those who, under civil sanction, are thus married."

Resolution 40: "When an innocent person has, by means of a court of law, divorced a spouse for adultery, and desires to enter into another contract of marriage, it is undesirable that such a contract should receive the blessing of the Church. Voting: for 87; against 84."

Resolution 41: "The Conference regards with alarm the growing practice of the artificial restriction of the family, and earnestly calls upon all Christian people to discountenance the use of all artificial means of restriction as demoralising to character and hostile to national welfare."

Resolution 42: "The Conference affirms that deliberate tampering with nascent life is repugnant to Christian morality."

23. As early as 1867 there had been the idea of a sort of "Consultative Council." The bishops had requested a "Spiritual Court of Appeal," but this did not eventuate. The American bishop of Olympia, Stephen Bayne, who became the first Anglican executive officer, created what he named an Anglican Consultative Council after the 1958 conference, but nothing was formally set in place until 1968.

24. Lambeth Conference 1920, Resolution 46: "Women should be admitted to those councils of the Church to which laymen are admitted, and on equal terms. Diocesan, provincial, or national synods may decide when or how this principle is to be brought into effect."

means to aid contraception was seen as "an invitation to vice."[25] The bishops called on Christians everywhere to bring pressure on governments to end the open or secret sale of contraceptives and the continued existence of brothels. The bishops believed that the use of such things "threatens the race."[26]

Remarkably, there is an undoubted echo of this viewpoint found in the response of the Church in Nigeria to the request of the 1998 Lambeth Conference that the Communion should listen to homosexuals as the Nigerian Church stated that such practice "threatens . . . the continuation of the race."

At the end of the 1920 Lambeth Conference, the assembled bishops wanted to express their thanks to the Archbishop of Canterbury and to his wife, Mrs. Davidson, for their hospitality. For the first time ever a woman stepped onto the platform and the then bishop of Pennsylvani,a in presenting her with a gift, said: "We don't want this to be taken as a sign that women will be admitted in the episcopate!" Little did they know that seventy-eight years later that would become a reality.

The 1930 Lambeth Conference still set its face against widespread birth control but its hard line against prophylactic methods had softened. The bishops still reaffirmed, that "the primary purpose for which marriage exists is the procreation of children."[27] But, if some restriction on family

---

25. Lambeth Conference 1920, Resolution 69: "The Conference must condemn the distribution or use, before exposure to infection, of so-called prophylactics, since these cannot but be regarded as an invitation to vice."

26. Lambeth Conference 1920, Resolution 68:
"The Conference, while declining to lay down rules which will meet the needs of every abnormal case, regards with grave concern the spread in modern society of theories and practices hostile to the family. We utter an emphatic warning against the use of unnatural means for the avoidance of conception, together with the grave dangers—physical, moral and religious—thereby incurred, and against the evils with which the extension of such use threatens the race. In opposition to the teaching which, under the name of science and religion, encourages married people in the deliberate cultivation of sexual union as an end in itself, we steadfastly uphold what must always be regarded as the governing considerations of Christian marriage. One is the primary purpose for which marriage exists, namely the continuation of the race through the gift and heritage of children; the other is the paramount importance in married life of deliberate and thoughtful self-control. We desire solemnly to commend what we have said to Christian people and to all who will hear."

27. Lambeth Conference, Resolution 13: "The Conference emphasises the truth that sexual instinct is a holy thing implanted by God in human nature. It acknowledges that intercourse between husband and wife as the consummation of marriage has a value of its own within that sacrament, and that thereby married love is enhanced and its character strengthened. Further, seeing that the primary purpose for which

size was required the bishops called for "deliberate and thoughtful self-control ... in intercourse." Though abstinence was their preferred method, they now resolved that "where there is a morally sound reason for avoiding complete abstinence ... other methods may be used"—though not for selfishness or mere convenience.[28] They did not make clear what other methods were possible to use while their ban on prophylactic was still in force but at least they seemed to be getting the important message that the world had changed and what they had decided on in earlier days would not stand the test of time.[29]

The Second World War interrupted the Lambeth timetable and it would not be until 1948 that the Conference would meet again. If the experience of the First World War had brought new ideas and serious questioning of traditional thinking, especially on sexuality issues, this second worldwide conflict had a cataclysmic effect on the whole of society in that area. It was impossible for the Church to escape from this vortex.

The 1948 Lambeth Conference, in a world reeling from the disaster that had just over taken it, and recognising that what had been revealed about the depths of depravity to which human nature could descend, demanded a Christian response.

The conference made statements about the spiritual nature of humanity and that, therefore, the terrible disorders and conflicts of the past, both distant and recent, are due to spiritual ignorance of the love and lordship of Christ.[30] They also denounced war as a Christian way of settling

---

marriage exists is the procreation of children, it believes that this purpose as well as the paramount importance in married life of deliberate and thoughtful self-control should be the governing considerations in that intercourse."

28. Lambeth Conference 1930, Resolution 15: "Where there is clearly felt moral obligation to limit or avoid parenthood, the method must be decided on Christian principles. The primary and obvious method is complete abstinence from intercourse (as far as may be necessary) in a life of discipline and self-control lived in the power of the Holy Spirit. Nevertheless in those cases where there is such a clearly felt moral obligation to limit or avoid parenthood, and where there is a morally sound reason for avoiding complete abstinence, the Conference agrees that other methods may be used, provided that this is done in the light of the same Christian principles. The Conference records its strong condemnation of the use of any methods of conception control from motives of selfishness, luxury, or mere convenience."

29. There was, however, strong opposition to this change of view and, though it was approved by a 3–1 margin, 67 bishops did not support it.

30. Lambeth Conference 1948, Resolution 1: "The Conference, believing that man's disorders and conflicts are primarily due to ignorance rejection of the true understanding of his nature and destiny as revealed by God in Jesus Christ ... affirms ... that he can attain full stature only as he recognises and yields to the love of

international disputes but conceded that sometimes it had to be the lesser of two evils.[31]

On the issues of remarriage, gender, and sexuality there was little change despite the revolution that had taken place in society, especially the growing number of divorces among church-going people. In one of its resolutions the bishops urged even those in painful and hurtful relationships to remain together for the sake of their vows,[32] and in another it affirmed that there could be no remarriage in church for those whose previous marriages had been recognised by the Church.[33] Divorcees who disregarded the teaching of the Church were put under discipline regarding their participation in the Eucharist.[34]

The Conference of 1958, while maintaining that the resolutions from the 1948 Conference on marriage were helpful and to be studied again and emphasised,[35] nevertheless recognised the reality of the practice of birth control among its members. Instead of condemning contraception, they now believed that methods "mutually acceptable to husband and wife in

---

God as revealed in Jesus Christ and to the influence of his Holy Spirit."

31. 1948 Lambeth Conference, Resolutions 9 & 10: "The Conference reaffirms Resolution 25 of 1930, 'that war as a method of settling international disputes is incompatible with the teaching and example of our Lord Jesus Christ.' . . . ' it recognises that there are occasions when both nations and individuals are obliged to resort to war as the lesser of two evils."

32. Lambeth Conference 1948, Resolution 92: ". . . It calls upon members of the Church and others to do their utmost by word and example to uphold the sanctity of the marriage bond and to counteract those influences which tend to destroy it. It is convinced that maintenance of the Church's standard of discipline can alone meet the deepest needs of men; and it earnestly implores those whose marriage, perhaps through no fault of their own, is unhappy to remain steadfastly faithful to their marriage vows."

33. Lambeth Conference 1948, Resolution 94: "The Conference affirms that the marriage of one whose former partner is still living may not be celebrated according to the rites of the Church, unless it has been established that there exists no marriage bond recognised by the Church."

34. Lambeth Conference 1948, Resolution 96: "Confirmed members of the Church who marry contrary to the law of the Church, as accepted in the provincial or regional Church to which they belong, should be regarded as subject to the discipline of the Church in respect of admission to Holy Communion. Their admission to Holy Communion lies within the discretion of the bishop, due regard being had to their own spiritual good and the avoidance of scandal to others."

35. Lambeth Conference 1958, Resolution 119: "The Conference believes that the Resolutions of the 1948 Lambeth Conference concerning marriage discipline have been of great value as witnessing to Christ's teaching about the life-long nature of marriage, and urges that these Resolutions, and their implications, should continue to be studied in every province.

Christian conscience" were acceptable.[36] There was a new recognition of the fact of the ever-decreasing numbers of men in its congregations[37] and the consequent need to encourage and enhance the ministry of women.[38]

On the matter of what to do in cases of polygamy, a matter that had been raised at the very first Lambeth Conference of 1867, the bishops made it clear that there was still no agreement on the best way to handle the pastoral problems encountered.[39]

The Lambeth Conference of 1968 continued the move away from requiring a rigid formal subscription to the Thirty-Nine Articles as a defining note of Anglican loyalty. Provinces were now free to decide whether to include them or not in their prayer books. Even if a formal subscription was to be made, it was now to be seen as a way of setting the breadth of the Anglican heritage in a historical setting.[40]

36. Lambeth Conference 1958, Resolution 115:"The Conference believes that the responsibility for deciding upon the number and frequency of children has been laid by God upon the consciences of parents everywhere; that this planning, in such ways as are mutually acceptable to husband and wife in Christian conscience, is a right and important factor in Christian family life and should be the result of positive choice before God. Such responsible parenthood, built on obedience to all the duties of marriage, requires a wise stewardship of the resources and abilities of the family as well as a thoughtful consideration of the varying population needs and problems of society and the claims of future generations."

37. Lambeth Conference 1958, Resolution 122: "The Conference believes that a most important answer to the crushing impact of secularism on family life lies in a return to the discipline of family prayer and in a faithful common Christian life in the household. It urges that the clergy work towards this end by teaching both the privilege and the means of such worship, and of Bible reading, in which fathers should take their due place with mothers and children as members and ministers of a worshipping community."

38. Lambeth Conference 1958, Resolution 93: "The Conference thankfully recognises the particular contribution of women to the mission of the Church; and urges that fuller use should be made of trained and qualified women, and that spheres of progressive responsibility and greater security should be planned for them"

39. Lambeth Conference 1958, Resolution 120: ". . . It acknowledges that the introduction of monogamy into societies that practice polygamy involves a social and economic revolution and raises problems which the Christian Church has as yet not solved."

40. Lambeth Conference 1968, Resolution 43: "The Conference accepts the main conclusion of the Report of the Archbishops' Commission on Christian Doctrine entitled 'Subscription and Assent to the Thirty-Nine Articles' (1968) and in furtherance of its recommendation:
    (a) suggests that each Church of our Communion consider whether the Articles need be bound up with its Prayer Book;
    (b) suggests to the Churches of the Anglican Communion that assent to the Thirty-nine Articles be no longer required of ordinands;

Th 1968 Conference also made it clear that it thought the pope was in error when, in his encyclical "Humanae Vitae," he condemned all methods of birth control except abstinence and the so-called rhythm method. The irony of this is, of course, that if the pope was in error now because of this teaching, the bishops themselves had also been in error when they resolved the same thing at their 1920 Conference.25, 26 Here was clearly yet another complete change of teaching and episcopal direction.

The 1968 Conference was also the first to come under pressure about the ordination of women. It was, in a way, a clear consequence of the admission of the declining number of men in the congregation and the consequent decline in male vocations. What was also clear was that the bishops were not ready to grasp this nettle.

While they agreed to lay participation in the newly formed Anglican Consultative Council, with its emphasis on the statutory inclusion of women, they expressed the opinion that the theological arguments for and against the ordination of women to the priesthood were "inconclusive," and asked that the member churches study the matter carefully and seek advice from the Consultative Council before doing anything rash.[41] The only thing that was rash was that resolution, and the thought that things could be held back like some King Canute attempting to restrain the incoming tide on the seashore.

In fact, when the Conference met again in 1978 the horse had already bolted. Ordinations of women to the priesthood had already taken place in the American Episcopal Church and also in Hong Kong, New Zealand, and Canada. Another eight provinces were also on the brink of following the lead that had now been set. The bishops could only now plead for unity and patience. What they did make was an important statement about the holding together of diversity within unity as being of the essence of Anglicanism.[42] This was to have important ramifications as the debate about human sexuality grew more volatile.

(c) suggests that, when subscription is required to the Articles or other elements in the Anglican tradition, it should be required, and given, only in the context of a statement which gives the full range of our inheritance of faith and sets the Articles in their historical context."

41. Lambeth Conference 1968, Resolution 34: "The Conference affirms its opinion that the theological arguments as at present presented for and against the ordination of women to the priesthood are inconclusive"

42. Lambeth Conference 1978, Resolution 21.7: "We recognise that our accepting this variety of doctrine and practice in the Anglican Communion may disappoint the Roman Catholic, Orthodox, and Old Catholic Churches, but we wish to make it clear (a) that the holding together of diversity within a unity of faith and worship is part of

What is evident here is a marked shift in thinking from the 1920 Lambeth statement on women's ministry in Resolution 48: "The order of deaconesses is for women the one and only order of the ministry which has the stamp of apostolic approval, and is for women the only order of the ministry which we can recommend that our branch of the Catholic Church should recognise and use."[43] Now there is a clear acceptance of the inclusion of women in the order of the diaconate on equal footing with men[44] and on to the ordination of women to the priesthood and, later, to the episcopate.

Even in 1978 the matter of human sexuality was seen as a "complex" issue that required further theological study.[45] While affirming heterosexuality as the scriptural norm, there was a serious attempt to bring the issue of homosexuality into open debate for the first time and to take seriously the discoveries of science and medicine in this area. There was also an admission of the needs and pastoral concerns of homosexuals, which had to be taken seriously through direct dialogue. The bishops applauded the fact that some parts of the Communion were already engaged in these things.[46]

---

the Anglican heritage; (b) that those who have taken part in ordinations of women to the priesthood believe that these ordinations have been into the historic ministry of the Church as the Anglican Communion has received it . . ."

43. Lambeth Conference 1920, Resolution 48.

44. Lambeth Conference 1968, Resolution 32, "The Ministry—The Diaconate": "The Conference recommends:
(a) That the diaconate, combining service of others with liturgical functions, be open to
  (i) men and women remaining in secular occupations,
  (ii) full-time church workers,
  (iii) those selected for priesthood.
(b) That Ordinals should, where necessary, be revised:
  (i) to take account of the new role envisaged for the diaconate;
  (ii) by the removal of reference to the diaconate as 'an inferior office';
  (iii) by emphasis upon the continuing element of 'diakonia' in the ministry of bishops and priests.
(c) That those made deaconesses by laying-on of hands with appropriate prayers be declared to be within the diaconate.
(d) That appropriate canonical legislation be enacted by provinces and regional Churches to provide for those already ordained deaconesses."

45. Lambeth Conference 1978, Resolution 10: "(1). The need for theological study of sexuality in such a way as to relate sexual relationships to that wholeness of human life which itself derives from God, who is the source of masculinity and femininity."

46. Lambeth Conference 1978, Resolution 10: "(3). While we reaffirm heterosexuality as the scriptural norm, we recognise the need for deep and dispassionate study of the question of homosexuality, which would take seriously both the teaching

With the aid of hindsight we now know that these decisions would cause much angry debate that continue until the present day and threaten the very existence of the Lambeth Conference and even the Anglican Communion itself.

The 1988 Lambeth Conference actually revealed the depth of the divisions that were fracturing the Communion. Phrases such as "the present impaired nature of Communion" were common. Provinces were asked to respect the decisions of other provinces, whether they agreed with them or not. A request was made of the Archbishop of Canterbury to appoint a commission with the task of following all that was happening around the world.

Bishops were encouraged "to exercise sensitivity, patience and pastoral care towards all concerned" and were "encouraged to seek continuing dialogue with, and make pastoral provision for, those clergy and congregations whose opinions differ from those of the bishop, in order to maintain the unity of the diocese."[47] No advice was given as to how they were to actually do that in practice.

---

of Scripture and the results of scientific and medical research. The Church, recognising the need for pastoral concern for those who are homosexual, encourages dialogue with them. (We note with satisfaction that such studies are now proceeding in some member Churches of the Anglican Communion.)"

47. Lambeth Conference 1988, Resolution 1, "The ordination or consecration of women to the episcopate": "This Conference resolves:
1. That each province respect the decision and attitudes of other provinces in the ordination or consecration of women to the episcopate, without such respect necessarily indicating acceptance of the principles involved, maintaining the highest possible degree of communion with the provinces which differ.
2. That bishops exercise courtesy and maintain communications with bishops who may differ, and with any woman bishop, ensuring an open dialogue in the Church to whatever extent communion is impaired.
3. That the Archbishop of Canterbury, in consultation with the primates, appoints a commission:
   a) to provide for an examination of the relationships between provinces of the Anglican Communion and ensure that the process of reception includes continuing consultation with other Churches as well; b) to monitor and encourage the process of consultation within the Communion and to offer further pastoral guidelines.
4. That in any province where reconciliation on these issues is necessary, any diocesan bishop facing this problem be encouraged to seek continuing dialogue with, and make pastoral provision for, those clergy and congregations whose opinions differ from those of the bishop, in order to maintain the unity of the diocese.
5. Recognises the serious hurt which would result from the questioning by some of the validity of the episcopal acts of a woman bishop, and likewise the hurt experienced by those whose conscience would be offended by the ordination of a

Movement Three: The Church as Anglican

It was this Conference that finally decided, after a struggle lasting 128 years, that converted polygamists and their multiple wives and children could be baptised and receive the Eucharist.22 This was a complete change in theology and practice from the situation in 1867, which had caused Bishop Colenso of Natal such heart searching.

In the introduction to the GAFCON we noted that the conservative American bishops, reeling from liberal advances in their own country and disillusioned with the possibility of bringing about internal reform, set about encouraging African bishops to throw their weight behind conservative agendas, and in particular the issue of homosexuality. Their strategy was to ensure that the African voice would be heard effectively at Lambeth.

Tolliday has noted that at previous Lambeth Conferences the bishops from the Global South had not been particularly influential. The stylised organisation of discussion at Lambeth did not suit an African form of discourse. He reminds us of a reflection by Michael Marshall on Lambeth 1988 noting the comment from one Ugandan bishop, "This is not our way of doing things, so we just leave it to you." Marshall himself reported: "With a few notable exceptions much of the drafting was the work of the English and American bishops, who still tended to dominate, especially in the plenary sessions."[48] As it happened, Lambeth 1988 would be the last time when bishops from the South would be lost for a voice at Lambeth.[49]

Hassett points out just how things had changed for Africans between Lambeth 1988 and 1998. In 1988 the African message had been essentially, "Africa has these problems, and the rest of the Communion and the world needs to respond to them." But by 1998, at least with regard to questions about human sexuality, the message from the South was, "The rest of the Communion has a problem, and Africa and the Global South are going to respond to it."[50] That they were able to get this message across is due, in the opinion of Hassett, to documents such as the Kuala Lumpur Statement and the Dallas Statement, both of which began to question the principle of provincial autonomy throughout the Communion. For example, the Kuala Lumpur Statement spoke of the need for "mutual accountability and interdependence" and of needing to "learn how to seek each other's counsel and wisdom in a spirit of true unity, and to reach a common mind

---

woman to the episcopate. The Church needs to exercise sensitivity, patience and pastoral care towards all concerned."

48. Marshall, *Church at the Crossroads*, 29.
49. Tolliday, "Global Witness: But of What Sort?"
50. Hassett, *Communion in Crisis*, 54.

before embarking on radical changes to Church discipline and moral teaching." They concluded that such precipitous actions could have deleterious consequences, since the way one province acts "can radically affect the mission and witness of the Church in another' province."[51]

The Lambeth Conference of 1998 was, therefore, very different and difficult, with sexuality being the subject that received most of the publicity and raising most of the anger. By this time, in different parts of the Anglican Communion, there were women ordained not only to the priesthood but to the episcopate.

In 1989 the reality of the first female Anglican bishop materialised when Bishop Penny Jamieson was consecrated as the seventh bishop of Dunedin in the Anglican Church of New Zealand. In the same year, the Episcopal Church in the USA consecrated Barbara Harris, an African-American woman, as bishop suffragan of the diocese of Massachusetts. The die had certainly been cast.

In August 1997 the Eames Monitoring Group[52] had issued a report in which they estimated that there were "well over 4,000" female priests in the Communion, as well as "10 women bishops of which 6 are diocesan bishops." The provinces of Australia, Burundi, England, Kenya, Philippines, Scotland, Uganda, Wales, West Africa, and West Indies accepted women as deacons or priests. Brazil, Ireland, Mexico, and Southern Africa had accepted, in principle, women to all three ministries of the Church: deacon, priest, and bishop. The provinces of Aotearoa, New Zealand, and Polynesia had joined Canada and the USA by actually having women functioning in all three levels.[53]

By the time of the 1998 Conference a majority of the provinces had decided to ordain women. There was now no real controversy about female deacons and priests. Female ordination had become almost a non-issue.

51. "Kuala Lumpur Statement."

52. Part 'c' of Resolution 1 of the 1988 Lambeth Conference had recommended that the Archbishop of Canterbury, Robert Runcie, appoint a commission to monitor female ordination. The main purpose of the group was to preserve the unity of the church during this critical time. There was considerable concern that one or more provinces would break away from the Anglican Communion. None ever did. The commission's formal name was the Archbishop of Canterbury's Commission on Communion and Women in the Episcopate. It became generally known as the Eames Commission because it was chaired by the Most Reverend Robin Eames, Archbishop of Armagh in Ireland. In 1994 the Commission was disbanded, but was replaced by the Eames Monitoring Group, which continued to observe the female ordination issue in the Communion.

53. "Ordination of Female Priests and Bishops."

In South Africa, for example, Bishop Duncan Buchanan of Johannesburg noted: "On the whole it has been a huge and wonderful non-issue and I mean that in the best way. It is not that people have gone the same way, but that people have respected each other's point of view. . . . Those of us who have ordained women to the priesthood have done so supported by an enormously loving brethren also in the episcopate who have disagreed with us."[54]

Eleven female bishops attended the 1998 Lambeth Conference. Eight were from the USA, two from Canada, and one from New Zealand. All but one had been ordained as priests between 1978 and 1984. They were thus pioneers from the beginning of their ordained ministries as deacons and priests. "Nearly all can tell tales of painful marginalization, even, in a few cases, of being spat upon, shouted at, verbally abused. . . . With each bishop, however, such tales are told only rarely and then reluctantly, and usually, only to illustrate how much progress has been made."[55]

There were certainly protests by conservative bishops, some of whom decided not to attend any worship services or Bible studies where female bishops were in attendance. Fifty bishops even decided to hold an alternative meeting and one even declined to be included in the official photograph if women were to be present.

It was a group of women bishops together with some conservative male bishops who prepared a resolution on female ordination. It stated that bishops should not be compelled to act against their conscience by ordaining or licensing female priests. It was, in fact, moved by Bishop Penny Jamieson of Dunedin in New Zealand.[56]

---

54. Skidmore, "Women's Ordination."

55. Sherrod, "First Female Bishops."

56. Lambeth Conference 1998, Resolution III.2, "The unity of the Anglican Communion": "This Conference, committed to maintaining the overall unity of the Anglican Communion, including the unity of each diocese under the jurisdiction of the diocesan bishop,
   a) believes such unity is essential to the overall effectiveness of the Church's mission to bring the Gospel of Christ to all people;
   b) for the purpose of maintaining this unity, calls upon the provinces of the Communion to uphold the principle of 'Open Reception' as it relates to the ordination of women to the priesthood as indicated by the Eames Commission; noting that 'reception is a long and spiritual process.' (Grindrod Report);
   c) in particular calls upon the provinces of the Communion to affirm that those who dissent from, as well as those who assent to, the ordination of women to the priesthood and episcopate are both loyal Anglicans;
   d) therefore calls upon the Provinces of the Communion to make such provision, including appropriate episcopal ministry, as will enable them to live in the

This enabled a parish that was opposed to women priests or bishops to be cared for by a second male rather than by their own diocesan bishop. This was a radical departure from Anglican tradition, which had always recognised the traditional authority of a single bishop within each diocese.

The most significant resolution of this Conference was what came to be known as "Lambeth 1:10" and concerns homosexuality. The bishops committed themselves "to listen to the experience of homosexual persons" and "assure them that they are loved by God and . . . full members of the Body of Christ." Homosexual practice was still rejected as "incompatible with Scripture," but "irrational fear of homosexuals, violence within marriage and any trivialisation and commercialisation of sex" were condemned. A number of protest resolutions referring to homosexuality as a "kind of sexual brokenness" and calling on bishops who ordain homosexual persons to repent were defeated. However, the bishops found that they could not "advise the legitimising or blessing of same sex unions nor ordaining those involved in same gender unions."[57]

---

highest degree of Communion possible, recognising that there is and should be no compulsion on any bishop in matters concerning ordination or licensing;
e) also affirms that 'although some of the means by which communion is expressed may be strained or broken, there is a need for courtesy, tolerance, mutual respect, and prayer for one another, and we confirm that our desire to know or be with one another, remains binding on us as Christians."

57. Lambeth Conference 1998, Resolution 1:10, "Human Sexuality": "This Conference:
a) commends to the Church the subsection report on human sexuality;
b) in view of the teaching of Scripture, upholds faithfulness in marriage between a man and a woman in lifelong union, and believes that abstinence is right for those who are not called to marriage;
c) recognises that there are among us persons who experience themselves as having a homosexual orientation. Many of these are members of the Church and are seeking the pastoral care, moral direction of the Church, and God's transforming power for the living of their lives and the ordering of relationships. We commit ourselves to listen to the experience of homosexual persons and we wish to assure them that they are loved by God and that all baptised, believing and faithful persons, regardless of sexual orientation, are full members of the Body of Christ;
d) while rejecting homosexual practice as incompatible with Scripture, calls on all our people to minister pastorally and sensitively to all irrespective of sexual orientation and to condemn irrational fear of homosexuals, violence within marriage and any trivialisation and commercialisation of sex;
e) cannot advise the legitimising or blessing of same sex unions nor ordaining those involved in same gender unions;
f) requests the Primates and the ACC to establish a means of monitoring the work done on the subject of human sexuality in the Communion and to share statements and resources among us;
g) notes the significance of the Kuala Lumpur Statement on Human Sexuality and the concerns expressed in resolutions IV.26, V.1, V.10, V.23 and V.35 on the

Movement Three: The Church as Anglican

Resolutions to try and preserve respect for diocesan boundaries and Communion unity were passed or reaffirmed. Bishops could not be a sign of unity while they encouraged division.

There was a cry for stronger leadership from the centre. The importance of the role of the Archbishop of Canterbury was reaffirmed and the primates were encouraged to "exercise an enhanced responsibility in offering guidance on doctrinal, moral and pastoral matters," and it was felt that they "should carry moral authority calling for ready acceptance throughout the Communion."[58]

---

authority of Scripture in matters of marriage and sexuality and asks the Primates and the ACC to include them in their monitoring process."

58. Lambeth Conference 1998, Resolution III.6, "Instruments of the Anglican Communion": "This Conference, noting the need to strengthen mutual accountability and interdependence among the Provinces of the Anglican Communion,
a) reaffirms Resolution 18.2(a) of Lambeth 1988 which 'urges that encouragement be given to a developing collegial role for the Primates' Meeting under the presidency of the Archbishop of Canterbury, so that the Primates' Meeting is able to exercise an enhanced responsibility in offering guidance on doctrinal, moral and pastoral matters';
b) asks that the Primates' Meeting, under the presidency of the Archbishop of Canterbury, include among its responsibilities positive encouragement to mission, intervention in cases of exceptional emergency which are incapable of internal resolution within provinces, and giving of guidelines on the limits of Anglican diversity in submission to the sovereign authority of Holy Scripture and in loyalty to our Anglican tradition and formularies;
c) recommends that these responsibilities should be exercised in sensitive consultation with the relevant provinces and with the Anglican Consultative Council (ACC) or in cases of emergency the Executive of the ACC and that, while not interfering with the juridical authority of the provinces, the exercise of these responsibilities by the Primates' Meeting should carry moral authority calling for ready acceptance throughout the Communion, and to this end it is further recommended that the Primates should meet more frequently than the ACC;
d) believing that there should be a clearer integration of the roles of the Anglican Consultative Council and the Primates' Meeting, recommends that the bishops representing each province in the Anglican Consultative Council should be the primates of the provinces and that—
   i) equal representation in the ACC from each province, one presbyter or deacon and one lay person from each province should join the primates in the triennial ACC gathering;
   ii) an executive committee of the ACC should be reflective of this broad membership, and;
   iii) there should be a change in the name of the Anglican Consultative Council to the Anglican Communion Council, reflecting the evolving needs and structures to which the foregoing changes speak;
e) reaffirms the role of the Archbishop of Canterbury as a personal sign of our unity and communion, and the role of the decennial Lambeth Conference and of extraordinary Anglican Congresses as called, together with inter-provincial

The period between the 1998 Conference and the first Conference of the new millennium was alive with controversy. The sexuality issue was constantly to the fore. In October of 2003 the primates requested the Archbishop of Canterbury to set up what became known as the Lambeth Commission on Communion in the light of current events that were fanning the flames of possible division.

> The decision by the 74th General Convention of the Episcopal Church (USA) to give consent to the election of bishop Gene Robinson to the Diocese of New Hampshire, the authorising by a diocese of the Anglican Church of Canada of a public Rite of Blessing for same sex unions and the involvement in other provinces by bishops without the consent or approval of the incumbent bishop to perform episcopal functions have uncovered major divisions throughout the Anglican Communion. There has been talk of crisis, schism and realignment. Voices and declarations have portrayed a Communion in crisis.[59]

As we have seen, the history of the Lambeth Conference demonstrates that the Anglican Communion has always been in tension over various differences; however, the commission felt that "The depth of conviction and feeling on all sides of the current issues has on occasions introduced a degree of harshness and a lack of charity which is new to Anglicanism. A process of dissent is not new to the Communion but it has never before been expressed with such force nor in ways which have been so accessible to international scrutiny."[60]

This was the reason why the Archbishop of Canterbury set a clear period of a year for the completion of the report and urged "urgent and deep theological and legal reflection' in his mandate to the Commission recognising that they were dealing with issues that could 'tear the fabric of our Communion at its deepest level, and may lead to further division."[61]

---

gatherings and cross-provincial diocesan partnerships, as collegial and communal signs of the unity of our Communion."

59. Lambeth Commission on Communion, *Windsor Report*, 4.

60. Ibid., 5.

61. Lambeth Commission on Communion Mandate (in ibid., 8): "The Archbishop of Canterbury requests the Commission:
1. To examine and report to him by 30th September 2004, in preparation for the ensuing meetings of the Primates and the Anglican Consultative Council, on the legal and theological implications flowing from the decisions of the Episcopal Church (USA) to appoint a priest in a committed same sex relationship as one of its bishops, and of the Diocese of New Westminster to authorise services for use in connection with same sex unions, and specifically on the canonical

Movement Three: The Church as Anglican

The long-awaited report of the Commission on Communion was eventually published in October 2004 as *The Windsor Report*. It contained several important recommendations as to how the Anglican Communion might be able to maintain the highest possible level of communion among Anglicans in the midst of the controversies that were seriously dividing it.

Among its recommendations was an enhanced role for the Archbishop of Canterbury as the focus of unity, mission, and teaching in the Communion, especially in articulating the mind of the Communion in areas of controversy. It further recommended that a "Council of Advice" be established to assist the archbishop "in discerning when and how it might be appropriate for him to exercise a ministry of unity on behalf of the whole Communion."[62]

It also endorsed the adoption by all churches of the Anglican Communion of a common "Anglican covenant," which would deal with common identity, the commitments of being in communion with one another, and the management of disputes that may arise. At the heart of such a covenant would be the principle that "what touches all should be approved by all."[63] The Commission supplied a draft proposal for such a covenant.

---

understandings of communion, impaired and broken communion, and the ways in which provinces of the Anglican Communion may relate to one another in situations where the ecclesiastical authorities of one province feel unable to maintain the fullness of communion with another part of the Anglican Communion.
2. Within their report, to include practical recommendations (including reflection on emerging patterns of provision for episcopal oversight for those Anglicans within a particular jurisdiction, where full communion within a province is under threat) for maintaining the highest degree of communion that may be possible in the circumstances resulting from these decisions, both within and between the churches of the Anglican Communion.
3. Thereafter, as soon as practicable, and with particular reference to the issues raised in Section IV of the Report of the Lambeth Conference 1998, to make recommendations to the Primates and the Anglican Consultative Council, as to the exceptional circumstances and conditions under which, and the means by which, it would be appropriate for the Archbishop of Canterbury to exercise an extraordinary ministry of episcope (pastoral oversight), support and reconciliation with regard to the internal affairs of a province other than his own for the sake of maintaining communion with the said province and between the said province and the rest of the Anglican Communion.
4. In its deliberations, to take due account of the work already undertaken on issues of communion by the Lambeth Conferences of 1988 and 1998, as well as the views expressed by the Primates of the Anglican Communion in the communiqués and pastoral letters arising from their meetings since 2000."

62. Ibid., 45–46.
63. Ibid., 48.

It recommended a moratorium on the election and consecration of any candidate to the episcopate who was living in a same-gender union until some new consensus in the Anglican Communion emerges. The Episcopal Church was asked "to express its regret" over the breach it caused by consecrating Gene Robinson as bishop of New Hampshire, and those bishops who took part in the consecration were asked to consider withdrawing themselves from any representative functions in the Anglican Communion.[64]

It also recommended a moratorium on all blessings of same-sex unions and a study of the biblical and theological rationale for and against such unions. It also recommended the provision of alternative pastoral oversight by sympathetic bishops for those congregations that dissent from their bishop's support of the ordination of non-celibate homosexuals and the blessing of same-sex unions.[65]

Not unexpectedly, *The Windsor Report* did not receive whole-hearted acceptance, especially from the more liberal sections of the Anglican Church. Bishop John Shelby Spong claimed that the report was ". . . what one would expect from a frightened leadership that thinks that the problem is one of maintaining unity rather than seeking to discern the truth . . . (it) is, therefore, nothing more than a pathetic ecclesiastical attempt at damage control. It will fail in its stated purpose today. It will . . . be nothing but an enormous source of embarrassment in the future."[66]

On the other hand, conservatives also criticised the report. Several primates, including conservative members of the Commission, issued statements endorsing the report as worthy of careful study. However, Akinola, who had announced his intention of forming a Nigerian-governed church in the United States, denounced the report and rejected its recommendation that he should express regret.

> Instead of a clear call for repentance we have been offered warm words of sentimentality for those who have shown no godly sorrow for their actions and harsh words of condemnation for those who have reached out a helping hand to friends in need of pastoral and spiritual care. . . . We have been asked to express regret for our actions and 'affirm our desire to remain in the Communion.' How patronizing! . . . We will not be intimidated. In the absence of any signs of repentance and reform from those

---

64. Ibid., 53–54.
65. Ibid., 58.
66. Clatworthy and Taylor, *Windsor Report: A Liberal Response*, x.

Movement Three: The Church as Anglican

who have torn the fabric of our Communion, and while there is continuing oppression of those who uphold the Faith, we cannot forsake our duty to provide care and protection for those who cry out for our help.[67]

With such conservative reactions ringing around the world it was not surprising that conservative feelings found a clearer focus in what became the Global Anglican Future Conference (GAFCON).

It is important for us to trace the evolution of this conference, which had such a major influence on the 2008 Lambeth Conference.

During the fifties and sixties of the last century Anglican evangelicals felt that they had a secure place within a church, which they saw as expressing principled comprehensiveness. Despite the activities of certain individuals who put forward radical and liberal views, none of the various elements that made up the Anglican Church seriously denied what were held to be the fundamentals of the faith and this enabled them to resist the pressures that were certainly brought upon them from outside of the Anglican Church[68] encouraging them to them to break away.

It is claimed that today two-thirds of the non-Western Anglican churches are Anglicans of the evangelical variety, with most of them being found in the churches of the African continent.

The first time this reality came to global prominence was the 1988 Lambeth Conference. Then in 1998 they made a stand for orthodoxy in the Communion's teaching on sexuality. Then in 2008 they boycotted the Lambeth Conference and, instead, they were some of the prime movers for the initiative that eventually produced GAFCON.

It is not possible to understand these developments without understanding the emergence of global non-Western Anglicanism, which has been slowly taking to itself a sense of responsibility for the whole Anglican Communion.[69]

---

67. Naughton, "Windsor Report calls for expressions of regret."

68. At a meeting of the Evangelical Alliance at Westminster Hall, London, on October 18, 1966, there was a famous confrontation between the acclaimed leader of Anglican evangelicals in the UK, Revd. John Stott, and the equally influential non-conformist Pastor of Westminster Chapel, London, Dr. Martyn Lloyd Jones. Jones called upon evangelicals to leave their "mixed" denominations (and this was a clear reference to Anglicans) and to join with all other evangelicals to form one evangelical church in the UK. This was dismissed by Stott on the grounds that the fundamentals of Anglicanism were evangelical at heart and that it was the non-evangelicals in the Anglican Church who were the deviationists. GAFCON clearly echoes this view today.

69. Samuel, "Why did GAFCON happen?"

Beating the Bounds

The theological divide that appears to have become a fissure across the whole of the face of the Anglican Communion reflects most clearly the profound demographic changes that have taken place in global Anglicanism during the past hundred years. Like much of the rest of Christianity, during the last century the demographic centre of Anglicanism has moved decidedly southward, where the faith is practised in a much more traditional fashion than in the generally more theologically liberal North.

In 1900, for example, more than 80 percent of Anglicans lived in Britain, and a mere 1 percent lived in Sub-Saharan Africa, according to figures from the World Christian Database. Today, a majority (55 percent) of the world's Anglicans live in Sub-Saharan Africa; by contrast, only 33 percent of Anglicans live in Britain. But this figure is deceiving, since, according to the Church of England's own numbers, average Sunday church attendance during this decade has dipped to approximately one million, or about 4 percent of the country's Anglican population.

During this same period, the USA branch of the Anglican Communion—the Episcopal Church—also has decreased in importance, going from 5 to 3 percent of the total Anglican population. And the decline of Anglicanism in the USA and Britain has occurred not only in relative but also in absolute terms; in recent decades there has been a decrease in the overall numbers as well. Britain has twenty-six million Anglicans today, which is three million fewer than in 1970; and the United States has two million Episcopalians, which is one million fewer than in 1970, according to the World Christian Database. In contrast, the Database puts the current number of Anglicans in Sub-Saharan Africa at forty-three million, which is thirty-five million more than in 1970. Despite being much smaller in relative size, the number of Anglicans in the Asia-Pacific region has more than doubled over this same period.[70]

This weighting towards Africa has caused several conservative Episcopal churches in the USA to look for alternative spiritual leadership after they became unhappy with the theological trends in the Episcopal Church. These breakaway parishes are now under the oversight of several African bishops. For example, the Convocation of Anglicans in North America (CANA) is undr the authority of the primate of Nigeria.

"Now that the Anglican Communion is majority African, and the vast majority of African Anglicans are theologically conservative, there

---

70. This constantly upgraded evidence is found at the website of the World Christian Database, http://worldchristiandatabase.org/wcd/home.asp.

Movement Three: The Church as Anglican

is a real question as to whether the historical ties of the Anglican Communion are strong enough to counter the forces that seem to be pushing the church."[71]

The consequence of such a seismic shift have been seized upon by those who wish to shake free from what they see from their point of view as the neocolonial shackles of a denomination that is still centred in England and whose figurehead is an English establishment figure. "A global Anglican Church based in Canterbury is almost over. There are now going to be competing centres of Anglican Christianity." These are the words of Jacob Olupona, Professor of African and African-American Studies and Religion in Harvard University's Faculty of Arts and Sciences and Harvard Divinity School.

Archbishop Robert Duncan of CANA was even more blunt in his assessment. "In the year 2000 the Archbishop of Canterbury was the second most important Christian leader in the world. In a short space of time that office has utterly been diminished. It shows that the British model of Anglicanism has failed. The new Canterbury will be in Africa. It is the realignment of Anglicanism and a new Reformation of Christianity sparked by Africa."[72]

Returning to the matter of Lambeth 2008 and GAFCON, Samuel also makes the point that it was the fact that the Archbishop of Canterbury, Rowan Williams, did not consult the Anglican primates over the invitations to Lambeth and, despite their pleas to postpone Lambeth, went ahead with inviting the consecrators of Gene Robinson to Lambeth, that triggered the decision to hold GAFCON.[73]

In the light of both *Windsor Report* reactions and the calling of the GAFCON conference, it was not surprising that the Lambeth Conference of 2008 was quite different from any of its recent predecessors.

At the heart of the Conference was a concept called "Indaba." The Archbishop of Canterbury described the Zulu word *indaba* as a ". . . meeting for purposeful discussion among equals. Its aim is not to negotiate a formula that will keep everyone happy but to go to the heart of an issue and find what the true challenges are before seeking God's way forward." He compared it to what ". . . Benedictine monks and Quaker Meetings seek to achieve as they listen quietly together to God, in a community

---

71. Lugo, Grim, and Podrebarac, "Global Anglicanism at a Crossroads."
72. "Christianity's New Center - Africa."
73. Samuel, "Why did GAFCON happen?"

where all are committed to a fellowship of love and attention to each other and to the word of God."[74]

Rowan Williams wanted to change the practice of the Conference of voting on resolutions, which often caused great division and difficulty. In fact no resolutions were passed. Instead, opting for the Indaba process enabled small group discussions to be designed to rebuild relationships and allow all voices to be heard.[75] Reflections from each group were then gathered and published but they did not have the force of resolutions but were to be used as the basis for further study within the Anglican Communion.

In his first address to the conference, Williams made it clear what he felt was needed:

> In institutional terms, we need renewal, and this is the moment for it. . . . The greatest need for the Communion now is for transformed relationships . . . new habits of respect, patience and understanding . . . [and] responsible agreement and search for the common mind. For this to be a reality we must be honest about how deep some of the hurts and difficulties currently go. We cannot ignore the pressures created by new structures that are being improvised in reaction to this pain and perplexity . . . pressures that are very visible in the form of irregular patterns of ministry across historic boundaries.[76]

Although no formal resolutions were promulgated, the Conference, in its *Lambeth Indaba* reflection document, certainly made its thinking clear on many issues. On the two central issues of unity in diversity and sexuality the conference not only reinforced previous Lambeth resolutions but took things further in the light of the growing divisions expressed at GAFCON and elsewhere.

The bishops present made it clear that those bishops who felt unable to attend Lambeth for reasons of conscience were much missed. "We have been diminished by their absence. We shall seek ways in which they may be drawn into our deliberations and held in communion. Our concern now is to rebuild bridges, to look for opportunities to share with them

---

74. Ibid., See also Makgoba, "Essence of Indaba," section on Indaba groups, 1–2.

75. "We have given these the African name of indaba groups, groups where in traditional African culture, people get together to sort out the problems that affect them all, where everyone has a voice and where there is an attempt to find a common mind or a common story that everyone is able to tell when they go away from it. This is how we approached it. This is what we heard. This is where we arrived as we prayed and thought and talked together" (Williams, "Archbishop of Canterbury: Better Bishops").

76. Ibid.

the experience we have had in Canterbury and to find ways of moving forward together in our witness to the Lord Jesus Christ."[77]

Those who had accepted the archbishop's invitation to attend had had it made clear to them in the invitation that they were to come with a heart to work with the recommendations of *The Windsor Report* and the draft covenant as a means of reshaping the Communion.[78]

The Indaba Reflection makes it clear that the Communion was not to be seen as a loosely federated collection of provincial churches, and neither was it to fall into the danger of over centralisation and a move to "a confessional church contrary to our historic identity."[79] Instead, the archbishop used a well-attested Anglican phrase as he spoke of the need to find a *via media* or "middle way" that would hold the Anglican Communion together. He saw the way to do this as being through the adoption of an Anglican covenant as had been suggested in draft form in *The Windsor Report*. This is an aspect we will come to in a later chapter. "Whatever the popular perception, the options before us are not irreparable schism or forced assimilation."[80]

The *Lambeth Indaba* reflections were honest about the problems this raised within such a diverse community. Although they were clear that ". . . as bishops in the Anglican Communion, we recognise and cherish four particular dimensions to our life in communion: that we are formed by scripture, shaped by worship, ordered for communion, directed by God's mission."[81]

They did not shrink from facing the real difficulties that these dimensions raised.

> We believe the scriptures to be primary and we read them informed by reason and tradition and with regard for our cultural context. We value the place of biblical scholarship as a critical tool, recognising nevertheless that this leads to divergent interpretations across our many and varied contexts, and of listening to our sister churches as they interpret the same scriptures. The over-arching issue with which we wrestle in relation to the scriptures is the interpretation of the Bible in our ongoing life.[82]

---

77. *Lambeth Indaba*, A:4.
78. Letter of invitation from the Archbishop of Canterbury, May 22, 2007.
79. *Lambeth Indaba*, A:13.
80. Williams, "Archbishop of Canterbury's Presidential Address."
81. *Lambeth Indaba*, G:99.
82. Ibid., G:100.

Beating the Bounds

This is the very heart of the divisions within the Communion, for different scriptural interpretations produce different attitudes to how the individual life of the Christian and the corporate life of the church are ordered. This is, of course, why ". . . the variety of ways in which Provinces are ordered—the different polities of our churches—can produce misunderstandings and confusions that need to be understood and addressed. We need to acknowledge that the whole is more than the sum of the parts and that each part of the Communion, when it acts, must do so in the knowledge of what it means for the whole."[83]

This sense of the role of the Communion was obviously central to the discussions on human sexuality. Bishops were reminded of the past deliberations of the Anglican Consultative Council, especially its declaration of 1976: "As in the first century, we can expect the Holy Spirit to press us to listen to each other, to state new insights frankly, and to accept implications of the Gospel new to us, whether painful or exhilarating."[84]

With this in mind the Conference reaffirmed Lambeth 1998 Resolution 1.10 but stressed what that resolution had said about the necessity for sensitive listening to those on all sides of the argument and wanted to take that further.[85] There was an encouragement for those who hold to traditional teaching on these matters to "understand or engage with a clear presentation of how people have come to a new understanding of scripture and pastoral theology."[86]

There was a clear recognition of some of the difficulties raised by this issue that are faced by Anglican Christians around the world where cultures are very different from each other.[87] While many wanted clear

---

83. Ibid. G:102.

84. Anglican Consultative Council, *ACC Trinidad*, 55.

85. *Lambeth Indaba*, H:107. "It is important therefore to be careful not to make dismissive judgements, because people have come to their decision after prayer and careful study of the Bible. Nor is there a monopoly on Christian charity: those who take different positions regarding this issue have often been the bearers of compassionate pastoral care to homosexual persons, though we must confess some failure in this regard. We come from different backgrounds, contexts and experiences. As Bishops we need to repent of the ways in which our hardness of heart toward each other may have contributed to the brokenness of our Communion at this present time. We need to repent of statements and actions that have further damaged the dignity of homosexual persons. People who have held traditional views on this matter have sometimes felt that they have been dismissed with ridicule or contempt."

86. Ibid., H:111.

87. Ibid., H:112. "The whole issue of homosexual relations is also highly sensitive because there are very strong affirmations and denials in different cultures across the world which are reflected in contrasting civil provisions, ranging from legal provision

and decisive action to be taken against those provinces that had strayed from the traditional teaching, there were also strong calls for further study and prayer and a desire to "keep walking, keep talking, keep listening together."[88]

Finally, Lambeth 2008 looked at the role of each of the Instruments of Communion and their contribution to keeping the channels of communication open and the conversations continuing within "the bonds of affection" that bind the Communion together.

While claiming not to be breaking away from the Anglican Communion, GAFCON's "Jerusalem Declaration" had made the revolutionary change from the 1930 Lambeth Conference Resolution 49 by stating, "While acknowledging the nature of Canterbury as an historic see, we do not accept that Anglican identity is determined necessarily through recognition by the Archbishop of Canterbury."[89] This clearly downgrades the traditional relationship with the Archbishop of Canterbury, which has always been a—if not *the*—major instrument of unity within the Anglican Communion.

Lambeth 2008, on the other hand, affirmed that "There is honour and respect for the office of the Archbishop of Canterbury. Being in communion with the See of Canterbury is one of the essential elements of belonging to the Anglican Communion."[90] However, the Conference did note that there was a need for further exploration of new possibilities for the role of the archbishop in the Communion as he exercises his apostolate.

What is clear from this look at the history and work of the Lambeth Conference is that what began as an initial hesitancy on the part of the bishops to pronounce on anything at all rapidly changed until, in later in the twentieth century, they gave an opinion on most of the contemporary issues in the society of their day.

What is most remarkable is the radical change in the positions the bishops have taken with regard to gender and sexuality. As Webber points out,

> In 1888, polygamists were not generally to be baptized; in 1988, they could be. In 1920, prophylactics were an "invitation to vice"; by 1958 they were "acceptable."

---

for same–sex marriage to criminal action against homosexuals. In some parts of the Communion, homosexual relations are a taboo while in others they have become a human rights issue."

88. Ibid., H:120.
89. GAFCON "Jerusalem Declaration."
90. *Lambeth Indaba*, K:148.

> Until 1948, divorced persons were never to be remarried in church and those who remarried in civil ceremonies were not to be admitted to communion; by 1958 this frequently stated position had been replaced by the suggestion that a procedure for defining marital status was needed and the separate churches and provinces should work on it. No more has been heard of that, and the Anglican provinces have found ways not only to give communion to the divorced and remarried, but also to perform second and even third marriages in the church.[91]

I think that one of the problems that has arisen regarding the Lambeth Conference is that many Anglicans see it as a sort of church council like the General Councils of the early church and expect it to act as such which, of course, it cannot and should not. That was never its purpose. To do otherwise would destroy what most Anglicans treasure about the ethos of the Anglican Communion.

Lambeth 2008 expressed a desire that the Lambeth Conference should meet more frequently, for a shorter period of time, with the particular suggestion of a ten-day meeting every five years. The reason for this sense of wanting to be together again so soon was the continuation of the Indaba process.

The question is whether or not the Anglican Communion can continue to function without some sort of more centralised authority with firmly constructed and defended definitions of doctrine. But would that be truly Anglicanism?

There was no problem surviving while Anglicanism remained inextricably linked with Britain, with its royal authority and unquestioned cultural traditions supporting the Church. However, when Anglicanism was thrust out into the world through the growth and development of the British Empire and then left to continue in the maelstrom of a postcolonial world of widely different cultures, it no longer has the supports it had previously relied upon. Inevitably, a variety of styles, theologies, liturgies, and polities have resulted.

One might have hoped that it could have been possible for Christians to embrace difference as the different facets cut into the brilliant diamond of the church. As Webber poignantly writes,

> One might imagine a community in which Christians were willing to accept strong episcopal authority in some places and strong lay leadership in others, narrow interpretation of the

---

91. Webber, "Brief History of the Lambeth Conference."

Bible in some societies and a more liberal interpretation in others. Why should African bishops have to dress like Victorian prelates and Japanese Christians be required to worship in Gothic buildings?

Yet these cultural trappings have been accepted and the more significant differences that might reflect a truly encultured gospel have left us badly divided and on the verge of dissolution.[92]

Webber sees this history as a salutary call for Anglicans to show more humility, "to be less sure of ourselves, more ready to listen, and more willing to leave a generous room for difference." He argues that if so many once-definitive statements of Lambeth have been so easily changed, how sure can we be that what we are saying now is right? "Might it be better to recognize that we might be wrong again and that we have yet to succeed in striking a proper balance between Biblical authority and cultural conditioning? Is it possible that we serve God's church best when we do least to divide ourselves and do most to center our common life on a pattern of worship that draws us closer to the redeeming love of God?"[93]

Of course, one could argue that that approach could lead to having no definitions about anything and losing any sense of a clear Anglican identity. However, that is clearly not the case. In fact such a position declares our identity as Anglicans and demonstrates a polity that, unlike the Roman Catholic Church, does not have to fear that admitting that some centrally issued dogmatic declaration was mistaken would raise the possibility of the whole façade of an authoritative magisterium tumbling down in disarray.

That is, of course, why many Anglicans, even from the conservative fundamentalist wing of the Church, are torn between demanding such authoritative statements on gender and sexuality and yet not wanting to give such authority to centralised bodies that might make other declarations they would not be happy with. Their answer seems to have been to create their own mirror image authoritative body in the form of the self-appointed GAFCON primates' council selected, of course, from within its own ranks and to which they have given an authority far beyond that given any other traditional Anglican council, even to the extent of operating within another Anglican jurisdiction.[94]

92. Ibid.
93. Ibid.
94. GAFCON, "Jerusalem Declaration": "We urge the Primates' Council to authenticate and recognise confessing Anglican jurisdictions, clergy and congregations and to encourage all Anglicans to promote the gospel and defend the faith. . . . We recognise the desirability of territorial jurisdiction for provinces and dioceses of the Anglican Communion, except in those areas where churches and leaders are denying the orthodox

This again is a direct infringement of the authority of the traditional Primates' Meeting within the traditional Anglican Communion.

This third Instrument of Communion was created in 1978 to try and bring some relationship and cohesion between the various international groupings within the Anglican Communion.[95] However, like the other Instruments of Communion the Primates' Meeting has not had more than a consultative and advisory authority although the Windsor Commission had indicated that it would like to increase its responsibility and authority in matters concerning doctrine, ethics and pastoral concerns.[96]

Lambeth 2008, however, expressed "some discomfort" about the role that the Primates' Meeting now finds itself exercising. Many think that it is overreaching itself in terms of the authority it seems to claim, while there are others who believe that the primates are the only ones who can bear the weight of our current challenges. "Perhaps their key role is in supporting the Archbishop of Canterbury. The primates should not exercise collectively any more authority than they have in their Provinces."[97]

Of the fourth Instrument of Communion, the Anglican Consultative Council, Lambeth 2008 admitted that there was

> . . . a lack of knowledge in the Communion about the Council and its members and therefore an uncertainty about its role. Some believe it exercises too much authority; others would like to see it reconstituted and given more. One suggestion was of a two-tier Council with a tier of Primates and another of clergy and laity with the inclusion of younger representation. There was a desire to enhance the presence of clergy and laity in decision making at the Communion level."[98]

Avis and Pickard seem to support Bruce Kaye's view that the sense of "enhanced authority" that has been slowly attributed to the primates has

---

faith or are preventing its spread, and in a few areas for which overlapping jurisdictions are beneficial for historical or cultural reasons."

95. Lambeth Conference 1978, Resolution 12: ". . . to initiate consideration of the way to relate together the international conferences, councils and meetings within the Anglican Communion so that the Anglican Communion may best serve God within the context of one, holy, catholic and apostolic church."

96. Lambeth Commission on Communion, *Windsor Report*, section C. It urged the Church to "consider proposals made at the Lambeth Conferences in 1988 and 1998, and reiterated in *To Mend the Net*, for the primates to have an '*enhanced responsibility* in offering guidance on doctrinal, moral and pastoral matters'" (ibid., 104).

97. *Lambeth Indaba*, K:151.

98. Ibid., K:150.

Movement Three: The Church as Anglican

begun to marginalise the ACC—"a development observed to some extent in a shift in focus from a conciliar/consultative to a collegial focus."[99]

The draft version of an Anglican covenant as proposed in *The Windsor Report* sparked much discussion at Lambeth 2008 and has been followed by much discussion and argument. There have been a number of different iterations of such a covenant as discussions have progressed.

What this chapter has demonstrated is that the heart of this disruption within the Anglican Communion reflects in a powerful way many of the issues facing the whole Church as it seeks to come to terms with the cultural transformation and paradigm shifts of postmodernism as well as the geographical shift of Anglican influence from North to South while, at the same time, seeking to remain true to its original ethos and mission.

Mark Oxbrow urges us to look beyond the simplistic headlines of the media, which see this conflict as revolving simply around the issue of human sexuality. He draws our attention to the fact that

> . . . in reality the fault lines run much deeper. In geological analogy the consecrated gay bishop, Gene Robinson, and Archbishop Peter Akinola's calls for a return to 'biblical faithfulness' are the constantly rising Alpine range, glistening in the sunlight; but deep below the oceans tectonic plates collide with unforgiving and immeasurable power. It may not be the Alpine snow or even the rocky crags that will shape Anglican future but rather the tectonic plates of ecclesial power and theological fire.[100]

It is to those concepts of ecclesial power that we now must turn as the first subject of the minuet gives way to the trio.

Trio: Politics, Power, and Persuasion

The trio section got its name during the baroque period, when a set of two dances would be followed by a repetition of the first dance. The second dance was known as a trio because it was usually played by three instruments. As the title indicates, the three "instruments" in use in this section are politics, power, and persuasion.

We have seen the Anglican Church's centre of gravity shift to the south, which has led to the development of the power of the African bishops within the Anglican Communion through the Lambeth Conference

---

99. Avis and Pickard, *Instruments of Communion*, 5.2.1.
100. Oxbrow, "Anglicans and Reconciling Mission," 8.

and the other corporate Anglican bodies as well as their high-profile involvement in the formation of GAFCON with its continuing influence in the Anglican Church. It is incumbent upon us now to look more closely at the political activity that lies behind this shift of influence, especially the influence of the extreme right of the conservative movement in the United States both in church and state. For it is in these murky waters that we discover that the motivation for the taking of the high moral ground by certain influential African bishops could well be fuelled less by theological persuasion and more by the promise of rewards in kind.

Matters of social justice and welfare have always been at the heart of the mission of the church since its beginnings, rooted as it was in the prophetic traditions of Israel.

> He has showed you, O man, what is good. And what does the LORD require of you? To act justly and to love mercy and to walk humbly with your God. (Micah 6:8)
>
> But let justice roll on like a river, righteousness like a never-failing stream! (Amos 5:24)

So it was that the New Testament church was recognised as a caring community where the needy had their needs met and the church members gave sacrificially to finance the work of social justice and welfare.

> All the believers were together and had everything in common. Selling their possessions and goods, they gave to anyone as he had need. Every day they continued to meet together in the temple courts. They broke bread in their homes and ate together with glad and sincere hearts, praising God and enjoying the favour of all the people. And the Lord added to their number daily those who were being saved. (Acts 2:44–47)

Such ministry continued throughout the history of the church alongside its evangelistic endeavours. The monasteries were not only centres of spirituality and learning but served an important role as places of love and care within the communities of the Middle Ages. In the nineteenth century the great missionary expansion of the church, especially throughout the British Empire and the lands colonised by other European powers, was accompanied by the building of hospitals and schools and the mission to raise the standard of living and future hope of those denied what were truly believed to be the benefits of Western civilisation.

Movement Three: The Church as Anglican

This emphasis within the mission of the Anglican Church is particularly evidenced through many of the Lambeth Conference resolutions concerning social justice and welfare.

The understanding of the negative aspects of colonialism dawned only slowly, both for the native African and for the church. A popular African statement became, "When the white man arrived, he had the Bible and we had the land; now, we have the Bible and he has the land."

To their credit, since the early 1960's, mainline Protestant and Catholic churches have worked to reverse the colonial errors and to empower oppressed people, including the poor, coloured people, and women.

It is true that most of this social justice work was emphasised by what could be called the more liberal wing of the church while the conservative, evangelical wing tended to oppose the liberal "social gospel" agenda, preferring to concentrate on evangelism and "winning souls for Christ."

> Traditionally African evangelicals' values are very different from those of the U.S. religious right. They have embraced the ideas of Liberation Theology from Latin America as well as Black Theology from South Africa and they have generally been far more progressive in their views of social justice than many of their evangelical counterparts in the U.S. They have often aligned with left-wing political movements because, for them, political and economic liberation are essential parts of the Christian Gospel.[101]

Kapya Kaoma, in his hard-hitting but well-argued report, *Globalising the Culture Wars: U.S. Conservatives, African Churches and Homophobia*, argues, from a clearly North American perspective, that there has been a total role reversal for liberal and conservative Christians and their related organisations active on the African continent. "For decades in Africa U.S. mainline Protestant churches joined struggles—opposed by the U.S. Right—to topple racist colonial regimes in Rhodesia (now Zimbabwe) and South Africa, and to empower oppressed people of all sorts."[102]

Now, Kaoma says, U.S. conservatives are attempting and having success persuading African Christians that these same mainline denominations and their continuing commitment to human rights are neo-colonialists making ". . . imperialistic attempts to manipulate Africans into accepting homosexuality—which they characterize as a purely western

---

101. Brouwer et al., *Exporting the American Gospel*, 268.
102. Kaoma, *Globalising the Culture Wars*, 3.

phenomenon."[103] This has been despite the overwhelming evidence that it is the mainline churches that have clearly demonstrated their opposition to neo-colonialism of any sort, particularly with their open commitment to advance the United Nations' Millennium Development Goals [104] and their support of a preferential option for the poor.

Kaoma identifies the main source of the promotion of homophobia in Africa as the Institute on Religion and Democracy (IRD), a well-funded neo-conservative religious think tank that actually opposed the African liberation struggles. Now, through secretive funding, scholarships for African clergy in theologically conservative training centres, together with ". . . the provision of orphanages, Bible schools, universities, and social welfare projects . . . U.S. conservatives have convinced Africans that they are the perfect partners."[105]

He describes how the African continent is saturated with propaganda denouncing the mainline denominations for rejecting the doctrine of the Trinity, the deity and the humanity of Christ, as well as the authority of Scripture, particularly in the area of sexual ethics.

Writing off whole denominations as heretical, many Africans accept these generalisations as true and so they then turn to U.S. conservatives for support, not a little encouraged by the promise of money from the rich West. This is a matter we will examine in some detail.

Why would U.S. conservatives go to these lengths? Kaoma lays out much clear evidence that for the IRD ". . . this campaign is part of a long-term, deliberate and successful strategy to weaken and split U.S. mainline denominations, block their powerful progressive social witness promoting social and economic justice, and promote political and social

---

103. Ibid., 3.

104. The Millennium Development Goals (MDGs) are eight goals to be achieved by 2015 that respond to the world's main development challenges. The MDGs are drawn from the actions and targets contained in the Millennium Declaration that was adopted by 189 nations and signed by 147 heads of state and governments during the UN Millennium Summit in September 2000.
- Goal 1: Eradicate extreme poverty and hunger
- Goal 2: Achieve universal primary education
- Goal 3: Promote gender equality and empower women
- Goal 4: Reduce child mortality
- Goal 5: Improve maternal health
- Goal 6: Combat HIV/AIDS, malaria and other diseases
- Goal 7: Ensure environmental sustainability
- Goal 8: Develop a Global Partnership for Development

See http://www.un.org/millenniumgoals/.

105. Kaoma, *Globalising the Culture Wars*, 8.

conservatism in the United States. Using African leaders as a wedge in U.S. conflicts is only its latest and perhaps most effective tactic."[106] He sees this mobilisation of African clergy as a tool in their domestic culture wars as a cunning use of the demographic shift of the centre of Christianity from the Global North to the Global South, increasing Africa's influence on Christianity worldwide.

American conservatives who are in the minority within the mainline churches depend on African religious leaders to legitimize their positions.

Jim Naughton, a retired senior priest of the Episcopal diocese of Washington, has written a telling report for that diocese called "Following the Money," in which he lays out the way in which the U.S. right has infiltrated and influenced the Anglican Church in many parts of the world, not least in North America, Africa, and the United Kingdom. "Millions of dollars contributed by a handful of donors have allowed a small network of theologically conservative individuals and organizations to mount a global campaign that has destabilized the Episcopal Church and may break up the Anglican Communion."[107]

So begins this report in which he concentrates on the financial activities of five secular organisations[108] and one individual who, according to the watchdog group the National Committee on Responsive Philanthropy, have ". . . made an extraordinary effort to reshape politics and public policy at the national, state and local level."[109] These foundations are noted for their contributions to political and religious organisations, particularly the U.S. mainline denominations. They have been responsible for much of the support of the American Anglican Council and the Institute on Religion and Democracy. Both of these organisations have worked together in opposing the Episcopal Church and pressurising the Archbishop of Canterbury to remove the Episcopal Church from the Anglican Communion and to support the more conservative bishops who have set up a new parallel province in North America which is very much linked with the GAFCON movement.[110]

---

106. Ibid., 3.

107. Naughton, "Following the Money," 1.

108. Naughton uses forms filed with the Internal Revenue Service and statements by the donor organisations themselves to list these foundations as: the Ahmanson and the Bradley, Coors, Olin, Scaife, and Smith-Richardson family foundations.

109. National Committee on Responsive Philanthropy, *Moving a Public Policy Agenda*.

110. Naughton, "Following the Money," 9.

Howard Ahmanson Jr., together with his wife Roberta, has been deeply involved in all the current Anglican controversies, supporting financially many organisations that are working for some very extreme right-wing policies, especially the movement against the Episcopal stance on homosexuality. They also support financially the Discovery Institute, the intellectual flagship of the Intelligent Design movement in the U.S.[111]

The Ahmansons powerfully supported the American Anglican Council in its work to influence the 1998 Lambeth Conference resulting in Resolution 1:10, declaring same-sex relationships as incompatible with Scripture. They also were very much involved behind the scenes in the Episcopal Church's General Convention of 2003, as well as making very generous contributions to British evangelical organisations, in each case trying to encourage them to oppose liberal or social justice issues.[112]

Following the consecration of the Rt. Rev. Gene Robinson as bishop of New Hampshire on November 2, 2003, things moved at quite a pace.

Naughton expresses the view that the attempt to remove the Episcopal Church from the Anglican Communion would have really diminished its stature and its membership, as ten dioceses and a number of parishes were already speaking of breaking with the Church. These actions combined would have produced a very monochrome and deeply conservative church.

Another development that came to light at this time was the fact that several of the influential primates in the developing world clearly wanted to change the nature of the Communion from that of a group of autonomous provinces held together in a relationship through "the bonds of affection" to the much more centralised curial form of government that had been suggested by the authors of the Ekklesia Society-sponsored publication *To Mend the Net*.[113]

American conservatives put pressure on Archbishop Rowan Williams to expel the Episcopal Church and replace it with the Anglican Communion Network, which later combined with the group Common Cause to form the Anglican Church of North America. This self-styled

---

111. Ibid., 2.

112. Ibid., 3–4. Naughton claims evidence from IRS Form 990 that three British evangelical organisations—Anglican Mainstream, the Church Missionary Society, and the Oxford Centre for Mission Studies—received substantial donations from the Ahmansons in 2003 and 2004.

113. The general secretary of Ekklesia was Bill Attwood, former canon in the Episcopal Church, who has now been consecrated a bishop in the Anglican Church of Kenya but operates in the United States.

Movement Three: The Church as Anglican

province is not recognised by the Anglican Communion although there is considerable pressure upon the Communion for recognition of ACNA as an Anglican province coming from conservatives such as Archbishop Peter Jensen and the diocese of Sydney together with the African primates.

In fact notes have come to light[114] from a meeting in London on November 20, 2003. In attendance were Archbishop Duncan, several American conservatives, and several primates sympathetic to their cause.

According to Duncan's notes, ". . . those present secretly agreed that the primates who supported the Network would announce their support to Williams, urge him to recognize the Network as the true expression of Anglicanism in the United States, and 'Tell Rowan that if he will not recognize the Network they will separate from him.'"[115]

These same notes recorded that "in the present crisis the issue of boundaries is suspended, meaning that bishops could claim the right to minister uninvited in one another's provinces and dioceses in clear contradiction of ancient as well as modern church canons."[116]

It was also suggested that the primates remove their recognition of any bishop who had participated in the consecration of Gene Robinson. This would have had the immediate effect of declaring thirteen American sees as vacant.

There was also a move to have Duncan regarded as equal to the Episcopal Church's presiding bishop at all international gatherings. In addition, Duncan's notes say, "We commit to the guerrilla warfare of the next year."[117]

There has been little indication up to the present time of writing that the archbishop will recognise the group as a province.

An important incident took place at the Dromantine Retreat and Conference Centre in February 2005 when the primates of the Anglican Communion met to discuss the issue of homosexuality and to try and force the Archbishop of Canterbury to take a much harder line against the Episcopal Church. The African bishops of Nigeria, Uganda, and

---

114. Naughton, "Following the Money," 5: "The notes came to light a year later, when two parishes in the Diocese of Pittsburgh sued Duncan and other diocesan officials, alleging that they planned to claim ownership of property held in trust for the national church. The suit was settled out of court in October 2005, but not before several memos and emails circulated among leaders of the AAC, the IRD and the Network appeared on the Web site of the Allegheny County (Pa.) prothonotary's office."

115. Ibid., 4.

116. Ibid., 4–5.

117. Duncan, "Mainstream Meeting Memo," Point F.

Argentina—Peter Akinola, Henry Luke Orombi, and Greg Venables—were there working with the leaders of the American Anglican Council, the Anglican Communion Network, the Ekklesia Society, and the Institute on Religion and Democracy, all of which were funded in greater part from the U.S. political right. [118]

> Activists took rooms nearby Newry and kept in touch with the Primates by mobile telephones which had been purchased for the Primates by the foundations and other donors. They also had easy access to the primates to influence them in any way they chose.
> ... Conservative American and British activists, and the press corps, quickly found that the Dromantine security guards were not a formidable obstacle to gaining access to the Primates, and would kindly ... pass notes to Primates if asked. ... Car traffic into Dromantine ... was busy throughout the week as conservative activists would take the Primates off-campus from the centre to dine and strategise.[119]

Indeed, on the night before the conference communiqué was presented at a press conference, a number of primates left the resort to attend a celebratory dinner hosted by Akinola and paid for by the American conservatives. Williams had tried his best to hold the meeting together, but he remonstrated with these primates when they returned.[120]

This interference in the running of the Primates' Meeting caused the presiding bishop, Frank Griswold, to express anger when he discovered that documents had been infiltrated into the conference from these outside agencies claiming various abuses of evangelical clergy and congregations by liberal bishops. He spoke later in an interview on this matter. "I spoke very frankly about where these pieces of paper came from, and why are these people down the road in constant communication with various of you, and whose agenda is this?"[121]

Colin Coward and Davis Mac-Iyalla (Changing Attitude England and Nigeria), Caro Hall (Integrity USA), and Scott Gunn (Inclusive Church) were present at a later Primates' Meeting at the White Sands Hotel in Tanzania during February 2007. They reported events that confirm

---

118. Naughton, "Following the Money," 4.

119. Conger, "Behind the Scenes."

120. Ibid.

121. Bishop Frank Griswold, in an interview with Deborah Caldwell of Beliefnet, cited in Naughton, "Following the Money," 4.

Movement Three: The Church as Anglican

the deep suspicions developed as they observed the visits by Archbishop Peter Akinola to the first-floor room where Martyn Minns, Chris Sugden, David Anderson, and other GAFCON organisers met all day, every day. They speculated that they were waiting patiently for Archbishop Akinola to come and report to them (quite improperly) what had been taking place in the Primates' Meeting next door.

They claim in their report[122] that they have evidence that reveals that they were clearly doing more than this. They were drafting material for Archbishop Akinola to take back to the Primates' Meeting. They prepared an alternative text for the final communiqué that Archbishop Akinola was given to present to the primates. The final press conference on the Monday evening was delayed until nearly midnight, almost certainly because Akinola was arguing at length with the other primates, desperately trying to force the Minns/Sugden/Anderson agenda on the other, mostly unwilling, primates.

We have already seen that the agenda was being set by powerful outside influences that were ultimately to result in the success of Resolution 1:10 at the 1998 Lambeth Conference. "The question leaders of the Communion have begun to ask since that conservative Episcopalians' highly visible role at Dromantine is whether they and their financial backers such as Howard F Ahmanson, Jr., are the real power behind a movement that outwardly claims to draw its strength from Africa and Asia. Who is paying the piper and who is calling the tune?"[123]

Naughton quotes Archbishop Eames saying that he was "quite certain" that African bishops were being offered money to cut their ties with the Episcopal Church. "Is it the might of finance that will influence a theological outlook, and then that outlook come to dominate the Communion? It raises a serious question for me: what is the real nature of their faith and their Anglicanism? It is certainly different from mine."[124]

Archbishop Akinola challenged Eames to provide evidence or apologise. Eames responded with a very luke-warm statement that was far from an apology. "I categorically state I have never believed that any financial offer was accepted by any of those who represent the Global South on any other than terms of Christian outreach."[125]

---

122. This report came in the form of daily bulletins from the Tanzanian conference (February 13–17, 2007) that were published on the Changing Attitude website. The first day's bulletin can be found at http://changingattitude.org.uk/archives/2139.

123. Naughton, "Following the Money," 7.

124. Ibid.

125. Ibid.

However, at the same time as Akinola was demanding his apology, his own director of communications for the Church of Nigeria, Canon Akintunde Popoola, was actually admitting that what Eames had originally said was really happening.

> For years, wealthy ECUSA churches like Trinity Wall Street bankroll churches in developing countries (and dare I say even the Communion) with no eyeballs raised. Some 'poor churches' feel it is immoral to collect money from those they do not agree with. Those that agree with the position of the poor are coming to their aid and some guys feel that is not moral....
>
> Before such statements are made, Leaders should consider what the poor are receiving and what they are missing. Which is greater?[126]

Kaoma has evidence of such bankrolling from the very heart of the church in Uganda. He personally interviewed Rev. Aaron Mwesigye, the provincial secretary in the Ugandan Archbishop Henry Orombi's office. In that interview Mwesigye confirmed that U.S. conservatives had been "contributing towards the remuneration and salaries of the provincial staff since 1998." He also added that "American conservatives provide money to Africans not as donors but as development partners in mission."[127]

Further evidence of such outside interference is given by Archbishop Njongonkulu Ndungane of South Africa in a letter to *Church Times* in the United Kingdom. He states that after a letter from some of the primates from the Global South that was very critical of the Archbishop of Canterbury was released, a number of the signatories attempted to distance themselves from its contents. He sees this as providing further evidence of American advisors pressurising Southern primates to do their bidding. In his published letter he complained that his delegate at the meeting, Bishop Johannes Seoka, had "... found himself excluded from meetings, including those at which the letter was discussed—despite the presence, it appeared, of others who were neither Primates nor, indeed, from the Global South."[128]

The fact of African leaders being used by American backers was seen when, in November 2005, Bishop Robert Duncan held a conference in Pittsburgh during which a Southern Cone bishop from Bolivia was called in to ordain clergy to work under his authority in the dioceses of Maryland

---

126. Ibid.
127. Kaoma, *Globalising the Culture Wars*, 9–10.
128. Ndungane, "Plea for Patience."

and Washington.[129] Most significant were the words used by Archbishop Akinola of Nigeria on that occasion when he addressed the congregation of about 2,500.

> Many of you have one leg in ECUSA and one leg in the Network. With that, my friends, comes disaster. While that remains, you can't have our support. Because, you see, as we speak here, we have all broken communion with ECUSA. If you want Global South to partner with you, you must let us know exactly where you stand. Are you ECUSA? Or are you Network? Which one?[130]

Here was a veiled threat that resources from "the Network" would only be available to those churches that separated themselves completely from the Episcopal Church in America. "The Network" refers to the Network of Anglican Communion Dioceses and Parishes, more usually known as the Anglican Communion Network (ACN).

The ACN was officially formed in January 2004 and its main intent is to provide a system to supply theologically conservative leadership and church oversight to Anglicans in the United States and Canada. It was formed ostensibly in response to the homosexuality issue but many of the issues behind it date back much further than that into liturgical reform in the Episcopal Church. In Canada the trigger was the approval of services of blessing for same-sex unions in 2003.

The most interesting thing is that most of the work in establishing the ACN was performed by the American Anglican Council, a group that we have already noted is very much funded and supported by the right-wing conservatives in the U.S. that have been the subject of this chapter.

The question might be asked why so much time has been spent on these matters of politics and power play within the Anglican Communion in a study concentrating on theological orthodoxy. The reasoning is simple. It seems clear from the evidence provided that when many of the African and other Third World bishops speak so strongly in the theological debates concerning orthodoxy and orthopraxis, they do so from positions that may possibly be compromised as far as their total independence is concerned.

The poverty and dire need that engulfs many of their countries and their church congregations, and the offer of strong financial and other practical support that emanate from conservative, right-wing groups in the U.S., must make it almost impossible for them to take any other

---

129. Duin, "Bolivian ordains Anglican clerics."
130. Boyer, "Church Asunder."

theological view than that espoused by their benefactors. This must be especially difficult when threats of withdrawal of support are made.

This also brings into question the fact that GAFCON makes much of the weight of support they have from the African and other Third World bishops for their cause. There is evidence that even the words spoken or written by African bishops are words that have been placed in their mouths by others.

For another example, let us consider a report in the respected *Church Times* that reported that Bishop Martyn Minns, not Archbishop Peter Akinola, was the principal author of a letter from the Church of Nigeria that was issued in Akinola's name.

> "A bishop in the United States has been revealed as the principal author of a seminal letter to the Church of Nigeria from its Archbishop, the Most Revd Peter Akinola, which was published on Sunday.
>
> The letter includes a suggestion that the Archbishop of Canterbury's status as a focus of unity is "highly questionable". It also refers to a "moment of decision" for the Anglican Communion, which is on the "brink of destruction".
>
> The document, "A Most Agonising Journey towards Lambeth 2008", appears to express to Nigerian synods the personal anguish of Archbishop Akinola over his attendance at the Lambeth Conference."[131]

Ashworth discovered that the use of computer tracking software suggested that the letter was extensively edited and revised over a four-day period by the Rt. Rev. Martyn Minns, who was consecrated last year by Archbishop Akinola to lead the secessionist Convocation of Anglicans in North America (CANA).

> "Close examination of the document, tracing the authorship, editing history, and timing of changes, reveals about 600 insertions made by Bishop Minns, including whole new sections amounting to two-thirds of the final text. There is also a sprinkling of minor amendments made by Canon Chris Sugden of the conservative group Anglican Mainstream. The significance of this development is not just the fact that Akinola had a ghostwriter; the leaders of many organisations, ecclesiastical and secular have staff members who handle writing assignments for them. What really matters is that what has long been portrayed

---

131. Quoted in Naughton, "Who speaks for Africa?"

Movement Three: The Church as Anglican

as the authentic voice of African Anglicanism is, manifestly, not African, and perhaps never has been."[132]

Of course such a view has been challenged. Through *The Church of England Newspaper* correspondent George Conger, (an American Episcopal priest who is a keen sympathiser with GAFCON), the Church of Nigeria's director of communications Archdeacon Akintunde Popoola was enabled to respond robustly that it was "very insulting and racist to infer that the Primate of All Nigeria is being dictated to." He argued that all these charges reflect is the fact that, on a visit to the United States, the archbishop used a computer registered to Bishop Minns. This accounted for the apparent involvement of Bishop Minns in the composition of the pastoral letter. Bishop Minns himself denies any involvement but states that he was simply being used as Archbishop Akinola's amanuensis.[133]

Although he is now retired, this accusation certainly damages Akinola's already sagging prestige in Nigeria, where he may now be perceived as having been a mouthpiece for wealthy Westerners. Certainly, Naughton notes, his fellow primates had been often made weary of his practice of interrupting their meetings to take counsel from Minns and Sugden. This actually provides a context within which the accusations sound believable. If nothing else, the possibility of such interference from outside must compromise the ministry and message of the office of Primate of All Nigeria and the standing of his successor.

The significance of these revelations is that they raise the very real questions: How real and authentic is the support from Africa that GAFCON claims, and how much does it actually represent the views of the rank-and-file members of these churches that claim so many members?

This latter point is also important because it has been pointed out that the authority of many of the archbishops in Africa is of a tribal nature and it is this tribal rule that is sometimes used to count adherents. *Makau Mutua, dean and distinguished professor at the State University of New York at Buffalo Law School and chair of the Kenyan Human Rights Commission, wrote concerning the involvement of church leaders in tribal matters in Kenya:* "In the wake of the demonic violence in 2008, the country is looking for a leader who is not captive to a tribal cabal. That's why I was shocked to see retired Anglican Archbishop David Gitari, a respected reformer, and

---

132. Quoted in ibid.
133. See *The Church of England Newspaper*, 31 August 2007, 7.

his Methodist counterpart Bishop Lawi Imathiu, co-chairing the Gema tribal conclave."[134]

There have been many other comments about the behaviour of African bishops, which includes their autocratic manner and demands for instant obedience in the style of tribal chieftains.

First Subject Re-Examined: Authority in Anglicanism

Having looked at authority in a rather general way in the first subject of the minuet, we need now to take a deeper look into what really is the particularly Anglican view of authority and examine in detail its history and praxis. Dr. Edward Norman, Canon Treasurer of York Minster, in a lecture to the Ecclesiastical Law Society during the Lambeth Conference in August 1998, spells this out clearly and it is this lecture that forms the basis of much that is written in this chapter.

Norman begins by noting that, contrary to common belief, the "birthday" of the church was not Pentecost. Jesus himself had founded it during his earthly ministry when he appointed the twelve teaching apostles and then the seventy evangelistic disciples.

Also contrary to contemporary practice, Jesus did not commit his teaching to writing as a religious text; neither did he appoint a priestly caste within a religious system to perpetuate his thought. Instead he chose to reveal his truth to a community of living people who, after his ascension, became the "body of Christ," his living presence in the world. As Norman says, "Precisely because the message was thus conveyed organically it remained permanently new: able to adapt to changing intellectual modes and social filtration, capable of bringing forward fresh insights in the successive cultural shifts of a progressive humanity."[135]

Whatever the more conservative and fundamentalist wings of the church say, written texts do not reveal fully understandable truth of themselves: they require interpretation again and again, often over long periods of time, if they are to fulfil their revelatory purposes. This interpretative work is constantly in process through the living community of people, whose focus is not a philosophical or ethical system but a person—Jesus Christ. This is a community that is forever changing yet forever the same.

This community must carry the hallmark of indefectibility just as Jesus does, because he himself made the promise that the Holy Spirit he would

134. Mutua, "Kenya: Can the Gema Community Rescue Uhuru?"
135. Norman, "Authority in the Anglican Communion."

give them would guide them into all truth. Thus, whatever the apostles were commissioned to do the church today has the authority to do.

In the third century, the successors of the apostles created a new canon of scripture by deciding which texts were to be recognised as authoritative. The authority they used is still present in the church. The magisterium or teaching authority of the church came before the written Gospels and remains, therefore, as the true dynamic for mission. Living testimony to Christ takes precedence over written text. What the church really means by "tradition" is "the succession of authentic representation of Christ carried through human cultures by those who seek obedience to Christ's first calling."[136]

The church is primarily not a support group for emotional cripples, although part of its ministry may encompass something of that purpose. Most specifically the church is actually and overwhelmingly an institutionalised teaching office. This means that it has authority to proclaim the truth at the same time as creating or recognising "developments" of doctrine.

> The Church can never invent or create doctrines, but it can define or declare them, with images appropriate to circumstance, so that truths implicit in the understanding of the first believers may only over centuries assume richer meaning. The smallest of seeds becomes the mustard plant; there is no way initially of telling which dimensions of Christ's teaching may assume importance in the history of society. It is a sign of the authority of Christ in his Church that the People of God are capable of defining the nature of his presence in contexts that are unavoidably transient.[137]

Most Christians have always believed this. As the new catechism of the Roman Catholic Church states, "Sacred Tradition; Sacred Scripture and the Magisterium of the Church are so connected and associated that one of them cannot stand without the others."[138]

Of course, in the past, where there has been controversy requiring clarification, General Councils have been called and attempted to discern the way forward by their *consensus fidelium*, having the mind of Christ. General Councils, therefore, are a valid source of teaching for those who stand in the tradition of the historic, but only as supplemental to the

---

136. Ibid.
137. Ibid.
138. *Catechism of the Catholic Church*, ch. 2, art. 2, III, 95.

pre-existing deposit of received truth. The Anglican Thirty-Nine Articles themselves recognise that even General Councils have made mistakes.[139]

This has led some Protestants, in the last five centuries, to believe that they can only establish their authenticity by reference to Scripture.

> The difficulty here is that the authority of Scripture derives from the body which selected and canonized it: the Church. A further difficulty is that nineteenth-century scholarship (historical and anthropological as much as theological) has rather compromised the reliability and integrity of Scripture as an infallible resource. It is also awkward for Protestants to argue consistency of teaching since they do not agree among themselves over an impressively wide range of points, and in the case of the Church of England these disagreements extend internally across the whole experience of its adherents.[140]

Even Hooker himself laid down clear limits for the authority of scripture. For him Scripture was not an authority to be used at random; like everything else, it had its own particular purpose. Scripture conveys the way of salvation revealed from God, it is, therefore, the ground for all doctrine. For Hooker matters directly concerning God's plan of salvation must be settled by reference to Scripture. However, that is the limit of Scripture's authority. Hooker explicitly rejects the Puritan position, as he understands it, on the omnicompetence of Scripture. [141]

The usual way of dealing with this internal problem has been to speak about and pursue the somewhat ethereal reality of an Anglican identity. The ecumenical movement has made this *de rigueur* as a pathway towards some form of unity. However, as we will see in more detail in the section on "Ecclesiology: The Key to a Distinctive Anglican Orthodoxy (Scherzo)," Stephen Sykes noted in 1978, "Anglican apologists have not always seen that their attempts to explain how all the various viewpoints co-exist in one communion raise extremely far-reaching issues about the nature of the Church."[142]

J. Robert Wright, Professor of Ecclesiastical History at the General Theological Seminary in New York City, also noted that ". . . as far as the taking of authoritative decisions is concerned, there is clearly a vacuum at

---

139. Article 21 (1571).
140. Norman, "Authority in the Anglican Communion."
141. Harrison, "Prudence and Custom."
142. Sykes, *Integrity of Anglicanism*, ix.

the centre, whether one chooses to evaluate it positively or negatively."[143] Indeed, when Professor Wright and Dr. Gillian Evans worked together on a collection of texts they called *The Anglican Tradition* in 1991 they felt it necessary at the beginning to issue a disclaimer stating that "no collection of Anglican sources can be 'authoritative' in any sense which can make it fully 'official.'"[144]

Dr. William Sachs issued a warning to the effect that ". . . uncertainty about the Church's identity has reached crisis proportions. . . . Anglicans have no coherent sense of identity and no apparent means to resolve their uncertainty. . . . A cacophony of voices with equal claim to being normatively Anglican has arisen without a means to mediate among them. Thus the history of modern Anglican life reveals a bewildering profusion of claims to be Anglican."[145]

The whole centre of gravity of the debate had shifted. In the past, the key question had been the place of Anglicanism as the *via media*, and the careful use of statements of fundamentals, like the Lambeth Quadrilateral of 1888, made good use of a type of reductionism that avoided the basic difficulty of defining an institutional source of authority.[146]

Anglicans used to claim their unity was embedded in their submission to the authority of Scripture, but scriptural authority, as already pointed out, has been consistently weakened by critical scholarship since the eighteenth and nineteenth century so that old certainties of the seventeenth century and before have been lost forever.

The use of the Prayer Book was also a foundation of unity, but it is probably true today that most Anglicans under the age of forty have probably never seen one let alone used one.

Even the Thirty-nine Articles of religion, which represent a snapshot of the issues of contention in the religion of the sixteenth century, are now seen by many parts of the Communion as redundant. Bishop Stephen Bayne is quite succinct: "I rather think of them as a kind of monument to an attempt on our part, centuries ago, to show how far we could go in the direction of a confessional attitude without actually adopting one. In any case, they are museum pieces now."[147] Ian Ramsey, one-time bishop of Durham, had a similar view:"We do not want to sweep the Thirty-Nine

---

143. Wright, J. R., "Authority of Lambeth Conferences."
144. Wright and Evans, *Anglican Tradition*, xv.
145. Sachs, *Transformation of Anglicanism*, 2, 4, 336.
146. Norman, "Authority in the Anglican Communion."
147. Bayne, *Anglican Turning Point*, 117.

Articles under the carpet but to send them to a stately home in England where we can visit them from time to time."[148]

Bishop Bayne goes on to give his considered summary of Anglican attempts at defining a basis of unity.

> We have no particular theological statement of our own to fence us off from other Churches. We have no international power structure which forces our younger Churches to conform to some alien pattern of life. We have no central executive power. We have no uniform Prayer Book. We have no common language. We have no laws which limit the freedom of any Church to decide its life as it will. We have no ecclesiastical colonies. We have no "Anglican" religion. We have no test of membership save that of Baptism itself. We have nothing to hold us together except the one essential unity given us in our full communion. And even that is not limited to Anglican Churches, for we share in the table of other Churches as well, in increasing number.[149]

In reality, Norman argues, Anglican involvement in ecumenism has merely maintained the myth that Anglicanism has been at the forefront of some great movement of Christian unity. The reality is quite different. In fact, if honesty prevailed, it would be crystal clear that all the churches involved still hold on to their different beliefs and ecclesiologies, even their views on authority. What has been seen as a movement towards unity is really a movement towards "... a sort of loose federalism in which spiritual camaraderie is mistaken for structural agreement about identifying who the People of God are."[150]

Problems of identity, unity, and authority were not solved by the expansion of the Church of England overseas and its transformation into the Anglican Communion. Norman derides Anglicans who sometimes speak as if the sheer scale of the Communion as a whole is a sort of proof that they are part of a truly universal church. Yet, for the church fathers it is clear that the concept of a universal church was not authenticated by mere numbers but rather by consistency of teaching. He reminds his readers that Christ himself sometimes suggested that he considered that the numbers of his real followers, in all societies, would always be small.[151]

---

148. Simpson and Story, *Long Shadows of Lambeth*, 145–46.
149. Bayne, *Anglican Turning Point,*, 271.
150. Norman, "Authority in the Anglican Communion."
151. For example: "Do not be afraid, *little flock*, for your Father has been pleased to give you the kingdom" (Luke 12:3, emphasis added).

As for the supposed authority of the Lambeth Conferences, we have already seen from the very beginning of the first Lambeth Conference in 1867 that Archbishop Longley made it clear that the gathering was a conference and not a synod, and that its resolutions would be purely advisory—they would have only the influence of recommendations.[152] That is, of course, the position as it remains to this day. Resolutions of Lambeth Conferences only have effect if enacted by synods in each constituent church of the Communion.

We have already seen that postmodern episcopal theologians such as Kathryn Tanner [153] see the solution of these problems within Anglicanism through a form of "dispersed authority," envisaging the existence of mutually conflicting theological beliefs and ecclesiastical orders as a species of creative unity.

Critics, including Norman, see this concept of the Church producing merely "an umbrella expression providing shelter for an exceedingly generous range of contentions and panaceas." Norman is scathing of Report IV of the Lambeth Conference of 1948, where "dispersed authority" was first spelled out as a substitute for Anglican ecclesiology. He is also critical of Stephen Sykes in his generous support of it when he describes it as "the most satisfactory public statement of the Anglican view of authority."[154]

For Norman, however, all this produces is what he calls "steady-state; permanent indecision." He admits that Sykes is right when he regards conflict in the identification of doctrine as unavoidable and the "Anglican history of the experience of conflict" as "of potentially great service."[155]

Norman, however, does not see as others do the positive advantages of the unavoidable existence of conflict. He takes refuge in Hooker's belief in the priority of error over controversy. Hooker wrote that it was better ". . . that sometime an erroneous sentence definitive should prevail, till the same authority perceiving such oversight, might afterwards correct or reverse it, than that strifes should have respite to grow."[156]

Norman uses the sharp edge of sarcasm to show his distaste for the notion of "dispersed authority," describing its outworking as producing nothing more than ". . . a crisis of identity, a crisis of unity, and an inability to adduce a coherent ecclesiology. It is hard to imagine that divine

---

152. Wright and Evans, *Anglican Tradition*, 328.
153. See section on "The Emerging Church" in the Second Movement.
154. Sykes, *Integrity of Anglicanism*, 88.
155. Ibid., 89.
156. Hooker, *Laws of Ecclesiastical Polity*, 194.

providence, disclosed in the guidance of the Holy Spirit, can have entrusted the presence of Christ in the World to such an ideological shambles . . . . a tortuous dialectic of truth alternating with error."

There is no doubt that Anglicans have a real issue to address. Norman asks very basic questions: "Do Christians have access to an infallible teaching office, as the historic Churches have always claimed, or are the Protestants right in supposing that only Scripture is indefectible?"

He sees no possibility of a *via media* here. He does see the greatest danger to the Church as the entry of alien ideology and secular moral orthodoxy into Christian ethical teaching. Thus he warns of the still real danger of the ancient problem of heresy and the desperate need for the Church to have a mechanism for distinguishing truth from error and protecting accepted teachings from corruptions. The big question is, of course, how this is to be done. He has no faith in the efficiency of self-correcting mechanisms, and the belief that somehow truth will inevitably emerge in a recognisable form. Anglicanism, he says, prophetically, ". . . may well be approaching the conjunction of a crisis of identity and a general cultural crisis, so that it will be obliged to address the problem with greater clarity than in the past."[157]

As this book is written these words are being fulfilled before our eyes.

The difficulty is that those who espouse the idea of a strong, central authority structure within Anglicanism have to contend with the clear biblical example of how authority was exercised by Jesus himself. There was certainly no sense of coercion in his dealings with others. Instead the New Testament notion of authority seems to imply not jurisdiction over others or coercive behaviour but rather the "holder's rightful freedom to act."[158]

John's Gospel makes it clear that this authority is given to all who are children of God in Christ,[159] therefore, in a biblical sense one individual's freedom cannot be used to infringe the freedom of another. It can only be used in a persuasive manner. Any teaching or opinion shared cannot be enforced but must be accepted by the one to whom it is directed.

With that sense of the history, structure, and current vicissitudes facing the Anglican Communion, it is now necessary to take a closer look at the whole matter of Anglican ecclesiology.

---

157. Norman, "Authority in the Anglican Communion."
158. Cunningham, *These Three Are One*, 312.
159. John 1:12.

Movement Three: The Church as Anglican

Ecclesiology—The Key to a Distinctive Anglican Orthodoxy? (Scherzo)

In later symphonies the minuet was replaced by a more mischievous scherzo and this might well be a better metaphor for some of the political manoeuvrings that have troubled Anglicanism in later years. The Italian word *scherzo* means a "joke" or "joking" and implies a more playful or, perhaps better in this context, a more expansive approach. This is not, however, to imply that the travail through which the Church is passing is to be treated as something light and trivial—far from it! Indeed, in later years the scherzo itself at times became dark and dramatic in its form and lost that sense of light heartedness. The composer Schumann himself, commenting on Chopin's scherzi and their sense of darkness, said, "How is 'gravity' to clothe itself if 'jest' goes about in dark veils?"[160] So it is that this book recognises the solemnity and seriousness of the current situation while, at the same time, expresses the lightness and hope that comes from a clear belief that Christ is the head of the church and he will keep it and protect it through all its difficulties.

First Subjext: Why Ecclesiology?

The inclusion of a chapter on ecclesiology may seem a little odd to some readers in a book that is dedicated to orthodoxy. That is why I have included it under the movement known as scherzo, which is, as described above, the most "quirky" of the movements. Having said that, it not to say that there is not a serious point being made here. The support of serious scholars and theologians for this will support the value of this methodology.

Paul Avis reminds us that ". . . Hans Kung speaks of ecclesiology as the theological expression of the Church's image. *The New Catholic Encyclopaedia* defines ecclesiology in a nuanced way as 'the branch of theology that seeks to give a scientific exposition of the faith of the Church concerning itself.' Ecclesiology is, therefore, reasoned and informed reflection on the nature of the Christian Church."[161]

If such a view of ecclesiology is accepted then it is clear that what is believed and practised as ecclesiology is as much a statement of doctrine as any other statement made on another doctrinal subject such as soteriology or pneumatology. Indeed, that seminal expression of Anglican

---

160. Cited in Niecks, *'Frederick Chopin as a Man and Musician'*, 494.
161. Avis, *Anglican Understanding of the Church*, 2.

ecclesiology, the Book of Common Prayer, is clearly and deeply soteriological in every expression of its liturgy. Everything about its worship arises from a clear conviction of the need for grace and mercy from a loving and forgiving God in the face of man's sinfulness and unworthiness. It centres absolutely on the person and work of the Lord Jesus Christ and his offering of a "full, perfect, and sufficient sacrifice, oblation and satisfaction for the sins of the whole world."[162]

While it is clear that matters of doctrine and ethics undergird the expression of orthodoxy found in the Jerusalem Declaration, what is also clear is that the way in which GAFCON seeks to influence or, as some would say, impose the wider acceptance their views on orthodoxy throughout the Anglican Communion is by undertaking quite dramatic shifts away from traditional Anglican ecclesiology. They have sought to create for themselves an Anglican structure that is, in their opinion, better able to promote and encourage the acceptance of the Jerusalem Statement and, with that, the authority of their own primates and gatherings over against those of the Anglican Communion as a whole and the Archbishop of Canterbury in particular.

In some ways this strategy is hardly surprising. As Bishop Pierre W. Whalon wrote in his unpublished but significant paper "Towards a Distinctive Anglican Doctrine of the Church,"

> Ecclesiology is a church's thinking and speaking about itself. . . . As part of systematic theology—reflections upon the faith organised around particular images —ecclesiology cannot be kept apart from a theology's explanations of grace, salvation, pneumatology, sacrament, church governance, and moral reflection. How we conceive of the Church invariably influences to a large extent how we speak about God, Christ, the Spirit, and ourselves in God's economy.[163]

If it is true that orthodoxy and ecclesiology are so inextricably linked then it would seem that it is important to ascertain whether there is such a thing as a clearly defined "standard" Anglican ecclesiology against which we can judge the innovations brought about by the supporters of GAFCON and others of a similar viewpoint.

---

162. Book of Common Prayer, 1662, Prayer of Consecration.
163. Whalon, "Towards a Distinctive Anglican Doctrine of the Church," 2.

Movement Three: The Church as Anglican

Development: The Complexities of Ecclesiology

Whalon reminds us that ecclesiology is a complex phenomenon, which involves mixed reflections on such sources as the New Testament images of the church; church history, both general and specifically focusing on particular churches and how they see themselves within that stream; the variety of statements of belief and doctrinal formulations; the polity; the witness of saints; and how various theologians have expressed themselves. All this must be seen as part of systematic theology.

The useful distinction made here between the church in general and a particular church within it allows us to differentiate, as Avery Dulles does, between ". . . an idealized concept of the community founded by Christ and the apostles, and 'the churches,' concrete historical Christian communities which hold various ideals of the Church."[164] Thus it can be said that different churches, whether by that is meant a local church community or a particular denomination, are seen for what they really are: groups of Christians who, to the best of their ability, attempt to hold on to what is their version of that "idealised concept."

There is no doubt that any view of the church (ecclesiology) that claims an imprimatur from the New Testament onwards is indeed "idealised." This point of view was made more clearly in the earlier chapter on the evolving orthodoxy of the early church.

New Testament scholarship has long noted that there are different ecclesiologies evident even in the Gospels themselves. Matthew, for example, has clearly a Jewish audience in mind when he stresses the fulfillment of Old Testament prophecies and the way in which Jesus seems to act like a new Moses, even claiming the authority to make changes in the Law with sayings such as, "You have heard it said . . . but I say to you." All that is so different from other gospel writers such Mark who, writing to a Gentile, not Jewish community, helpfully offers explanatory notes about some of the intricacies of Judaism and its practices for his Gentile readers. While neither author tells us this directly, it is clear that an unspoken and often partially hidden ecclesiology is often something that permeates and influences a particular set of beliefs but whose existence can only be inferred from careful study of the text and style of the author.

Whalon suggests four reasons why ecclesiology seems to be such an elusive concept. Firstly, he sees that there is the problem of subjectivity when examining our own church's ecclesiology. It is sometimes easier to understand another church's ecclesiology than our own. Secondly, he

---

164. Dulles, *Models of the Church*, 17.

argues that the inextricable link between ecclesiology and the other great themes of systematic theology means that what a person believes about election or grace, for example, will undoubtedly affect directly how they view what constitutes the church. Thirdly, he makes the observation that our ecclesiologies are often more akin to ideology than theology. An ecclesiology may be used as just another way of expressing the exclusive—or inclusive for that matter—view of salvation that a particular group holds. Fourthly, Whalon concedes that, in the end, ecclesiology, like all matters pertaining to the church, must be seen as mystery. This word, used in its New Testament sense, refers to the inability of the human mind ever to grasp more than dimly the action of God in Christ, uniting the divine and the human. As Paul writes, "This is a profound mystery—but I am talking about Christ and the church" (Eph 5:32).[165]

Avery Dulles sums it all up succinctly: ". . . [T]he reason for this lack of intelligibility is not the poverty but the richness of the Church itself. Like other supernatural resources, the Church is known by a kind of connaturality (as Thomas Aquinas and the classical theologians called it). . . . Furthermore, the Church pertains to the mystery of Christ; Christ is carrying out in his Church his plan of redemption."[166]

Daniel Hardy, one-time Van Mildert Professor of Divinity in Durham University, speaks of this as a sort of paradox involving the fact that "wholeness" and "not-wholeness" are the simultaneous, constant, and expected experience of the church.

> In fundamental respects, Anglicanism is formed through its worship, through "praying the Scriptures," through a eucharistically-formed corporate life, and through a complex ministry and mission in the world, each of these deeply interwoven in different spatio-temporal circumstances. Rooted in the infinite identity of the Lord, it has a "relative identity," but it is always also implicated in the world, implicated in every aspect of life in the world. So its identity is traceable to the divine identity, but it is also implicated in the complexity and messiness of the world, its actions are always contingent, and they are—or should be—directed to the coming of the Kingdom of God. Such wholeness as it has—as formed through worship, etc.—is also a "not-wholeness" because the world in which it is implicated is not whole; we are not whole, and cannot presume that we are.[167]

165. Whalon, "Towards a Distinctive Anglican Doctrine," 3–4.
166. Dulles, *Models of the Church* , 17.
167. Hardy, *Anglicanism in the Twenty-First Century*.

Movement Three: The Church as Anglican

Second Subject: The Anglican Distinctive

If this is true, then what can we say then of the concept of a distinctive Anglican theology and, more particularly in this context, a distinctive Anglican ecclesiology? It is a pertinent question because it is often said that Anglicanism has no doctrines of its own but that it holds to a "mere Christianity," the core of the doctrines of the church when it was unified in antiquity.

Henry R. McAdoo, in his book *The Spirit of Anglicanism: A Survey of Anglican Theological Method in the Seventeenth Century*, seems to agree with this assessment.

> There is no specifically Anglican corpus of doctrine and no king-pin in Anglican theology such as Calvin, nor is there any tendency to stress specific doctrines such as predestination, or specific philosophies such as Thomism or nominalism or any other one of the several medieval brands of philosophy. ... Anglicanism is not committed to believing anything because it is Anglican but only because it is true. Perhaps the most important thing about Hooker is that he wrote no Summa and composed no Institutes, for what he did was to outline method. What is distinctively Anglican is then not a theology but a theological method.[168]

This premise is, however, now challenged by those who feel that it is possible to define a distinctive Anglican theology through what is clearly the most distinctive doctrine of Anglicanism, namely its Anglican ecclesiology. The blossoming of ecumenical relationships and the consequent need for those involved to know more clearly what lies behind why participating churches take the form that they do has created a need for this distinctly Anglican doctrine to become more formally stated.

The issue is not just one of interest to interested outsiders. It is not too much of a stretch to suggest, as Whalon does, that the real issue lying under the current tensions in the Anglican Communion finds its root in competing ecclesiologies that each claim to be Anglican. That makes the need for a clear statement of what is Anglican ecclesiology the more urgent. "While the presenting issues seem to be sexuality and territorial invasions creating new non-geographical jurisdictions like the Convocation of Anglicans in North America, the real issue is ecclesiology. The broader challenge facing Anglicans around the world is to re-commit

---

168. McAdoo, *The Spirit of Anglicanism*, 1.

to and live out in new ways the distinctive Anglican ecclesiology—what makes us Church."[169]

Stephen Sykes has written extensively on this subject and has argued strongly for the existence of an Anglican systematic theology, and sees the exposition of a distinctive Anglican ecclesiology as a significant emphasis within that theology. Taking Richard Hooker's statement that the church is both a society and a "society supernatural,"[170] Sykes sees the image in 1 Corinthians[171] of the different spiritual gifts bestowed by the Holy Spirit on individual members of the church as reflecting an ecclesiology where "It belongs to the heart of this theology that we maintain that God's action in the world involves an affirmation both of created sociality and that which is new, surprising, and unique."[172]

This leads to the acceptance within such an ecclesiology that the "... natural mode is to allow disagreement, debate, and conflict as a natural part of its life. It will provide a structure of the God-given gift of insight and leadership and for understanding and consent; and that structure will be appropriate to differing patterns of authority in different cultures at various times."[173]

Sykes does not mean here that anything goes. Indeed Sykes launches an attack on what he saw as doctrinal relativism masquerading as the traditional Anglican virtue of comprehensiveness. He calls, instead, for an Anglican systematic theology to define limits to comprehensiveness.

Variation One: The Place of the Thirty-Nine Articles of Religion

Of course, in the past it was the Thirty-Nine Articles of Religion that were the foundational roots of Anglican ecclesiology. However, the authority of the Articles within the Anglican Communion as a whole has been very much diminished. Many Anglicans now see them in a different way: as a strange mixture of propositional statements of belief, often totally coloured by an historical situation of intense religious bigotry and violence and rooted in the superstition and pre-scientific era of the sixteenth century. It

---

169. Whalon, "Towards a Distinctive Anglican Doctrine," 3–4.

170. Hooker, *Laws of Ecclesiastical Polity*, I.xv.2.

171. 1 Cor 12:7: "Now to each one the manifestation of the Spirit is given for the common good."

172. Sykes, *Genius of Anglicanism*, 239.

173. Ibid., 240.

is no longer acceptable to many to see these Articles, fossilised in the 1662 Book of Common Prayer, as a litmus test for orthodoxy.

Sykes sees clearly that, with the decline of the authority of the Articles, a vacuum has appeared, precisely in the area of ecclesiology, and thus, in Anglicanism's sense of its own identity.[174]

The options open to Anglicans now in terms of identity seem to be either to rewrite the Articles or to seek for some other, more relevant way to establish a distinctive Anglican identity.

Clearly the Articles need reforming, whether in the light of closer attention to the language of Scripture, in rereading in the light of scientific knowledge, in the light of modern historical scholarship about Paul and Judaism, or in the ways we seek to influence our reading of one text in the light of another, or allowing one text to be crucial and relativising another as merely contextual.

To do anything else than continue the reformation would be to place the Articles over Scripture as an unchanging hermeneutical key, and deny Scripture the power to offer fresh challenges to what are really Tudor formulations of the faith. But the problem for the Church is, in the real world, which individual or group would feel adequate to do that and who would be acceptable to the whole Anglican Communion?

Ultimately that is why the Articles can never stand as a test of orthodoxy. They are certainly part of our Anglican inheritance but they themselves point to the Scripture as normative—as an authority above their own. Stranded in the life, scholarship, and devotion of the past as they are, they cannot adjudicate between competing understandings of Scripture for the Church seeking to proclaim the gospel afresh in each generation. Indeed, even the Church of England and many other provinces of the Anglican Communion now ask only that licensed ministers accept them as bearing their historic witness to the "faith uniquely revealed in the Holy Scriptures and set forth in the Catholic creeds."

That is a role in which we can receive them with grateful thanks as critical friends who remind us from where we have come but who cannot be allowed to restrict where we are going. They are too rooted in their own time and place to be universal, too ready to admit error even to a General Council to be infallible, and too aware of their own submission to Scripture to be unreformable. A true faithfulness to them demands that they be transcended in some way or other.

---

174. Sykes, *Anglicanism and the Doctrine of the Church*, 103–7.

Beating the Bounds

Variation Two: Other Distinctive Features

The question then is, what other means do we have to form our Anglican ecclesiological identity? Sykes puts forward some of the ideas that he believes create the "ecclesial instinct" that have informed Anglicans. The first is the church as a "sign," in clear contrast to the Orthodox idea of the church as "icon" or the Roman Catholic view of the Church as "sacrament." In the word "sign" are subsumed all the many and varied biblical metaphors for the church found in the New Testament. Seeing the church as "sign" enables believers to see the church as God intends it to be and how God uses it despite it failings to be all that it should be. The church fundamentally belongs to the sign-character of God's activity in human history.

For Sykes, a second facet of the church as "sign" is that it gives to baptism its rightful primary status in contrast to the historic overemphasis often given to the Eucharist. The Anglican welcome given to other Trinitarian church traditions to the Eucharist makes a clear statement that it is baptism that "makes" a Christian. Baptism in the name of the Trinity is the way in for a person to enter the eucharistic community. The one, holy, catholic, and apostolic church is far greater than all the Anglican churches together. That is why Anglicans (with certain Anglo-Catholic exceptions) have generally accepted the validity of the orders of non-episcopal churches. Indeed, in the first hundred years of the English Reformation, non-episcopally ordained clergy were allowed to minister in the Church of England without reordination while, at the same time, still holding on to the concept of the threefold ministry of bishop, priest, and deacon, as Hooker did, as the optimum polity for the Church.

Sykes sees this openness and welcome to others, rather than feeling the need to "unchurch" them with quite different beliefs and practices, as being rooted in the context of Article 19, which states that all Christian churches, even the most ancient, have wandered into error, including the Anglican Church. Herein lies that innate humility that is truly Anglican and which recognises the reality of its own fallibility.

He emphasises that the centre core of this self-criticism is found in the laity, whose open access to and increasing knowledge of the Scriptures enables them to examine critically the preaching and teaching ministry of their clergy. This is the baptismal right and authority of every member of the Church, who together are corporately a royal priesthood. There is in Anglicanism, therefore, an inbuilt creative tension between the laity and the clergy who are called to equip them.

Movement Three: The Church as Anglican

Thus the sources of the authority of the Church are many. They are, in the words of Lambeth 1948, "... distributed among Scripture, Tradition, Creeds, the Ministry of the Word and Sacraments, the witness of saints, and the *consensus fidelium*, which is the continuing experience of the Holy Spirit through His faithful people in the Church."[175]

Paul Avis shares with Sykes the rejection of the view of Anglicanism as having no specific doctrines. He too sees the distinctively Anglican doctrine being one concerning the church. He concludes that "... there is indeed a tacit Anglican ecclesiology—though it is not static and needs to be disentangled from various historical frameworks, particularly those that I have designated the 'erastian' and 'apostolic' paradigms."[176]

By the "erastian paradigm" Avis is speaking of when the church senses its identity through being set in a particular Christian country, in which both an allegiance to the monarch and church membership are seen as two sides of the same coin. It was this notion that had been crucial to the concept of Christendom. This paradigm was defended vigorously in England by Richard Hooker and others. The Civil War and the republican Commonwealth period under the Puritans, however, took their toll on that view. The social and political tolerance of Roman Catholics and other Non-Conformists inflicted a mortal wound and, to all intents and purposes, this paradigm is moribund today.[177]

In the nineteenth century in England the "apostolic paradigm" was developed by the members of the Oxford Movement, or Tractarians, who saw in the political events of the time an opportunity to counter what they saw as erastian attacks on the Church. Theirs was a strong reaction to the decision by a secular parliament to take upon itself the authority to change the diocesan structure of the Anglican Church in Ireland through the Irish Church Temporalities Act of 1833.

At the time the Church of Ireland accounted for only 12 percent of the Irish population, yet was served by no less than twenty-two bishops, many of whom received handsome salaries for serving tiny dioceses with a couple dozen parishes. No diocese was untouched by the amalgamations except Meath and Limerick, which were home for large numbers of Protestant farmers in those days. The act produced a storm of protest in England. Turning away from the Protestant character of the Church of England, the Tractarians invested the church's legitimacy entirely in the

---

175. "Meaning and Unity of the Anglican Communion," report to Lambeth 1948 quoted in Sykes, *Authority in the Anglican Communion*, 285.

176. Avis, *Anglicanism and the Christian Church*, xvii.

177. Ibid., 300–303.

apostolic succession of its bishops. That legitimacy was focused almost exclusively on the episcopate as guarantor of the efficacy of the sacraments.

Avis, in a similar vein to Sykes, sees the urgent need for a new ecclesiological paradigm to strongly assert the distinctive theology and legitimacy of Anglicanism. Avis also favours a strongly baptismal ecclesiology, as expressed in the Appeal of the 1920 Lambeth Conference: "... the vision which lies before us is that of a church, genuinely catholic, loyal to all truth, and gathering into its fellowship 'all who profess and called themselves Christian."[178]

Variation Three: The Value of Comprehensiveness

What are we to make of the long-celebrated Anglican comprehensiveness? Avery Dulles defined it as "the legitimacy of keeping irreducibly distinct theologies alive within the same ecclesiastical communion."[179]

We have already noted that Sykes believed that that comprehensiveness had degenerated into relativism. Avis, on the other hand, historically records the rise in the seventeenth century and the later contemporary developments of the low-church, broad-church, and high-church party positions. What is interesting is that neither Sykes nor Avis gives a very clear argument for comprehensiveness as a central feature of Anglican ecclesiology.

That task is taken up by Tim Bradshaw, whose strength of argument for Anglican comprehensiveness is unusual in a clearly self-identified evangelical.

After analysing different Anglican ecclesiologies Bradshaw, as one would expect, suggests that an evangelical or low-church ecclesiology is most likely to be the distinctive Anglican ecclesiology. However, this is no evangelical rant or polemic. Bradshaw roots his ecclesiology in the deeply biblical concept of *covenant*. This was something that God brought into being in order to create a people for himself. Bradshaw sees such a covenant demanding a response of trust and obedience from men and women. Indeed this is the Apostle Paul's central theme. "The covenant relationship, for Paul, is pure grace. It is communicated in comprehensibly spoken promise, received in faith and obedience."[180]

The church is seen through the biblical image of adoption. There is a new family with Jesus at its head as the "new Adam," and men and women are "born again" into it. All this is only made possible by the death and

---

178. Ibid., 310.
179. Dulles, *Models of the Church*, 5.
180. Bradshaw, *Olive Branch*, 131.

resurrection of Jesus. His resurrection life is able to bring new life to this new family of God.

Bradshaw shifts from the more "incarnational" view of some Anglican ecclesiologies that emphasise the church as Christ's body and his bride. This view, he says, sees the church as the "church in Christ." Bradshaw, from his low-church, evangelical perspective, prefers to see Jesus as Jesus as the head of the body—Emmanuel, "God with us." This is a distinct shift from the incarnational "church in Christ" view to "Christ in the church." The reformed ecclesiological emphasis is on the covenant people with Christ dwelling in their midst, not the church as an extension of the incarnation. Jesus is a corporate person but is yet distinguishable from the church's individual members. This all comes about through the action of the Holy Spirit in the lives of the visible church's members. Here clearly then is a divide between the visible church present throughout history and the invisible church known only to God.[181]

While the sacramental life of the church is vital and carries the full weight of dominical authority, the issue of polity is secondary. Following Richard Hooker, Bradshaw has a utilitarian view of Episcopacy as a commendable and historical but not essential form of ecclesiology. For him the bishops are not seen as the successors of the apostles. They could never continue the unique role played by those first witnesses to the resurrection. Individual Christian faith comes through believing their witness to Christ. He denies the Roman view that Peter would be the rock upon which the church would be built. It was, rather, Peter's confession of faith in Jesus as "the Christ" that was the rock upon which the church would be built. It is that same confession made by each individual member that constitutes the building blocks of the church.[182]

His emphasis on covenant, which for someone from a Reformed tradition becomes the basis for (paedo-) baptism, provides another baptismal ecclesiology. Alongside this, Bradshaw's firm defence of the primacy of Scripture, especially the New Testament, with its clear teaching, through examples of how differences of opinion and divisions are to be handled in the light of the truth of the gospel, lead him to a strong defence of comprehensiveness.

> Leave to God the things that are God's, to the church the things that are the church's, bearing in mind that the church is more than merely the present moment in her history. Disagreeing with Rome

---

181. Ibid., 197–200.
182. Ibid., 146–56.

and the Radical Reformation tradition, the Anglican evangelical refuses to make spiritual declarations on things permitting legitimate variation. This allows recognition of the great church in many denominations, however distorted and unclear some may be.[183]

Bradshaw's s deep ecumenical interests and commitments, as an Anglican who has served on many boards concerning "faith and order" issues and as a member of the International Anglican Orthodox Theological Commission, have led him to be constructively critical of those of his own churchmanship. He feels deeply that too much emphasis on individual piety has resulted in the loss of the family identity, especially in the sacramental life of the church and its moral teaching. "The greatest danger is that the evangelical, confident in being declared right with God, will only listen, and fail to act; will neglect the gospel in social and political life."[184]

These three writers—Sykes, Avis, and Bradshaw—have given us glimpses of possible facets of a distinctive Anglican ecclesiology. The question still remains as to whether there exists an overarching doctrine of the church held by all Anglicans. One feature of this would have to be the rationale for allowing Anglicans to hold differing, even contradictory views on the theology of the church.

Pierre Whalon is acting provocatively when he writes,

> It may be that, in fact, there is no "mere Anglicanism"; that the tensions involved in the Elizabethan Settlement are irreducible and irreconcilable. The features of Anglicanism will be found not to translate to a global level, but to be only a peculiarly Anglo-Saxon phenomenon. In that case, John Newman's submission to Rome, joining one of the Orthodox churches, or the move toward a purely reformed church like the Reformed Episcopal Church may be the only options honest Anglicans have.[185]

Reading further, however, it is clear that he does not really believe that.

> The issue is far from settled, however. The hard work of self-definition of a global Anglicanism has only just begun. The extraordinary missionary vitality of the African, Asian and South American churches suggests that there is a permanent achievement of the Holy Spirit in Anglicanism beyond the Anglo-American context, that it is not merely a political compromise

---

183. Ibid., 196.
184. Ibid., 200.
185. Whalon, "Towards a Distinctive Anglican Doctrine," 24–25.

papered over with theological decoration. The blood of the thousands of recent Anglican martyrs gives a fresh testimony to the reality of the Risen Christ. In myriad mundane ways, as well, ministries of Anglicans worldwide bear witness to the power of the Spirit to bring forward first fruits of God's Realm within the Anglican churches.[186]

In speaking of comprehensiveness Whalon recognises that it is "within a visible, settled Church that comprehensiveness can most easily flourish." When churches are in hostile situations and facing persecution then tolerance of difference is a luxury they cannot easily afford. That, of course, is an insight with significant importance in a church that has provinces in many different parts of the world.

Above all, from the very beginning, the Church has been one and, as Whalon points out,

> One conundrum that Anglicans have had to face since the first intimations of the break with Rome is how to be the One Church when unity is no longer. Of the four "notes" of the Church, unity is first. "Is Christ divided?" Paul sarcastically asked the Corinthians (I Cor. 1:13). That would be obviously absurd. Yet unity has been broken. The Reformed way of solving this conundrum—that the true Church had disappeared for centuries—was not open to the first Anglicans. They were the Catholic Church in England. They knew in their bones that their church was . . . no sect. At the same time, the Roman solution . . . was unacceptable as well. Anglicans have not been able in good conscience to see themselves as the One True Church, all others being more or less fraudulent.[187]

From the start the Church of England knew itself still to be part of the Catholic Church. As such it also knew itself to be that society which offered its members salvation in Christ through their participation in its worship and sacramental life led by a legitimate clergy teaching the Scriptures and the creeds. In the light of that fundamental belief about itself it is possible to see that one of the most basic and enduring features about Anglican ecclesiology is the awareness of "the absurdity of being a fragment of the whole Church, one shard of the mirror, as it were, shattered by Christian disunity."[188]

---

186. Ibid., 25.
187. Ibid., 26.
188. Ibid., 27.

This awareness has produced within the Anglican Church a real desire to work for unity. This has been expressed through a deep Anglican commitment to the ecumenical movement, in which Anglicans have had a leading role. There has been much ecumenical work done between the Anglican and Roman Catholic Churches attempting to overcome the two communions' mutual estrangement. The Anglican-Roman Catholic International Consultation has produced some detailed and significant work over the last three decades.

A tangible result of these ecumenical discussions and relationships has been the emergence of *koinonia* ecclesiology, which, as it has developed, seems to have become central in discussions about a distinctive Anglican ecclesiology over the years.

Ecumenically, the notion of *koinonia* has been seen as a very good place to start interdenominational discussions. It had a good New Testament pedigree, especially in the Pauline writings. Consequently all the major documents of the Anglican Communion written to respond to recent stresses and strains within the Anglican Communion, which will be examined in due course (namely, *The Virginia Report* and *The Windsor Report*, and of course the proposed covenant), sought to establish *koinonia* as the common ground upon which hopes for a restoration of unity might be pinned.

Phillip Groves, however, notes that the word *koinonia* has itself been somehow elevated from a simple term into an ideal concept and this he sees as a problem.

> This is echoed in a paragraph defining the Fellowship of Confessing Anglicans: "We are a fellowship of people united in the communion (*koinonia*) of the one Spirit and committed to work and pray together in the common mission of Christ." The use of brackets and transliterated Greek conveys a notion that there is a biblical state of "fellowship" or "communion" defined by the true *koinonia* that needs to be recovered in the present era. *Koinonia* is presented as a concept that defies translation, rather than a word with differing meaning in different contexts.[189]

Of course, what the Fellowship of Confessing Anglicans, like every other group, wants is for the reader to accept their unstated definition as an umbrella term for everything else that they stand for.

The truth is that when this term is used without definition it can be made to mean whatever the writer wants it to mean. If this notion of *koinonia* is to have any value at all, it must actually refer to what we are

189. Groves, "Model for Partnership," 153.

Movement Three: The Church as Anglican

genuinely affirming in common, as well as for the different meanings we derive from it. If we persist in using the same phrases to refer to what are actually different realities, our dialogue will not genuinely progress.

It is clear that *koinonia* is expressed in the relationship of the local and universal church; or, to say it more directly, the universal church is a communion of local churches, in each of which the fullness of the church resides. The tangible signs of this *koinonia* are the shared confession of the apostolic faith in the creeds and a common participation in baptism and the Eucharist. Without these, *koinonia* in its fullness cannot exist. With these tangible signs in place we can at least affirm together that the church, in its universal dimension, is a *koinonia* of local churches—a unity in diversity, a diversity in unity.

The fact is, of course, that different groups understand differently how "local churches" relate to the one universal church, and therefore do not agree as to what "local churches" refers to. In Anglicanism some see "local churches" as the provinces within different countries, with their own history, culture, and character. Others use "local churches" only to refer to the local, street-level congregations. However, our common affirmation of universal and local levels, and of unity in diversity, still has significance, and needs further exploration.

Any distinctive Anglican ecclesiology must, therefore, begin with that declaration of the unity of the catholic church of which Anglicanism is truly a part. This is the reality of *koinonia* tangibly expressed in all we affirm in the creeds and should be demonstrated in a sacramental life that expresses openness, hospitality, and welcome. This unity, however, is a unity in diversity, which leads us on to the next facet of a distinctive Anglican ecclesiology: "comprehensiveness."

In the fractal-like economy that is the universal church, what is true of the whole has to be true of its parts. So within a distinctive Anglican ecclesiology unity in diversity must prevail; that is, a willingness to tolerate some variation of doctrine.

While it is clearly true that this may have been at times merely for the sake of peace, at heart it is a true recognition of the appropriate ecclesiology for a fragment of the catholic church. The 1948 Lambeth Report on Authority, which we have already mentioned, with its assertion that authority in Anglicanism is dispersed among several sources, is one of the recent attempts to explain and defend this particular aspect of Anglicanism.

One of the primary marks of this comprehensiveness is a clear place for the vocation and ministry of the laity. Stephen Pickard makes this clear: "Anglicans stand in this long tradition of theology as the active pursuit of wisdom and its radical transformative impact. It is clearly not an optional extra, nor a luxury the church can ill afford, nor the preserve of an elite—clergy, seminarians, the experts or 'professionals'. It is a task for the baptised enshrined in their baptismal vows and a corollary of their diverse ministries in the world."[190]

Pickard sees this encapsulated in the Good Friday Collect from the 1549 Book of Common Prayer written by Thomas Cranmer. If ever there was a clear description of this facet of Anglican ecclesiology this is it:

> Almighty and everlasting God, by whose Spirit the whole body of the Church is governed and sanctified; Receive our supplications and prayers, which we offer before thee for all estates of men in thy holy Church, that every member of the same, in his vocation and ministry, may truly serve thee; through our Lord and Saviour Jesus Christ, who liveth and reigneth with thee, and in the unity of the same Spirit, ever one God, world without end. Amen.

In a footnote Pickard notes that "this Collect points to a profound mutuality in ministry wherein each ministry bestows life and energy on other ministries."[191]

Whalon reminds us that in order for the laity to exercise this vital ministry,

> ... they need unfettered access to the Scriptures, the primary tradition, so as to be formed by the mind of the Trinity. The people need to be able to pray in a way that will mould them more and more into the image of Christ—to become holy people. The laity need to have their share in the governance of the Church. Only together do we possess the mind of Christ (I Cor. 2:16) and therefore only therefore will the Holy Spirit lead us into all truth. Paradoxically, that requires a great deal of individual freedom. This is the heart of the English Reformation, of the protestant character of Anglicanism.[192]

When this freedom to study the Scriptures for themselves is given to the laity and if the teaching, tools and encouragement they need are provided through the clergy and others, the church clearly opens itself up to the real possibility of disagreements over doctrine and interpretation.

---

190. Pickard, "Theology as a Power," 86–87.
191. Ibid., 87.
192. Whalon, "Towards a Distinctive Anglican Doctrine," 29.

Movement Three: The Church as Anglican

The question then arises, which doctrines are considered to be primary and which are seen as *adiaphora*?

It could be thought that the creeds provide the basic minimum of core doctrines. It is, however, more likely that those of a more conservative and propositional view of orthodoxy will have a far fuller and more detailed answer up their sleeve. However, encouraging Christians to think through their faith does require time and patience and some flexibility. Whalon points out that, if we consider the Anglican Articles, they are very circumspect in applying too much detail in their definitions. For example, Article 6, which Whalon says ". . . draws a hermeneutical circle around the Scriptures, saying that they '*contain* all things necessary to salvation' without spelling out what those 'things' are. Furthermore, the Article draws another circle around each individual Christian that no ecclesiastical power can force anyone to believe what Scripture does not *contain* or what can be clearly and convincingly proven therein."[193]

This brings us back to that *esprit critique* Sykes so valued as a ministry of the biblical informed laity.

One further aspect of Anglican comprehensiveness is the acceptance of the concept of probability rather than that of certainty when it comes to knowledge of the truth. This attitude of humble awareness of our human frailty means that, although we declare Jesus Christ to be the Truth, our human formulations of that Truth can never encompass it in all its fullness but can only feel the way towards it. Therefore, although the church is not infallible, because the truth of its doctrine points, however incompletely and falteringly, to Christ, the church believes God will not let it fall into fatal error. This so-called indefectibility gives a certain theological ground for confidence in the ideal of comprehensiveness.

After all, Christ did say concerning the church, "I will build my church, and the gates of Hades will not overcome it" (Matt 16:18)

Of course, the question arises about where the boundaries of comprehensiveness lie. Anglicanism has always tended towards requiring of its members and, by definition more publicly its clergy, doctrine that is encapsulated more in the way the church worships rather than in some strictly confessional documents.

This principle, *lex orandi lex credendi*, enables the church to maintain foundational doctrine alongside allowing individual believers the freedom to offer their own interpretation of them. This is the situation that early church history supports. It leads away from arguments about doctrine to

---

193. Ibid., 30.

disputes about right worship. Moreover, freedom on the matter of forms of worship has existed since the 1637 Scottish Book of Common Prayer. This trend has accelerated immensely in recent days, with each province now producing its own liturgies.

This development is implicit in Cranmer's opening sentence of the introductory notes entitled "Concerning the Service of the Church" in the Book of Common Prayer where he lays out the need for the constant revision of the liturgy: "There was never anything by the wit of man so well devised, or so sure established, which in continuance of time hath not been corrupted."

Such continuing liturgical work requires another clear characteristic of Anglican theology, namely openness not only to what can be learned from the early church but also an openness to investigate seriously the contribution of current scholarship. From its inception Anglicanism has argued that there is no one source of Christian truth but that Scripture, reason, and tradition must all be taken into account. One decisive step in the process that led to the break with Rome was Cranmer's advice to Henry VIII to appeal over the head of the pope to the consensus of theological opinion within the universities of Europe. Hence Anglicanism came into being with the insight that a true understanding of Christian sources was a matter for scholarly research.

One immediate consequence of the Reformation in Britain was a dramatic expansion of the grammar schools in Britain and the revival of the universities. The Elizabethan ordinal insisted that the clergy must be "godly and well-learned" and the idea grew up that there must be an educated person or "parson" in every village; to teach the faith and to be responsible for education. In a church that values scholarship it was and is inevitable that diversity of opinion should exist. The church has nothing to fear from theological disputations.

Bishop John Jewel of Salisbury, for instance, pointed out that since modern scholarship (of his day) has made the Scriptures available, along with other ancient writings, Rome's charges of heresy and schism against the Church of England may be easily disproven. In fact, they prove, he says, that Rome is itself the source of heresy and schism.[194]

Another feature of Anglicanism is the way that, in many countries, it views itself as ministering to the whole nation. This is not in an arrogant way or in an attempt to become the established church as it is still in

---

194. Jewel, *Apology of the Church of England*, 18.

Movement Three: The Church as Anglican

England. It is, rather, in a spirit of service to the nation or land where God has been pleased to plant it.

F. D. Maurice, the nineteenth-century theologian, made some assertions about the need for the church as a universal society to respect the need for people to live in families and, by extension, in nations.[195] While the Church of England, as the established church, is clearly the church of the nation, that notion seems to have been carried over into some younger Anglican provinces even if this was somewhat diluted after independence.

Anglicans bear in mind the pastoral and cultural needs of the country in which God has placed them as well as acknowledging the authority of the Scriptures, the weight of historic tradition, and the findings of current scholarship. The Lambeth 1988 Resolution 26 to allow African polygamists to keep several wives after conversion to Christianity is a good example of this that has already been noted in an earlier chapter.

In summary then, any distinctive Anglican ecclesiology, reflecting as it does the orthodox theological basis of the Anglican Church, has its origins in that untenable situation that Anglican thinkers have found themselves in, struggling with the theological oxymoronic position of being a fragment of the church that should be a whole and yet is not. Of course, such a position is not alien to Christianity. It could be said that Christianity itself is rooted in the most outrageous oxymoron of all in that it is centred on the *deus-homo*, the one described in the Definition of Chalcedon as "truly God and truly man." The creedal statement strikingly affirms that divinity and humanity are not only non-destructive polarities but, more positively, creative polarities. This creative tension produces the light and life that is at the heart of all Christian ecclesiologies. However, creativity is a risky business and, in such a situation, confusion and error are bound to appear. This is inevitable as mere human beings wrestle with truths that are undoubtedly beyond human understanding. Whalon, in a clear reference to the wheat and the tares, sees that "We need to leave much alone for the time being, for orthodoxy and error are intertwined. Patience and gentleness are necessary to disentangle them. And we need to have confidence that this situation will end some day when God shall do the final sorting."[196]

He also asks whether the baptismal ecclesiology of Sykes, Avis, and others, and the eucharistic *koinonia* ecclesiology so favoured now by Anglican theologians, could not be simply two sides of the same coin: that coin being our searched-for reality of a distinctive Anglican ecclesiology.

195. Maurice, *Kingdom of Christ*, 235–36.
196. Whalon, "Towards a Distinctive Anglican Doctrine," 32.

Roman Catholic theologian George Worgul has something useful to say in this regard: "Baptism is Eucharist begun, Eucharist is baptism completed." An ecclesiology, therefore, that is biased in one direction—towards *either* baptism *or* Eucharist—is less than complete. It fails to promote fully both the evangelistic and sacramental priorities that create a full-orbed version of the church's life. This fullness of life in which all Christian are called to share actually constitutes the very being of the church.[197]

The distinctive Anglican ecclesiology will therefore affirm features of various baptismal and eucharistic theologies of the church while at the same time almost negating or eliminating them by declaring them to be important elements in a dialectic process that preserves them as partial elements in a synthesis. It will affirm the real value of episcopal polity without in any way denying the essential validity of non-episcopal churches. It must also defend the comprehensiveness that is so necessary for a pilgrim church to continue the journey. On top of all these, Anglicanism benefits constantly from the new rich insights from the experience of the Third World churches at the same time as engaging creatively and generously with its ecumenical partners.

Someone might ask what all the purpose of this is. Whalon sums it up well: "One day, God willing, the distinctiveness of Anglicanism which this doctrine of the Church expresses will be subsumed into a larger, even richer whole, to the glory of God the Holy Trinity, in whom all people live and move and have their being."[198]

This reflects the views of Archbishop Michael Ramsay, who wrote:

> While the Anglican Church is vindicated by its place in history, with a strikingly balanced witness to gospel and Church and sound learning, its greater vindication lies in its pointing through its own history to something of which it is a fragment. Its credentials are its incompleteness, with the tension and travail in its soul. It is clumsy and untidy, it baffles neatness and logic. For it is sent not to commend itself as 'the best type of Christianity', but by its very brokenness to point to the universal Church wherein all have died.[199]

He went further when, in "The Anglican Spirit," having masterfully described and defended a distinctive Anglican ecclesiology as an expression of its orthodoxy, he humbly asserts that Anglicanism does not exist

---

197. Worgul, *From Magic to Metaphor*, 188.
198. Whalon, "Towards a Distinctive Anglican Doctrine," 34.
199. Ramsay, *Gospel and the Catholic Church*, 220.

for itself and that perhaps the time will come when it will have to dissolve to make way for the greater good of the one, holy, catholic church.

It seems to me that, when seeking to define orthodoxy, Anglicanism is starting from a deep conviction that doctrine is not an end in itself but a beginning: the beginning of an ongoing conversation. Knowledge of God and knowledge of self and the world go hand in hand. Indeed knowledge of self and the world are facets of our knowledge of God our Creator. Anglican orthodoxy sets limits by making a commitment to an ongoing conversation with Scripture, reason, tradition, and one another so that together we may continually be converted, following the traditional Benedictine greeting, "Please pray for my conversion as I pray for yours."

Brian McLaren, one of the Emerging Church leading lights, attempts to define orthodoxy.

> For most people, orthodoxy means right thinking or right opinions, or in other words, "what we think," as opposed to "what they think." In contrast, orthodoxy . . . may mean something more like "what God knows, some of which we believe a little, some of which they believe a little, and about which we all have a lot to learn. Or it may mean "how we search for a kind of truth you can never fully get into your head, so instead you seek to get our head (and heart) into it." Most people are too serious, too knowledgeable, and busy for such an unorthodox definition of orthodoxy.[200]

McLaren describes two approaches to orthodoxy that, he says, are popular but nevertheless incorrect. The first he describes as the "minimalist" approach, which, looking for what might be called the lowest common denominator, limits orthodoxy to a few core essentials mostly taken from the Nicene-Constantinople Creed and the Apostles' Creed, and anything other than those cannot be claimed as orthodox. McLaren argues against this view, seeing creeds as something other than weapons with which to wage a theological war. He also reminds us that the Scripture is itself "above the creeds" and that ". . . the Holy Spirit may use Scripture to tweak our creedal understandings and emphases from time to time, so that new creeds are needed to give voice to the cry of faith today."[201]

The second approach is what he calls the "accumulating-opinion" approach to orthodoxy. Here the legal approach of the historical accumulation of precedents creates an ever increasing, heavy burden of dos and don'ts that

---

200. McLaren, *Generous Orthodoxy*, 32.
201. Ibid., 32.

take us way beyond anything found in the New Testament or early church. McLaren is not saying that the linking of the notion of practice with orthodoxy is wrong—far from it! Indeed, for him orthodoxy is consistently linked with the "practice of *humility, charity, courage* and *diligence.*"

For him *humility* is that grace that allows us to admit that in the past we might have been wrong in our understanding of the faith and our current understandings may have to be changed. *Charity* is the approach we should to take to those who understand things differently, and perhaps more clearly, than we do. *Courage* speaks of perseverance and faithfulness to this approach even when criticised. *Diligence* is that determination to be continually seeking after truth recognising that we are all on a spiritual journey that will only find its fulfilment when we reach our destination.

What McLaren is clearly saying here is that our orthodoxy is mediated through and exposed to the light of true examination through our orthopraxy. Indeed he rounds off this argument with the statement that is as simple as it is profound. He sees our "orthopraxy as the point of orthodoxy."[202]

This is, of course, a similar approach to that taken by the liberation theologians. Genuine theology, for them, cannot be just a reflection on truth, or a philosophy, but more radically it is a way to live. This is what Gutierrez refers to as praxis. Richard Gillingham described this approach in his article "Praxis and the Content of Theology in Gustavo Gutiérrez's Theological Methodology: A Comparative Critique."

> Theology and praxis far from being distinct actually form a symbiotic and determinative relation on the other. Christian praxis without theology ceases to be Christian praxis and, likewise, theology without Christian praxis ceases to be theology, that is, an (active) explication of the divine will. This in turn has a direct effect on liberation theology's conception of truth. Truth is no longer a mere metaphysical concept to which our beliefs may or may not correspond. Instead, after the model of the incarnation, truth aspires to becoming enfleshed (John 14:6) and theology does not merely reflect upon the world "but rather attempts to be part of the process through which the world is transformed."[203]

Gutierrez defines theology as "critical reflection on historical praxis." In saying that he reminds theologians that they are engaged in a dynamic not a static process. It cannot be simply engaged in while remaining safely

202. Ibid., 34–35.
203. Gillingham, "Practice and Content."

Movement Three: The Church as Anglican

locked away in the ivory towers of academia. It can only flow from a deep and personal involvement with the world and its ongoing life, especially concerning the oppressed and the marginalised. Indeed it is that involvement that must be primary for the living situation actually becomes the source of new theological truth.[204]

Professor Daniel Hardy also leans towards emphasising orthopraxy when he defines Anglicanism as "a practical *idea,* one given us by God, which is realised in the ways we are related to each other." For him there are three dimensions that serve to identify and hold together the reality of Anglicanism.

The first dimension is something that is a given and over which we have no choice and, as such *"antecedently conditions* our life together." Alongside this is the second dimension of being *"immersed"* in the historical and contemporary complexities of just living in the world and so impinges on our everyday life. Both of these dimensions are governed by the third and perhaps most important dimension, that of God's purpose for the future. Hardy calls this an *"ultimate aim."* He sees the church as constantly having to correct its "sociality" by reference to what it might be or become. Thus the ultimate aim exerts a moral force upon present action.

He sees these three dimensions as being sustained ". . . by a practical *habitus,* a 'practice of practices' in which each of us has to be nurtured throughout our lives, not so much for ourselves and our relationships as in and for the world. Our mission is to identify ourselves so closely with others that they will be brought to the same hope that sustains us."[205]

Thus, for Hardy, the ecclesiology of Anglicanism acts like a funnel channelling our worship of God, especially in the Eucharist, together with the needs of the world through the prism of Scripture the regular reading of which, of course, has always been at the heart of Anglican liturgy. Hardy's view of Scripture sees it as having ". . . a 'density' of meaning that—like God—always exceeds our capacity to understand it, or to translate it into simple moral precepts. First, last and always, therefore, we are engaged with God for God's sake, not in order to instrumentalise God in supporting our own views."[206]

This ensures that this ecclesiological orthopraxy is bathed in the "mystery of God's infinite identity" and "God's ultimate purposes for the world"

---

204. Gutiérrez, *Liberation Theology.*
205. Hardy, "Anglicanism in the Twenty-First Century," 4–5.
206. Ibid., 5.

rather being used to promote some personal or group views on orthodoxy or even as a slogan for some possibly politically motivated theological movement. Hardy quotes his favourite mentor from history, Samuel Taylor Coleridge, to support his views. "He, who begins by loving Christianity better than Truth, will proceed by loving his own Sect or Church better than Christianity, and end in loving himself better than all."[207]

Hardy senses that when the Communion is in crisis this notion of "antecedent" Anglicanism as well as the focus on God's ultimate purposes tend to be submerged and forgotten in the pain and perplexity of the struggle. It is, he says, similar to the way in which those who suffer physically or psychologically can lose their own sense of integrity in the experience of the suffering.

If nothing else, McLaren's rather radical definition of orthodoxy and Hardy's more esoteric theological approach both support the view that "The greatest threat to Anglicanism today is that . . . the personal will (what each person wants), and the will of sectional interests in the Church are displacing love for the truth. By the logic of Coleridge's aphorism, the result can only be a downward spiral to self-love."[208]

This, of course, brings us full circle back to my criticism of GAFCON and its supporters. They, like so many before them, have attempted to "capture" Anglicanism in a particular historically liturgical and doctrinal "form" by attempting to provide "universal norms" for its practice. Hardy sees two possible dangers in this. They run the risk of ". . . assigning to the future what properly belongs to the past, or 'limiting' the ultimate aim of Anglicanism to what has appeared in the past."[209]

These are certainly difficult waters to swim in, with strong currents that ebb and flow. What is clear is that Anglican orthodoxy rests on certain givens such as the central authority of the Scriptures and the interpretation of those Scriptures expressed in the ecumenical creeds, the Thirty-Nine Articles, and the Book of Common Prayer.

However, these interpretative givens are foundational only in the sense that they tell us how, where, and why Anglicanism began and where it has been as it has travelled on its continuing pilgrimage. They are snapshots of particular battles fought throughout centuries of grappling with mysteries beyond our human understanding, always coloured by the

---

207. Coleridge, *Aids to Reflection*, 107.
208. Hardy, "Anglicanism in the Twenty-First Century," 5.
209. Ibid., 10.

Movement Three: The Church as Anglican

social and historical situations current at their writing. Francis Schaeffer's comment about truth is relevant:

> It is an important principle to remember, in the contemporary interest in communication and in language study that the biblical presentation is that, though we do not have exhaustive truth, we have from the Bible what I term *true truth*. In this way we know true truth about God, true truth about man, and something truly about nature. Thus on the basis of the Scriptures, while we do not have exhaustive knowledge, we have true and unified knowledge.[210]

This acknowledgement that our knowledge is "true" but not "exhaustive" supports the view that all these givens act as lights from behind casting our own long shadows of darkness—(for "darkness" read "ignorance" or "intransigence")—in front of us. Light for the way ahead can only come from our contemporary wrestling with what we think we know in the light of what Hardy calls the "ultimate aim" of God's purposes for the church and for the world.

Brian Haymes writes in his essay "Baptist and Pentecostal Churches,"

> In the last analysis, all our ecclesiologies are provisional. This too is a truth about the church. We all pray for a future not yet achieved, for a fulfilment not yet given. Risking, perhaps unwisely, a crude analysis, the churches which are strong on order, priesthood and creation are churches of the Father; those whose passion is for salvation and the coming of the Kingdom are churches of the Son; those who are less concerned with orders but rejoice in the power and new life from God are churches of the Spirit. How do we become together the Church of the Holy and undivided Trinity?[211]

This will clearly be painful and difficult process that, like the striking of a flint against stone, applies the spark of argument and debate to the tinder of what has gone before, which, when blown upon by the wind of the Holy Spirit, produces something beautiful and new. This is true, godly, and productive theological creativity and doctrinal diversity.

This notion of theological creativity was made when we examined the contemporary and Emerging Church and its link with Hiebert's fourth "self"—that of self-theologising. It is also the hallmark of the history of the Lambeth Conference as we have seen the growth and development

---

210. Schaeffer, *Escape from Reason*, ch. 2.
211. Cited in Avis, *Christian Church*, 130.

of "new" provinces within Anglicanism bringing their own theological thinking to bear on the traditional teaching that was exported from the mother country during the colonial period and the times of great missionary expansion.

We have so far attempted to clarify what might be considered a distinctive Anglican orthopraxy, namely its ecclesiology. At the beginning of this section it was made plain that ecclesiology must be seen clearly as a matter of doctrine or orthodoxy. What Christians do reflects what they believe. Paul Avis reminded us of Hans Kung's phrase concerning ecclesiology that it is "the theological expression of the Church's image" and how it is "the branch of theology that seeks to give a scientific exposition of the faith of the Church concerning itself."[212]

In this chapter, therefore, we have metaphorically knocked on the front door of the Anglican Communion as it presents itself to the world through its ecclesiological forms and structures. When this door is opened we are able to discern, as Sykes reminds us, the theological and doctrinal content that undergird those structures, namely, its orthodoxy.[213] If Anglican ecclesiology is distinctive, as it has been shown to be, then the orthodoxy undergirding it must also be distinctive in its own way.

---

212. Avis, *Anglican Understanding of the Church*, 2.
213. Sykes, *Integrity of Anglicanism*, 46–49.

Movement Three: The Church as Anglican

Summary of Orthodoxy in the Third Movement

a) The minuet begins with a straightforward description of history and structure of the Anglican Communion with particular reference to the Instruments of Communion. Of these Instruments most time is given to the Lambeth Conference, whose resolutions carefully noted here show clearly that differences and division on doctrinal and moral issues have always been evident from its beginning. Of even greater significance is the fact that the Anglican Communion has literally changed its mind on major theological and moral issues over the years. Examples of these are polygamy, divorce and remarriage after divorce, contraception, the place of the Thirty-Nine Articles, and the ministry of women.

b) These major theological shifts have coincided with a demographic shift that has seen the numerical power base of the communion move from north to south with a particular emphasis on Africa. Beneath the surface of the current battle raging in the Anglican Communion there is evidence of underhand and ethically questionable ways in which conservatives are fighting to restrain and destroy any attempt to reinterpret the Scriptures and traditions of the Anglican Church to accommodate more contemporary views on what might be included within the boundaries of orthodox Anglicanism. These include a well-financed campaign to change the relationship that has hitherto always existed between the mainline denominations and the leadership of the African churches. Some of this undue influence is traced to the GAFCON leadership. Evidence has been shown that this malign influence has been felt in all levels on leadership in the Anglican Communion, not least to influence the Primates' Meeting and to compromise the independence of the powerful but poor African bishops, especially concerning their influence at the Lambeth Conference. This raises the question of how authentic is the African insistence for an orthodoxy that is in line with the ultra-conservative orthodoxy of evangelicalism in the United States and elsewhere.

c) Jesus committed his teaching to a community of living people whose focus is on a person—the Lord Jesus Christ. It is this focus that gives to this community alone the character of indefectibility through the power and presence of the Holy Spirit. Therefore the magisterium of the church precedes the gospel as the dynamic of mission. Testimony takes precedence over text. The church is a community with an institutionalised teaching office having the authority to create or recognise the development of doctrine. Those who claim that only Scripture can define doctrine have to deal with the argument over the priority of the magisterium—the arguments of modern scholarship that seem to undermine the infallibility and integrity of the Scriptures and the unpalatable fact that even those Christians with an ultra-conservative view of scriptural authority cannot agree on matters of doctrine or practice and continue to divide from each other. This dilemma is especially true within Anglicanism, where, even though it is one denomination, there is no central body that can claim to be authoritative.

d) It is easy to see why there is on the part of some a desperate cry for some central authority—but of what kind? The GAFCON view is that any authority needs to be coercive with sanctions against those who ignore or defy it. This, however, has never been the way the Anglican Communion has worked, and even in the early days of the reformation in the Church of England it never really worked, as we have already seen. Any teaching or opinion must be freely accepted rather than being forced.

e) The ecclesiology of the Anglican Communion may be said to reflect what it considers to be orthodox because what is practised as ecclesiology is as much a statement of doctrine as any other statement on issues such as grace, salvation, soteriology or sacrament. That is why what GAFCON has done in attempting to change the ecclesiological structure of Anglicanism, especially with their own primates' meeting being given such strong disciplinary powers, has huge doctrinal implications.

f) The authority of the Scriptures over the Thirty-Nine Articles is stressed here. They are not to be used as some sort of hermeneutical key for expounding the Scriptures and neither are they to be a test for orthodoxy. In fact, a case is made for their reformation or even their removal by some. Some Anglican provinces have relegated them to nothing more than endnotes in their prayer books.

g) Anglican comprehensiveness expresses the true humility that recognises that the Reformation truth of the freedom of the individual to search for truth guided by the Holy Spirit will inevitably require the toleration of difference or, at least, the acceptance that probability rather than certainty is all we can hope for this side of eternity. Such a view requires not only humility but charity towards those who hold differing views, together with courage to hold on to this position when criticised. The challenge is to diligently continue to seek after truth in the frustrating knowledge that it will always be partial and therefore our orthodoxies must, of necessity, always be partial and thus open to change.

h) Light from past orthodoxies behind us casts dark shadows before us. Light for the way ahead comes only from wrestling in the present with what we think we know in the context of contemporary living in eschatological hope.

4

Movement Four: The Church as Community
(Allegro Molto—Presto)

Quo Vadis Anglicanum?

Theme: The Sense of an Ending

THE FINAL MOVEMENT OF a symphony should be its culmination. In many ways the first three movements all predict the finale and the finale often starts with the quotation of the themes of the previous movements. It has become the role of the fourth movement to carry the weight of the whole symphony. The centre of gravity in the symphony has moved towards the end and, in doing so, is often fast or hurried, using the tempo descriptions of *allegro molto* (very fast) or *presto* (even faster), usually again in sonata or rondo form and stressing the urgency of that sense of an ending.

Professor Jeremy Begbie, in a lecture recorded at UC Berkley,[1] takes up the theme of a book by Frank Kermode, one of the most distinguished critics of English literature, entitled *The Sense of an Ending*. Kermode sees the notion of an ending as something that gives a story a unity and gathers the all the themes and chords together. The expected ending will show that all the chaos of events that have happened are, in fact, linked and all will be revealed at the end and thus sense will be made of it all.

Begbie sees the same as being true of music, at least in its Western tonic form. It is always moving towards an ending. It is in some form of permanent sonic future tense moving regularly from equilibrium through tension and into resolution. Its cadences lead the listener from home to

1. Begbie, "Sense of an Ending."

Movement Four: The Church as Community

away from home and then back home again creating a forward feel with a sense of incompleteness in the present. Music creates a dynamic desire or appetite for closure, a hunger for the "eschaton." This ending, however, is not just an exact repetition of where things began but rather it is better, greater, far beyond anything that could have been imagined at the beginning.

Scripture also has this musical movement from beginning to end. It recounts the equilibrium of Eden, which is then disturbed by tension but finds resolution through the coming of the prophets and ultimately in Jesus Christ. At its literary end the Bible speaks of an ending which it calls "a new heaven and a new earth,"[2] which will be a much better, richer, dynamic "home" than Eden could ever have been but which could only be achieved through the dramatic tensions and resolutions through which the whole spectrum of the drama of the Scriptures take us.

Begbie reminds us, however, that any sense of hope in an ending is suspect today. Postmodernism, with its denial of any metanarrative that can direct us to a destination or hope, is seen by many to have destroyed a sense of an ending or even a sense of continuity having broken the anchor chains that linked us to our origins, where we came from, and thus any link to where we are going.

In this context Begbie claims that we must say farewell to the confident modernist self, secure and self-assured, believing in its own ability to create some new world order that will bring confidence and security and put the world right as he alone knows how. For within the postmodernist paradigm this is anathema, an open door to the oppression through the many -isms that have arisen from this modernist approach. A catch phrase used is, "Great hopes often result in old hell." Like communism or socialism, even Christianity itself is not immune from this criticism with its history of the often violent oppression of slaves, women, Jews, heretics and other minorities and support of racism in some countries. The very word "resolution" sounds very like the "Final Solution" of the 1930s and 40s.

It is clear with the benefit of hindsight that the machinations of the Anglican Communion were to prove far too slow and not drastic enough to please the GAFCON ecclesiological revisionists. Sharing Begbie's "sense of an ending," in their frustration they seek, as did the Puritans in their own day, to bring about the final ἔσχατον by their own efforts. They see it as their mission to purify and purge the Communion of what they see as

---

2. Rev 21:1.

corruption before the "great and terrible day" arrives.³ We now examine what those machinations have been.

As befits a final symphonic movement, events in the Anglican Communion seem to have moved incredibly fast in the last four decades. We have already seen that the Anglican Communion came under great tension with the ordination of women to the priesthood and then, as hoped for by some and feared by others, they became bishops. What has been the straw that broke the camel's back has been the unilateral action taken in some provinces to try and include in a more full and active way gay and lesbian people. Attempts have been made to create and use liturgies celebrating the union of same-sex couples but, of course, the precipitating factor was the consecration of an openly gay partnered bishop for the diocese of New Hampshire in the Episcopal Church of the United States. This has caused a furore and conservative backlash that has resulted in the current great divisions within the Anglican Communion.

The problem is that, as we have already seen in the section on Anglican Authority, the Anglican Communion has no form of centralised, papal-like authority structure enabling it to exercise sanctions as a disciplinary measure within its international communion. The Communion has done what it always seems to do in these difficult situations and has set commissions in place to produce reports for Communion-wide study and response. These, it is hoped, will encourage "building structures within which the 'bonds of affection' may be able to flourish."⁴

International Anglicanism has always tried to carefully steer its way between being simply a colonial anachronism reflecting the culture of the United Kingdom as well as the more strict theological confessionalism that has been the pattern of the other European churches that were the fruit of the Reformation. Instead it has tended, in general up to the present, to focus simply on the statements in the Chicago-Lambeth Quadrilateral, which centres on the Scriptures, the historic creeds, the sacraments of baptism and Eucharist, and the historic episcopate.⁵ Anglicanism was never devised as a system created to be defined only by what it was against but rather as one that embraced whole-heartedly those things that had been agreed by the universal church. As it became more and more international, a form of bonding around common purpose within the

---

3. I am reminded of these words of Oliver Cromwell as he addressed the Barebones Parliament in July 1653: "You are as like the forming of God as ever people were . . . you are at the edge of promises and prophecies." Cited in Fraser, *Cromwell*, ch. 16.

4. Groves, "Model for Partnership," 10.

5. Lambeth Commission on Communion, *Windsor Report*, 73.

communion was created, which was to come to be known as "the bonds of affection."⁶

Problems arose for the Communion prior to the 1978 Lambeth Conference. The provinces of Hong Kong, Canada, the United States, and New Zealand had gone ahead and actually ordained women to the priesthood unilaterally. There were also another eight provinces that appeared to be on the brink of doing so, having agreed that theologically there was no bar to women's ordination. It was inevitable that this would cause tension at that conference. There was an attempt to persuade the conference to accept the then-novel idea of having two integrities accepted within the one church: those who accepted women's ordination and those who opposed it.

"(Bishop Bowles) asked the conference to make a commitment to ongoing unity 'without rancour, discrimination or excommunication.' He also saw the need to repair and maintain good relationships with the Roman Catholic Church and the Orthodox. His argument referred back to New Testament diversity linked with a very humble confession that the Anglican Communion was on a steep learning curve."

Groves also notes that ". . . even the respected Professor John Macquarrie, speaking at a side meeting at Lambeth 1978, argued for a 'hierarchy of truths' where central doctrines required common assent, and where peripheral issues existed in a grey area. He argued against the notion that '. . . the ordination of women priests in a Church is a sufficient ground for people to leave that Church and set up a schismatic body.'"⁷

It was the astute chairmanship of the Archbishop of Canterbury, Donald Coggan, that redirected the conference towards what was the crux of the problem, namely, the nature of authority in the Communion. Groves sees this refocussing as the driving force for setting the direction of the recently created Doctrine Commission.⁸

Ten years later at Lambeth 1988 the following resolution was passed.

"That the new Inter-Anglican Theological and Doctrinal Commission (or a specially appointed inter-Anglican commission) be asked to undertake as a matter of urgency a further exploration of the meaning and nature of communion; with particular reference to the doctrine of the Trinity, the unity and order of the Church, and the unity and community of humanity."⁹

---

6. Bayne, *Anglican Turning Point*, 10.
7. Groves, "Model for Partnership," 113.
8. Ibid.
9. *Truth Shall Make You Free*, 216.

Beating the Bounds

Variation One: The Virginia Report

The Virginia Report was produced in 1998 under the chairmanship of Archbishop Eames. It began with a reminder that, in John's Gospel, the Lord Jesus Christ prayed for his disciples to be at one as a reflection of the unity between the Father and Son within the Trinity and as a means of bearing a clear witness to the gospel in the world.[10]

Recognising the difficulty of such a calling and that the biblical record shows that the people of God have never found that perfect unity throughout their history,[11] the report goes on to suggest that some factors that have brought about the differences of opinion within the Communion concerning the contemporary troubles relate directly to "... our particular cultural context, our way of interpreting the Bible, our degree of awareness of being part of a wider human community, and our attentiveness to the response of other ecumenical partners and to the concerns of those of other faiths."[12]

The first chapter ends by setting a number of questions that the commission felt needed to be answered urgently in the light of the disarray of the Communion.

> When Christians find themselves passionately engaged in the midst of complex and explosive situations, how do they avoid alienation from those who by Baptism are their brothers and sisters in Christ, who are embraced in the communion of God the Holy Trinity, but who disagree? How do they stay in communion with God and each other; how do they behave towards each other in the face of disagreement and conflict? What are the limits of diversity if the Gospel imperative of unity and communion are to be maintained?[13]

Groves points out something very significant in chapter 2 of *The Virginia Report*. It is here that the first expression of the idea of relationships within the Communion based on a covenant is put forward. The Old

---

10. "My prayer is not for them alone. I pray also for those who will believe in me through their message, that all of them may be one, Father, just as you are in me and I am in you. May they also be in us so that the world may believe that you have sent me. I have given them the glory that you gave me, that they may be one as we are one: I in them and you in me. May they be brought to complete unity to let the world know that you sent me and have loved them even as you have loved me" (John 17:20–23).

11. Anglican Consultative Council, *Virginia Report*, 1.2.

12. Ibid., 1.5.

13. Ibid., 1.8.

Testament covenants of creation, post-flood, and Mosaic are referred to with the relational aspect of God, with naming himself to his people as "I AM" seen as particularly important.

Thus, the Commission did not see the significant covenant relationship in the law, but in "God's sacred relationship with his chosen people," articulated in Deuteronomy 7:6–8a. They saw the notion of being a chosen people in a relationship as vital.[14]

This emphasis on covenantal relationships was further developed by the prophets with the encouraging promises of restoration after times of great difficulty. "God's gracious gift of steadfast loving kindness was from the beginning known by the people of God in the form of covenant. From the prophets came the conviction that God's faithfulness was never-ending even when God's people were forgetful and betrayed the divine trust."[15]

Chapter 3 of *The Virginia Report*, "Belonging Together in the Anglican Communion," contains a simple reminder of what has come to be known as the "Anglican Way." That is the distinctive Anglican method we have already mentioned earlier of discerning God's will and purpose, or what might be called the mind of Christ, through the acceptance of the authority of Scripture read in the light of tradition and reason.[16]

This chapter also grasps the nettle of what it calls "the creative tension of provincial autonomy and independence."[17] Most significantly it raises the probable need for what is to some members of the Communion a threat and to others a reform that is a long time overdue: an international decision-making body that has some authority, even if it has only a moral authority.

> The life of the Communion is held together in the creative tension of Provincial autonomy and interdependence. There are some signs that the Provinces are coming to a greater realisation that they need each other's spiritual, intellectual and material resources in order to fulfil their task of mission. Each Province has something distinctive to offer the others, and needs them in turn to be able to witness to Christ effectively in its own context. Questions are asked about whether we can go on as a world Communion with morally authoritative, but not juridically binding, decision-making structures at the international level.... At the end of the decade one question for Anglicans is

---

14. Groves, "Model for Partnership," 123
15. Anglican Consultative Council, *Virginia Report*, 2.1.
16. "Anglican Way."
17. Anglican Consultative Council, *Virginia Report*, 3.28.

whether their bonds of interdependence are strong enough to hold them together embracing tension and conflict while answers are sought to seemingly intractable problems.[18]

One of the most significant innovations of this report, as noted by Groves, is the introduction of the principle of subsidiarity. No knowledge of the provenance of the theory of subsidiarity is shown, but the report quotes the Oxford English Dictionary definition: "Subsidiarity—a central authority should have a subsidiarity function, performing only those tasks which cannot be performed effectively at a more immediate or local level."[19]

The Virginia Report takes the subsidiarity theory on board almost without question.

> The Holy Catholic Church is fully present in each of its local embodiments. Decisions about the life and mission of the Church should be made in that place and need only be referred to wider councils if the matter threatens the unity and the faithfulness of teaching or practice of the Church catholic, or where the local church encounters genuinely new circumstances and wishes advice about how to respond.[20]

Groves notes, however, that a subsequent paragraph overturns the call for subsidiarity by yet another argument for a centralised authority system. "Is not universal authority a necessary corollary of universal communion?"[21]

There was, of course, no such "universal authority" in the Anglican Communion when the Episcopal Church in the United States proposed to consecrate Gene Robinson, an openly gay partnered man, as bishop of New Hampshire. This provoked an emergency Primates' Meeting, which produced the following statement.

> If this consecration proceeds, we recognise that we have reached a crucial and critical point in the life of the Anglican Communion and we have had to conclude that the future of the Communion itself will be put in jeopardy. In this case, the ministry of this one bishop will not be recognised by most of the Anglican world, and many provinces are likely to consider themselves to be out of Communion with the Episcopal Church (USA). This

18. Ibid.
19. Ibid., 4.8, quoting the *Oxford English Dictionary*.
20. Ibid., 5.17.
21. Ibid., 5.20.

will tear the fabric of our Communion at its deepest level, and may lead to further division on this and further issues as provinces have to decide in consequence whether they can remain in communion with provinces that choose not to break communion with the Episcopal Church (USA).[22]

This meant that another commission was required, this time to think deeply about what it means to have broken or impaired communion. Archbishop Eames was again asked to chair it.

Variation Two: The Windsor Report

This second report, known as *The Windsor Report*, moved on from *The Virginia Report* in that it made a clear and direct call for an Anglican covenant.[23] The report did not directly address the issues that had caused the tension and difficulty with the Communion. Instead it focussed on the life and relationships within the Communion in the face of real division.

Echoing the structural form of *The Virginia Report*, this report shares its view of the value of the principle of subsidiarity but goes further by including the notion of *adiaphora*, which was seen as by some Anglican theologians as an innovation foreign to traditional Anglicanism. In reality, however, as Groves points out, ". . . when the concept of *adiaphora* is combined with subsidiarity and authority this understanding is reversed. The report states that essential items need to be decided at a higher level and the decisions need authority."[24]

We have already seen clearly that any ideas of authority within Anglicanism were never formalised with concepts of different distinct levels. Indeed Anglicanism has always stressed the right, privilege, and indeed the responsibility of believers to read the Scriptures for themselves and to take personal responsibility for their own faith and belief. We already met this emphasis in the chapter on Anglican distinctives where Stephen Sykes reminded us that ". . . the centre core . . . is found in the laity, whose open access to and increasing knowledge of the Scriptures enables them to examine critically the preaching and teaching of their clergy. This is of the essence of the baptismal inheritance of every member of the Church, who together are corporately a royal priesthood."[25]

22. "Statement by the Primates."
23. Lambeth Commission on Communion, *Windsor Report*, 62–64.
24. Groves, "Model for Partnership," 137.
25. Sykes, *Authority in the Church of England*, 198.

Beating the Bounds

The Windsor Report also recommended that the Primates' Meeting should have "enhanced responsibility" and become the "Primates' Conference—the Lambeth Standing Committee." Another recommendation was that the Archbishop of Canterbury should have an authoritative role supported by a "Council of Advice." The report also recommended the adoption of an Anglican covenant. The covenant would, they argued, "Make explicit and forceful the loyalty and bonds of affection which govern the relationships between the churches of the Communion. The covenant could deal with: the acknowledgement of common identity; the relationships of communion; the commitments of communion; the exercise of autonomy in communion; and the management of communion affairs (including disputes)."[26] All this promoted the push for the adoption of a covenant.

Groves maintains that a ". . . consequence of *The Windsor Report* was the forming of a 'Panel of Reference'" to settle disputes "that were deemed to require a 'higher' authority to solve disputes that were intense and impossible to resolve at the local level." This initiative failed because its authority was not recognised, and those who deemed themselves the ones who lost out through its decisions simply went over their heads to appeal to another authority, even secular ones. It was disbanded in 2008.[27]

Variation Three: The Anglican Covenant

Clearly following from *The Virginia* and *Windsor Reports*, the Anglican covenant first appeared in the Nassau Draft form in 2007. It was followed in 2008 by the St. Andrew's Draft, and that was followed by the Ridley Cambridge Draft in 2009. Each of these drafts in turn was circulated around the Communion for discussion and comment.

The part of the final draft that proved to be the most contentious was section 4. This had been preceded by three sections that had outlined various ways in which the Communion should and could act together as autonomous churches seeking to bear common witness to their life in Christ. This included ". . . seeking a shared mind though engagement with the Instruments and Commissions of the Communion, acting with care and caution and, in situations of conflict, to participate in mediated conversations."[28]

26. Lambeth Commission on Communion, *Windsor Report*, 118.
27. Groves, "Model for Partnership," 139.
28. Ibid., 146.

Archbishop Jeffrey Driver of Adelaide makes it clear about what he feels is needed here. "It was clear that any covenant would need to be morally persuasive rather than coercive, advisory rather than punitive, and aspirational rather than juridical. What was recognised was a need for a clear and agreed process of conflict resolution between autonomous churches based on mutual self-limiting rather than ceding of autonomy."[29]

The vital question has to be about the procedures that need to be followed when all other avenues fail to bring agreement. This is what section 4 is meant to deal with. The relevant sections of the covenant outline that the following action should then be taken.

> (4.2.1) The Joint Standing Committee of the Anglican Consultative Council and of the Primates' Meeting, or any body that succeeds it, shall have the duty of overseeing the functioning of the Covenant in the life of the Anglican Communion. The Joint Standing Committee may nominate or appoint another committee or commission to assist in carrying out this function and to advise it on questions relating to the Covenant.
>
> (4.2.2) If a question relating to the meaning of the Covenant, or of compatibility to the principles incorporated in it, should arise, the Joint Standing Committee may make a request to any covenanting Church to defer action until the processes set out below have been completed. It shall further take advice from such bodies as it feels appropriate on the nature and relational consequences of the matter and may make a recommendation to be referred for advice to both the Anglican Consultative Council and the Primates' Meeting.
>
> (4.2.3) If a Church refuses to defer a controversial action, the Joint Standing Committee may recommend to any Instrument of Communion relational consequences which specify a provisional limitation of participation in, or suspension from, that Instrument until the completion of the process set out below.

The draft covenant kept to the idea of the necessity of a centralised response to conflict, in line with the implications of subsidiarity and, in doing so, it provoked a very prophetically worded but negative-leaning summary in 2009 by Groves. "It has been shown that the principle of subsidiarity has no biblical basis, is not argued for theologically, has not been tested within the Christian tradition, and has not had universal consent in the secular world, but it is the driving force for section 4."[30] As such,

---

29. Driver, "Towards an Anglican Future."
30. Groves, "Model for Partnership," 148.

section 4 of the covenant is unlikely to be a sufficient bonding material to cement relationships within the Anglican Communion. The lack of consensus indicates that there are potential problems ahead for the widespread adoption of the covenant as it presently stands.

The various provinces of the Anglican Communion were not asked for a quick response to the draft proposals. They were, however, asked to indicate their inclinations for or against adopting the covenant by November 2012. Anglican polity being what it is, the process is inevitably going to slow and, as already been indicated, there have been some major negative responses so far. In the Church of England, for example, despite the positive encouragement of the Archbishop of Canterbury, Rowan Williams, it has been found impossible for the proposal to secure the support of the twenty-two dioceses needed for the measure to be debated in General Synod. The covenant cannot now be discussed in the life of the current quinquennium, which ends in 2015. This, of course, creates a very difficult situation for the Archbishop of Canterbury, who leads a Communion where discussions still continue about the status of the covenant while his own church has rejected it.[31]

For some observers the actual results of the discussions around the world are of little importance because, for them, the whole exercise of producing a covenant is seen as futile. Bruce Kaye, for example, has written extensively and carefully in order to support his view that the covenant is a bad idea for Anglicans. Kaye gives four reasons for his view:

1. It is against the grain of Anglican ecclesiology (what we think the church is)

2. It is an inadequate response to the conflict in the Anglican Communion

3. In practical terms it will create immense and complicating confusion about institutional relationships and financial obligations.

4. It does not address the key fundamental issue in this conflict, how to act in a particular context which is relevant to that context and also faithful to the gospel.[32]

When Kaye speaks of "Anglican ecclesiology" he recognises that, even though certain patterns of practices are found throughout the Anglican tradition, not all Anglicans give the same significance to each particular. An example he gives is the almost universal practice of having a "threefold

---

31. *The Church of England Newspaper*, March 30, 2012, p. 1.
32. Kaye, "Covenant Is Not a Good Idea for Anglicans."

order of ministry disciplined in some way by an ecclesial judicature."[33] Over time these traditions or practices have become fixed into institutional forms that often clash with developments in theological thinking. Kaye sees this as a key feature of many of the present disputes within the Anglican Communion.

Although there have been changes in institutional arrangement over history, for example the re-emergence of synodical government in the nineteenth century, the present covenant proposal "to entrench a form of judicature for inter-provincial relations" is, according to Kaye, "... novel in that it is applied to inter-provincial relations. This means that there is little precedent to refer to and not much readily available theological argument to call upon in evaluating it."

Kaye sees it as vitally important that "any proposed arrangements must satisfy the general foundational qualities of the life of any Christian church," and that means that they must be seen to "facilitate or encourage the pre-eminence of love in relations in the church."

When it comes to the case of Anglican Church more specifically, Kaye argues that "... institutional innovations or reforms need to be able to show some reasonable continuity with the historic practices in that tradition and have arguments that might support the proposed innovation." For Kaye the covenant as proposed reflects far more than it should of "... the current of external cultural notions of authority and power and has led Anglicans to lose focus on the essential elements of their ecclesiological traditions and its underlying values."[34]

The covenant will, therefore, have the potential to support and encourage the clear intentions manifestly expressed by GAFCON and its protégé, the Fellowship of Confessing Anglicans, to control the perceived deviations of others by the exercise of juridical discipline. Thus the covenant will, as Kaye argues,

> ... multiply the institutional expressions of differences between provinces. There are many and various differences between provinces at the moment, to say nothing of those within provinces. There is nothing essentially wrong with that. Indeed it is to be expected as provinces seek to be faithful in their own context to their Anglican tradition of faith. The covenant has the potential to bring some of those differences into institutional

33. Ibid.
34. Ibid.

expression and in so doing re-shape the dynamics of relations between those provinces.

Kaye reminds us that Anglican history is littered with issues that many people felt were "gospel issues" at the time but which have now passed into history without the breaking of communion fellowship that seemed to be so imminent at the time.

We have already seen in this book how conflict is endemic in Christianity. Often these disagreements are resolved through agreement but, even when agreement is not possible, resolution comes through a commitment to live together in love within the shared framework of their tradition. Kaye reminds us that even Saint Paul, when dealing with division at Corinth, did not demand agreement but rather ". . . accentuated the divisions by naming the differences as of divine origin. They were gifts. He offered the model of a body as a way think about difference and coherence."

Instead they were to choose that more excellent way that was even greater than faith or hope: the way of love.

> Jesus said that it was more worthy to invite into your home those who would not invite you back, that is to say, those with whom you did not have a continuing close social relationship. Rather hospitality was to be open-ended and driven by open ended love. Love is the gospel dynamic that enables Christians to live positively and creatively and openly with those from whom we differ and with whom we are in conflict.[35]

Such a vocation to love is all but suffocated in the rush to juridically deal with conflict and difference rather than helping Anglicans to live with their differences and resolve them. Groups like GAFCON and the Fellowship of Confessing Anglicans see themselves as judge and jury over the rest of Anglicanism and, in so doing, institutionalise the conflict in exactly the same way as Kaye believes the covenant will.

It was deeply ironic that, while the Church of England's General Synod was in the process of giving the Anglican Covenant a free pass in its first step toward acceptance by the Archbishop of Canterbury's own church, the Church of England, GAFCON, an alliance presumed to be the greatest beneficiary of the covenant, was dismissing the pact as inadequate. The Oxford Statement of the GAFCON Primates' Council in November 2010 said that the GAFCON primates had decided that, ". . . while we acknowledge that the efforts to heal our brokenness through

---

35. Ibid.

the introduction of an Anglican Covenant were well intentioned we have come to the conclusion the current text is fatally flawed and so support for this initiative is no longer appropriate."[36]

In fact irony is not the real feature here. What we see here is pure power play. This statement makes great claim ". . . to link with those who not only form the majority of Anglicans in the world, but also those who affirm Biblical theological foundations of what Anglicans have always believed and practised can provide concrete relationships and meaningful partnerships that are of more substance than the structures that have shown themselves to be flawed or compromised."[37]

These claims from GAFCON are questioned in an incisive article, "Constructing the Boundaries of Anglican Orthodoxy: An Analysis of the Global Anglican Future Conference (GAFCON)." These writers make it clear that a very selective process was involved in the issuing of invitations to GAFCON in order to produce an appearance of unity. This meant that even some clearly conservative evangelical leaders who could not be trusted to toe a party line were not invited.

> However, the lack of clarity about who was invited to GAFCON . . . contributed to charges that a select group of people was claiming the right to define what constitutes Anglican orthodoxy. The mystery around the invitation process served to fuel perceptions that organisers only issued invitations to those "orthodox" Anglicans who they felt were inclined to agree with their vision for GAFCON, intentionally excluding conservative voices that would potentially disrupt the image of movement unity. For example, one evangelical Church of England bishop who was not invited to GAFCON explained his exclusion as follows:
>
> "I think there's a real issue that, when they gathered in Jerusalem, they invited who they wanted to invite and that made it very easy for them then to produce a fairly unanimous statement because if you invite people who are going to agree with you, you can easily appear united to the world . . . But had the invitation been wider, I suspect . . . the statements at the end might have been a bit different."[38]

---

36. GAFCON, "Oxford Statement," para. 5.
37. Ibid., Introduction, para. 3.
38. Sadgrove et al., "Constructing the Boundaries."

There was clearly some nervousness about what delegates might be tempted to say to the press if questioned and so strict instructions were given to lay delegates about not speaking with the press or researchers.

> Although bishops and other leaders were prepared to give statements to journalists, most delegates became reluctant to speak to outsiders after the first days of the event. When this was broached with various Church of England delegates, they replied that they had been told very clearly and repeatedly not to speak to the media, researchers, or other outsiders. Several delegates who had agreed to be interviewed at the beginning of the week refused once GAFCON organisers had made their position on contact with outsiders clear.[39]

The researchers for this article conclude that there is little evidence that any unity of purpose or acceptance of a leadership from the Global South among FCA members would continue once the battle concerning homosexuality finds some resolve and fades into history. They see it as being doubtful

> ... whether the FCA can prove attractive to a wider range of self-identified conservative or orthodox Anglicans who did not participate at (or were not invited to) GAFCON and who have not subscribed to the Jerusalem Declaration, or whether the FCA's tight boundary structure will preclude a broader participation from some parts of the Communion. For example, although a number of Anglo-Catholics in North America have found affinities with the GAFCON movement, English participation in GAFCON/FCA has primarily been by those with evangelical orientations, with many English Anglo-Catholics remaining notably sceptical of the grouping and its version of orthodoxy.[40]

It is probably true to say that the GAFCON/FCA primates have a particular brand of Anglicanism that actually gives them their raison d'être and which, therefore, they will continue to proclaim as the only way for Anglicanism to go. As Sadgrove and her colleagues suggest, "... the movement's goal, however, is clearly not to be *ecclesiola in ecclesia* (a church within a church), but rather to have its particular orthodox vision become the standard for Anglicanism itself."[41]

---

39. Ibid., 197–98.
40. Ibid., 204–5.
41. Ibid., 205.

The really big question to which we have no answer at the moment is what the results of a GAFCON/FCA success would be or what would happen to the GAFCON/FCA grouping if the covenant was adopted by the majority of the Anglican Communion.

A GAFCON success would alienate many less strident conservatives and vast numbers of more liberal Anglicans who would have to reconsider where they would find their spiritual home and with whom they could relate in fellowship.

A GAFCON failure would, no doubt, increase the martyr complex and that sense of being a faithful remnant that must hold on to the very end. There would certainly be an exodus from the existing Communion but it is highly unlikely that some of the tenuous strands that hold the members of the FCA together at the moment would stand the test of time. Many within this grouping come from very different contexts with different priorities and differing senses of Anglican identity. If and when the final break came it is highly likely that some would not be prepared to jettison their sense of belonging and Anglican heritage for the unknowns of a rigid GAFCON/FCA "police state" structure.

Neville Hoad argues that the really deep underlying problem expressed in the current crisis within the Communion is a clear power struggle about who it is who actually speaks for and represents the "Anglican universal." Is it Africans or Europeans? Is it Global North or Global South? Is it liberals or conservatives? His rather depressing conclusion is that the end result could be a proliferation of differing and distinct "Anglicanisms," each claiming to be true to a universal heritage of orthodoxy.[42] As Jeffrey Driver says, declarations of that nature would probably be ". . . little more than the very tedious debates of churches talking to themselves about their own survival . . . a sad conversation on the way to a funeral."[43]

A Counter-Melody: Anticipated Eschatology

Usually the main themes and variations in a classical composition like a symphony are what the ear naturally attunes to. However, often the composer writes another melodic line that is played at the same time as the main themes but is often understated and easily missed or taken for granted. Such a counter-melody is found in some of the documents we have already discussed here and in earlier sections.

42. Hoad, *African Intimacies*, 65.
43. Driver, "Towards an Anglican Future."

Stephen Pickard, the acting chairperson of the third Inter-Anglican Theological and Doctrinal Commission (IATDC), which met in Kuala Lumpur and produced a report entitled *Communion, Conflict and Hope* in 2008, believes that the report "offers an alternative tradition of construing orthodoxy and its dynamic compared to the Virginia and Windsor Covenant." His view is that that the tension concerning the orthodoxy issue ". . . is not simply between conservative and liberal but that there is a third voice or tune being played which is more illusive and nuanced and for this reason fragile and easily smothered."[44]

This notion of an unrecognised or ignored theme is found in a paper published by Scott MacDougall in which he contrasts *The Windsor Report* in which the idea of an Anglican Covenant was first raised, with the IATDC Kuala Lumpur report. He criticises the usual questions raised in discussions about the proposed covenant. Rather than asking whether or not the covenant is "confessional, contractual, conservative, centralising or punitive," it is more important to affirm what kind of relationships are the appropriate ones for member churches of the Anglican Communion. Then the covenant should be examined in the light of that response as to whether or not it would encourage or hinder such relationships.

MacDougall emphasises what he calls "anticipated eschatology," seeing the ultimate eschatological fulfillment of God's purposes including the bringing to perfection of failed relationships. MacDougall has a different perspective on that "sense of an ending" taken at the beginning of this chapter by Professor Jeremy Begbie. The church, he says, has a calling to be the image of that reality in the world in its relationships as individuals and as churches. He suggests five characteristics of an "anticipated eschatology" approach.

The first is a sense of "dynamic tension" between the now and the not-yet in our communal life. God's work in the church is an ongoing story and there can be no claims to present perfection. On the contrary, what is required is a humble acknowledgement of the limited knowledge we now have and the transient nature of our understanding.

Secondly, such an approach makes it necessary to be always open to the possibility that the Holy Spirit may be teaching the church something new and inevitably challenging to the status quo.

The third follows naturally from the second: namely, the requirement laid upon the church to accept the risk that healthy development might well undermine our present understanding of what is orthodox or truly "gospel."

---

44. Comments made in a personal email to the author, March 11, 2012.

Movement Four: The Church as Community

Fourthly, it requires trust in the best intentions of other Christians. As we saw in Movement One, many of those denounced as heretics in the early church were often certainly not satanic agents determined to undermine a pure church but were, rather, sincere Christians honestly seeking the truth and ways to explain the mysteries of God in fresh ways. That they failed in their explanations or that their understanding was flawed does not take away the good intentions of their hearts. Trust is also required in God himself to bring about all that he has promised to his church.

The fifth characteristic has to be the realities of hope and joy that such a trust produces, which enables Christians of differing understandings to work together in the expectation of God's fulfillment of his mission and purpose for his people.

MacDougall is clearly not in favour of the Anglican covenant approach. For him it lacks any sense of "anticipated eschatology" and is, therefore, not consistent with a truly Anglican understanding of the church. It would, in reality, he believes, inhibit the maintenance of the "bonds of affection" that have held the Anglican Communion together until now. Like Hardy, who we have already seen believed that these relational concepts are too often and too easily submerged in a time of crisis, our current tensions should not mean that the Anglican Communion should turn its back on those ideals by seeking a false unity through some form of "containment," but instead efforts should be made to strengthen them all the more. This is neither the time nor the place for the introduction of any quasi-judicial processes. [45]

---

45. MacDougall, "Covenant Conundrum," 17.

Summary of Orthodoxy in the Fourth Movement

a) Orthodoxy is a matter of heart and mind and will not be brought about by attempting to bring about some form of "realised eschatology" by human effort and brute force of discipline. The perfection and purity of the people of God will only be realised at the eschaton.

b) Responses to the covenant reflect in large measure from two very different visions of what the purpose of the covenant should be. While the *koinonia* between the Anglican provinces is seen as important, the very nature and purpose of the Anglican Communion is seen different ways.

c) The *confessional* view requires agreement about the fundamentals of Christian faith and life, believing that communion grows from and expresses a shared faith and form of life; in other words, conformity to an agreed definition of orthodoxy.

d) The *pluralist* view sees the communion growing from and expressing itself through its common forms of worship and service. Such a view is happy to subsist in a situation of quite different expressions of belief and moral practice. Common worship, hospitality, mutual aid, and partnership in mission are what produces communion. Confessional orthodoxy is not required.

e) *The Windsor Report* used the teaching of Ephesians and First Corinthians, which see the *koinonia* of Christians within the body of Christ as an expression of the life of the Trinity and as an aspect of God's aim to unite all things in heaven and earth in his Son.

f) While seeking to balance both the confessional and pluralist views, the covenant stresses the need for each church to put the needs of the global fellowship before its own. The problem still remains, however, of how to decide whether or not an action on the part of an individual province that offends some is not, in the end, something that is in fact for the good of all. This is, after all, precisely what TEC argues concerning the consecration of Gene Robinson. Although it is a scandal to some, to them, it is seen to be, in the long run, for the good of all.

g) One way to resolve these issues of orthodoxy is to engage in a type of conciliarism that operates through the practice of mutual subjection within the body of Christ. Forbearance and restraint

Movement Four: The Church as Community

(rather than juridical structure) provide time for actively seeking a common understanding of Holy Scripture—one that issues from testing by the historic episcopate, the Instruments of Unity, and the synodical and common life of the church.

h) Pluralists reject the idea of mutual subjection that is called for when unrest threatens the unity of the church. Instead they call for tolerance of differences of understanding of orthodoxy rather than forbearance and restraint for people who hold different views. This, they argue, becomes the real strength that sustains and enriches communion in times of stress.

i) Confessionalists object that some versions of Christian belief and practice distort the testimony of the church so much that tolerance, rather than protecting communion, eats away at its foundations. Only fixed forms such as liturgies and catechisms can maintain orthodoxy. However, the Anglican Communion has no agreed framework for liturgical revision.

j) Often truth and unity are seen as competing virtues. Those who emphasise one accuse the advocates of the other of betraying the heart of Christian belief, life, and witness.

k) History teaches us that divisions concerning orthodoxy, seemingly about things seen in the past as "gospel issues," have slipped into the mists of history without the catastrophic breakdown of communion that seemed to be so inevitable at the time.

l) Conflict is endemic in Christianity. Often these disagreements are resolved through agreement, but even when agreement is not possible resolution comes through a commitment to live together in love within that part of the framework of their tradition they do share.

m) The two reports and the covenant have not humbly grasped the necessity and true value of an "anticipated" eschatological approach, which would enable true unity in diversity and which was foreshadowed in *Communion, Conflict and Hope*, but of which they failed to take note.

5

Coda Finale

Conclusions

The Jazz Theology Approach

HAVING COMPLETED THE FINAL movement of the symphony, what is patently obvious is that the symphonic form, while it has been a useful tool for analysing and systematising the material used here to aid thinking about orthodoxy, is not able to bring us to real conclusions. It can make statements based on historic events and the history of theological and ecclesiological thought, but there is clearly something else at work here that defies the classical music framework.

Carl F. Ellis says,

> Like classical music, the classical approach to theology comprises the formal methods of arranging what we know about God and his world into a reasoned, cogent and consistent system. Classical theology interacts in the critical dialogue with the philosophies of the world. It investigates the attributes of God and communicates primarily through a written tradition.
>
> ... We are forever indebted to those who have codified and systematized the substance of our faith. Classical theology has done much to build our faith by helping us to see that there are good reasons and not just reasons that sound good for our faith. Classical theology and classical music reflect God's oneness. The unity of God's purpose and providence is reflected in the consistent explanations and consonant harmonies of classical music

and classical theology. The genius of classical theology is in the theology as it was formulated.[1]

Yet, as already indicated, if theological orthodoxy is nothing more than propositions and proposals and cerebral reasoning then something deep and significant is missing. Classical theology is vitally important but it is incomplete.

It is at this point, therefore, while maintaining the musical structure, that it is necessary to move away from the classical form to the jazz form. Jazz can be very difficult to define but Travis Jackson has proposed a broad definition of jazz as music that includes qualities such as swinging, improvising, group interaction, developing an individual voice, and being open to different musical possibilities.[2]

Classical music is formal music performed from written scores with the aim of a perfect reproduction of what the composer was hearing in his head as he wrote down the notes. The skill of the musician is seen in his or her ability to reproduce the original exactly. *Jazz music, on the other hand, is best described as d*ynamic music that can never be reproduced exactly the same way because at its heart is the musician's skill or ability to improvise.

Carl Ellis describes this difference as it can be applied to theology:

> Theology bears analogy with music in that it too can be approached as formal or dynamic. Classical theology is concerned with propositions while Jazz theology is concerned with what happens when those propositions interact with pain, life and the moment . . . *God in the moment . . . God moments: Theomoments.*
> . . . Jazz theology invites us to participate in the propositions. To enter in to the Biblical story and know the truth so that the truth can set us free. . . . Jazz theology is a participation in the basic patterns revealed in biblical life situations. It inquires not only what God did and said but how he said and did it. Further more, it expects him to do it again in a similar way in our lives.

When examined closely, jazz as a musical form seems to exist simply to deliberately break the accepted rules of classical musical form. The way jazz musicians do this is often very creative and, to jazz lovers, very attractive. It has the deliberate aim of encouraging that which does not obviously fit in to the accepted forms and in a revolutionary way raising questions about the way things are.

1. Ellis, *Free At Last?*, 38.
2. Elsdon, Review of *The Cambridge Companion to Jazz*.

Beating the Bounds

Wesley White describes it as "... an expression ... of that imaginative ability which allows human beings to protest the given, encouraging alternative ways of responding to dominant ideology. Jazz, it might be said, is playful protest music, and breaking at least some of the musical rules is its mode."[3]

Breaking the rules, of course, is not the usual form of behaviour expected of biblically orientated individuals. Yet White reminds us that the Bible is full of stories of individuals not keeping the accepted rules, and these transgressions end in a good result to the glory of God and the benefit of the people. From the Old Testament through to the New Testament, examples are quoted with the climax surely being that of Jesus himself who broke, for example, the accepted Sabbath day traditions among others.

George Steiner argues that

> The status of the future of the verb is at the core of existence. . . . It shapes the image we carry of the meaning of life and of our personal place in that meaning. . . . It essentially reflects an instinctual but nonetheless deliberate disregard for the givenness of the present that allows tomorrow to be imagined. In the course of re-imaging the future, the human community can entertain the possibility of change, but it requires a range of language that concedes the place of disparaging words when referring to existence that is narrowly defined by the present.[4]

Jazz embraces harmonic clashes and dissonance because, as Craig Werner suggests, "... jazz transforms noise into music, challenges us to *hear* the music in the noise, open our ears, our minds, our lives to things we hadn't thought about."[5]

Jazz somehow, by breaking the rules of a fixed order that exists only to impose limits rather than allow freedom, enables us to reach forward to a future that has long been hoped for. The heart of jazz is the skill of improvisation. Improvisation is instant composition, the instant creation of a new melody. It could be compared to the difference between the forms of liturgical and extempore prayer.

> When the improvised melody is not related to another song it is called **free** improvisation. In jazz the improvisation is most usually related to a previously written melody. In most cases the improvisation follows the chord progression of that song. In the

---

3. White, "Jazz and the Mode of Hopeful Transgression."
4. Steiner, *After Babel*, 202.
5. Werner, *Change Is Gonna Come*, 133.

early days of jazz, improvisation was a skill purely guided by the ear. Although this approach is still used by some, most jazz players now use their knowledge of chords, chord progressions and chord-scale relationships as the basis of their improvisation.[6]

In the end, the deeper the musical knowledge and skills acquired, the more expanded become the musician's creative and imaginative horizons.

In jazz, familiarity with the works of other musicians, knowledge of musical theory, and constant experimentation on an instrument will define the musical context in which free expression becomes valuable and enriching to both player and listener. Listening to many different musicians, analyzing what is heard, and practicing as much as possible are important but the final ingredient, the inspiration, can only be a gift.

The progressions we have seen mirror the way in which it is important for all Christians to deepen their understanding of biblical and systematic theology together with the writings of the early fathers and the creeds. However, this should be in the knowledge that that these initial "grammars" become the foundational tools for mature, creative, and imaginative application of those skills to the contemporary situation in which the church finds itself. If not it remains an anachronism with little relevance to the present day.

So it is with the matter of orthodoxy. In the light of this whole symphonic analysis taken together with the special perspective of dynamic jazz theology, we can now draw together our conclusions. These conclusions will be the basic "chord sequence" from which it will be possible to improvise our contemporary Anglican orthodoxy, ". . . which as any musician knows doesn't mean playing out of tune or out of time but rather discerning what is appropriate in terms of the story so far and the story's intended conclusion."[7]

There can, of course, only be one clearly known and intended conclusion, that of *soli Deo gloria*. It is to this eschatological end that the creation is moving. In a book structured by musical form it is a most suitable emphasis, written as it was on the many works of Johann Sebastian Bach and George Frideric Handel. As to the matter of the story so far, to those with distinctly conservative and biblicist leanings whose focus might be restricted solely to the simple reading of the biblical narrative, D. C. Toedt reminds us that "With all this in mind, you don't have to be a cultural

6. Furstner, "Primer."
7. Wright, "Bible and Tomorrow's World."

relativist to be unconvinced that the folk tales of a single small people are truly the central narrative of the universe."[8]

Indeed, as we have already seen, one of the glories of Anglicanism is its ability to hold the centrality of the Scriptures and their constant reinterpretation for each generation within the context of the development and insights of human thought, scientific knowledge, and social development, and there has been much development of insight and knowledge since the days when the Bible was written. Therefore, in the light of this I feel able to make the following conclusions.

Conclusions

The History and Nature of Orthodoxy Itself

History clearly teaches us that any notion of there being a golden age when a fixed understanding of orthodoxy or any selection of propositional statements, even when agreed at an ecumenical council, were understood in exactly the same way by all Christians has never existed in reality.

Orthodoxy has always had a dynamic nature and can never be viewed a closed or fixed system. A pilgrim church is always on a journey of faith and cannot be encumbered with the weight of having to carry the thought patterns and conclusions of earlier generations when so much has changed in society, culture, and scientific knowledge. The ongoing development of doctrine is a sign of the vibrant life of the church, and the church that is dynamically engaged in such "right thinking" is truly orthodox. Those who choose to be locked into patterns and statements of a previous time with a very different intellectual and theological climate have stopped right thinking and have become an anachronism and deserve the epithet of being irrelevant. They have also abandoned their congregations to the secularism of modern culture by failing to provide them with the intellectual and theological tools necessary to be able to maintain a relevant and vibrant belief in such a modern climate. The Holy Spirit has not retired since the closing of the canon or the Reformation. He is still at work teaching and leading the church "into all truth." Inspired improvisation is still the continuing order of the day.

---

8. Toedt, "NT Wright's Lambeth Lecture."

The Usefulness of Heresy

While, thankfully, we Christians no longer burn people at the stake for holding what we consider to be heretical views, the demonisation and unloving treatment meted out to those who hold views contrary to what has been traditionally believed, however, still go on to the severe detriment of the witness of the Christian faith in the world.

The definition of heresy as "other" puts the matter plainly. It is simply another way of looking at the truth, which has resulted in some Christians coming to different conclusions to those previously espoused by the majority or, more probably, by those who wield the most power. Rarely is the motivation for these different views malevolent; indeed the majority of "heretics" are simply trying to find ways to make the Christian faith more understandable, more acceptable, or more relevant. The fact that these views are held sincerely does not, of course, mean that these views cannot be challenged but it does mean that they deserve to be treated with respect and love as befits the behaviour of all who claim to follow Christ.

Such continuing dialectic conversations can only produce good as those involved are made to rise to the challenges of defending their points of view but also of coming to understand and respect the views of those who differ from them and being open to the possibility of learning something from them. The too frequently adopted ghetto mentality or attempts to silence those who differ merely demonstrate the failure to recognise that none of us has the monopoly on the truth because we all "see as through a glass darkly" while we live out our earthly Christian life. That godly man John Milton wrote well when he affirmed in 1644,

> . . . and though all the winds of doctrine were let loose to play upon the earth, so Truth be in the field, we do injuriously by licensing and prohibiting to misdoubt her strength. Let her and Falsehood grapple; who ever knew Truth put to the worse in a free and open encounter? . . . There must be many schisms and many dissections made in the quarry and in the timber, ere the house of God can be built.[9]

To those of the GAFCON, FCA, or similar conservative persuasion, as indeed to us all, the power of these words of Oliver Cromwell are relevant: "I beseech you in the bowels of Christ think it possible that you may

---

9. Milton, *Areopagitica 1644*, 41.

be mistaken."[10] This could be true even concerning our understanding of the vexed matter of homosexuality.

The Essential Freedom of the Postmodern Paradigm

The instinctive conservative reaction to postmodernism is negative and totally suspicious because of the postmodernist's distrust of unified theories and metanarratives. Postmodernism sees such theories and narratives as covering a multitude of tensions and contradictions all disguised under the cover of a smooth, harmonious whole.

Postmodernism contributes two important perspectives about culture and religion, including how these ideas interact with each other. These ideas are seen then not as something orderly, unitary, and stable, but rather as a miscellany of differing and often conflicting perspectives and attitudes that are constantly being contested and challenged. Culture is not a thing but rather a process that is not fixed and settled once and for all, but is always in flux. The same is true of religion, and of its impact upon the formation of culture. This shifting nature of things is not something to be feared but embraced with a confidence in an unchanging God. It is certainly a challenge but can bring great rewards.

The words of James Boyd White are so relevant: "When we discover that we have *in this world* no earth or rock to stand or walk upon but only shifting sea and sky and wind, the mature response is not to lament the loss of fixity but to learn to sail."[11]

Secondly, postmodernism emphasises the role of power and domination in what does and does not get counted at any given time and place as the accepted orthodoxy. This book has examined the plentiful and stark evidence of the often arbitrary, secretive, devious, and injurious methods that have been used to make sure that a certain conservative view prevails in the higher echelons of governance within the Anglican Communion.

If, as has already been affirmed, truth will always overcome falsehood in the end, it is important that those who claim to know the truth eschew falsehood and underhand methods of any sort and trust in the power of what they claim to believe. It is also shameful that some of the religious leaders from rich developed countries of the northern hemisphere are prepared to exercise their material influence upon the bishops and people

---

10. In a letter to the General Assembly of the Church of Scotland, 1650. Found in Carlyle, *Oliver Cromwell*, 149.

11. White, *When Words Lose Their Meaning*, 278 (emphasis added).

of the poorer South in order to get their own way. It is also sad that some bishops are prepared for their voices and their churches to be manipulated in this way.

The GAFCON primates' council has already said that, in their view, territorial diocesan boundaries cannot be allowed to stand in the way of gospel truth. Yet this is absolutely contrary to the oaths that they swore at their consecrations that committed them to maintaining those boundaries. Thus there is the anomaly of bishops who have sworn to observe these territorial jurisdictions, at the same time transgressing that same rule in other places. This then becomes not just a matter of legality but of honesty and integrity.

Fundamentalism and Legalism

The examination of fundamentalism demonstrated that, as a descriptor, the word has shifted its meaning. It no longer simply refers to those who hold to certain fundamentals of the faith but now has gathered connotations of an uncompromising literal biblicism. When this is combined with a rigid legalism that builds walls, sets boundaries, and brands all other views as "the enemy" it becomes a dead hand stifling all development of thinking.

It is this view that is now demanding the strict application of "law" and discipline within the Anglican Communion and thus has rejected the Anglican covenant as not going far enough in this area. Whatever view is taken of the value of the covenant, a rejection on these grounds is unacceptable. Any change of heart within any province of the Anglican Communion, or indeed in any individual, can never be brought about by edict, command, or order even if the Anglican Church had such a process, which it does not. Such change can only come about by the power and ministry of the Holy Spirit mediated by a form of osmosis through loving and faithful persuasive dialogue with others.

The Folly of Separatism

Being part of a worldwide communion should mean that it is almost a logical impossibility to embrace a notion of separatism. Nevertheless it seems that this has been within the genetic makeup of GAFCON/FCA since its inception.

By calling a great conference—whatever was claimed to the contrary—to be a spoiler for Lambeth 2008, GAFCON deliberately caused a raft of episcopal absentees from Lambeth and thus undermined any possibility of real cross-party discussion of any significance on the really vexatious issues troubling the Anglican Communion.

GAFCON 2008 ended with the publication of the Jerusalem Declaration. The documentation issued with the Jerusalem Declaration set up a rival primates' meeting that was given unprecedented powers to declare and pronounce whether this province or that was to be accepted as orthodox and thus acceptable to them.

It also encouraged Anglicans to sign up to the Jerusalem Declaration as a "rule of faith." This seems to be despite the fact that the Book of Common Prayer of 1662 is recognised as foundational for worship. Many supporters of GAFCON/FCA will never have read it or even found a copy available in many of their churches. Indeed, much of their worship today is barely liturgical. It also claimed that the Thirty-Nine Articles of Religion are authoritative for Anglicans.[12] Again, many of the younger supporters of this movement will never have read them and, if they have, might well question whether they can really uphold the teaching they proclaim. For example:

- The place of the Apocrypha in worship—Art. VI
- Pre-destination and election—Art. XVII
- The calling of General Councils—Art. XXI
- Baptismal regeneration— Art. XXVII
- Hearing the homilies regularly—Art. XXXV
- The death penalty approved—Art. XXXVII
- The Queen of England as Supreme Governor
- Pacifism condemned

It would be interesting to know if the majority of the self-declared "orthodox" clergy who attended GAFCON, including the bishops, actually

---

12. GAFCON, "Jerusalem Declaration":

Art. 4: "We uphold the Thirty-nine Articles as containing the true doctrine of the Church agreeing with God's Word and *as authoritative* (my emphasis) for Anglicans today."

Art. 6: "We rejoice in our Anglican sacramental and liturgical heritage as an expression of the gospel, and we uphold the 1662 Book of Common Prayer as a true and authoritative standard of worship and prayer, to be translated and locally adapted for each culture."

uphold all the Articles and accept all the teaching of the 1662 Book of Common Prayer.

With this possible double-mindedness, GAFCON, through its own primates, is still willing to "unchurch" those who do not dot all the GAFCON 'i's and cross all the GAFCON 't's. For them such conformity is the key test for orthodoxy.

While claiming to be true Anglicans they separate themselves off from the Anglican Communion, seemingly oblivious to the fact that history teaches that separatism almost always leads to decline and further division. We have already seen in an earlier chapter how the fate of the Nonurors and the Continuing Church Movement of the 1960s bears adequate witness to that truth in an Anglican setting. The Reformation itself, whatever good might be seen to have come out of it, was the stimulus for the greatest movement for division the Christian church has ever known, and that Protestant characteristic of separatism continues to the present day.

The possibility is that many good people with the most holy motives will align themselves with this separatist movement that plagues the Anglican Communion today and will end up in some sectarian backwater having been deceived by those who have led them.

The Essence of Anglicanism

Anglicanism has never attempted to portray itself as the only truly acceptable form of Christianity. It sees itself rather as a unique but valid part of the catholic church having developed itself from, as the Lambeth Quadrilateral implies, the priorities of Scripture, creeds, sacraments, and episcopal order.

The use of the word *Communion* when describing worldwide Anglicanism implies a close relationship that allows for both autonomy and responsibility. Believing itself to be under the guidance and direction of the Holy Spirit, it also demands of its members mutual respect, openness, and integrity coupled with patience in times of stress.

Anglicans believe themselves to be called to live a particular type of mutual life. Anglicanism does not have a centralised, papal-like leadership and indeed has, since its inception, eschewed a confessional structure similar to those of its European counterparts. This itself necessitates a high level of mutual respect and care in the light of the scriptural injunction to be "eager to maintain the unity of the Spirit in the bond of peace."[13]

The great upheavals of recent years that have brought into being *The Virginia Report* and *The Windsor Report* have ultimately produced the Anglican covenant, which, as we have already seen, is being debated at this time within the Communion.

For some Anglicans this is a development faithful to Anglicanism's evolving theological and ecclesiological tradition and identity, providing an agreed structure for future debate, diversity and development within mutually agreed commitments.

For others the current Instruments of Communion are seen to be adequate for those who would be willing to accept and live within a communion that has room for divergent views and differing understandings. The idea of a covenant is an innovation that has appeared out of the blue and is alien to the Anglican tradition, containing, as they see it, notions of centralised power, authority, and discipline. The covenant would mark as second-class Anglicans those who, in all good conscience, cannot sign up to in and instead wish to build bridges between Anglican churches with different traditions for understanding Scripture. It would also allow foreign bishops to extend their jurisdiction into other provinces around the world.

Even some others who see the idea of a covenant as having some value find the current one on offer too weak. They believe it should be abandoned for the GAFCON vision of confessional Anglicanism based around the Jerusalem Declaration. Many Anglicans, even if against the covenant, see such a confessional vision as a recipe for disaster that would simply result in further fragmentation and the ultimate breakdown of the Communion.

Archbishop Rowan Williams commends the covenant strongly, arguing that it will enable the Communion to agree "on ways of limiting damage, managing conflict and facing with honesty the actual effects of greater disunity."[14]

Although I now live in Australia and have been working for the Diocese of Adelaide in the Anglican Church of Australia, I remember well my ordination in 1972 as a deacon and subsequently a priest in the Church of England. The preface to the Declaration of Assent in the Church of

---

13. Eph 4:3.
14. Williams, "Archbishop of Canterbury's Advent Letter," sec. 7.

England, which was required of all bishops, priests, and deacons prior to my ordination, was as follows:

> The Church of England is part of the One, Holy, Catholic and Apostolic Church worshipping the one true God, Father, Son and Holy Spirit. It professes the faith uniquely revealed in the Holy Scriptures and set forth in the catholic creeds, which faith the Church is called upon to proclaim afresh in each generation. Led by the Holy Spirit, it has borne witness to Christian truth in its historic formularies, the Thirty-nine Articles of Religion, *The Book of Common Prayer* and the Ordering of Bishops, Priests and Deacons. In the declaration you are about to make will you affirm your loyalty to this inheritance of faith as your inspiration and guidance under God in bringing the grace and truth of Christ to this generation and making him known to those in your care?

This declaration has come to mean so much more to me in subsequent years as I have, hopefully, matured. What that growing understanding has become I find is most eloquently expressed by Paul Avis.[15]

He makes it clear that the Anglican Church (and here he notes that this preface, or one with very similar wording, is used throughout the Anglican Communion) sees itself as just a part of the universal church and makes no attempt to unchurch or pass judgement on other churches and their ministries. It is graciously humble in its affirmation.

It is clearly centred on Trinitarian theology, as indeed are the Thirty-Nine Articles of Religion, without delving too deeply into any speculation about the details of such a theology and what a candidate for the ministry must affirm as their belief.

The same generosity is applied to the Scriptures, which are described as a vehicle of revelation for the faith of the church. Once again no detailed system of belief concerning a theory of revelation or even of biblical inspiration is required. The Scriptures, in the Articles, are said to "contain all things necessary for salvation" or, as the Lambeth Quadrilateral puts it, they are the "rule and ultimate standard of faith." However, what the "all things" are, or what the "rule and ultimate standard" means, is never actually spelled out.

The faith then is revealed in the Scriptures and "set forth" or made manifest in the creeds, but those creedal statements cannot be a once and for all thing because, as the preface quoted above states, the church is

---

15. Avis, "Keeping Faith with Anglicanism," 11–13.

called to "proclaim afresh in each generation." This must speak of the possibility or even the necessity of reinterpretation or re-expression of previous understandings of both the Scriptures and creeds in order to make the faith relevant to the contemporary generation.

The historic formularies to which Anglicans are called to bear witness to are not to be seen as an end in themselves as if they are the last word allowed on any subject. They merely testify to the truth and how those in the past have understood it. Candidates affirm their loyalty to this inheritance of faith as inspiration and guidance under God for bringing this truth to their own generation. The words are carefully chosen here.

An inheritance speaks of something valuable handed down from the history of the past which is gratefully received. Yet, there is clearly a further mandate here to make this inheritance our own, for our time and for our people. An inheritance can be either a dead weight from the past or a resource that can fuel further development in the history of the church. The inheritance is, according to the preface, to be used as inspiration and guidance. These words themselves imply a continuing moral and spiritual quest rather than blind obedience and submission.

The quality of loyalty that is required to fulfill that mandate is a word about character and moral quality. It is certainly not implying an unquestioning submission to dogma and the stifling of continuing theological exploration and development.

The bishop, priest, or deacon then makes his or her personal affirmation as follows.

Declaration of Assent

> I, A B, do so affirm, and accordingly declare my belief in the faith which is revealed in the Holy Scriptures and set forth in the catholic creeds and to which the historic formularies of the Church of England bear witness; and in public prayer and administration of the sacraments, I will use only the forms of service which are authorized or allowed by Canon.[16]

This declaration then, while affirming the inheritance, clearly allows scope for reinterpretation and exploration. Anglicanism has always been open to the richness of theological study and modern scholarship. This is most certainly a "dynamic orthodoxy" and not a static or lifeless reiteration of

---

16. *Common Worship*, xi.

historic statements. It is vital and flexible enabling it to speak afresh to the very different context of our postmodern world.

Even the Roman Catholic Church with all its dogmatic and authoritative structures makes a similar point: ". . . even if revelation is already complete . . . it has not been made completely explicit; it remains for Christian faith gradually to grasp its full significance over the course of centuries."[17]

There are real problems, as I see it, with a "puritan" approach to the biblical text and biblical theology. The utopian view that argues for a biblical theology in which there are no problems because God has laid out a predetermined plan for this world, and has laid it out in detail for all his people to see, and has commanded them to go into the world and fulfil it in detail, cannot be true. On the one hand, the variety of interpretations and beliefs that claim to know God's perfect plan are legion. On the other hand, and perhaps more importantly, Scripture has proved itself to have much more depth of meaning in it than can ever be taken captive and metaphorically put in a measured box by any group of Christians.

Anglicanism has always recognised the human frailty and sinfulness of the human mind even in the greatest saints. The most appropriate approach to take regarding the Scriptures is to humbly recognise them as a gift from God and to seek to study and reflect on them but not fix their meaning or mark boundaries for them. Traditional Anglicanism's views of development of doctrine and the idea of reception allow for the ongoing development of individual understanding. Anglicanism and its dynamic orthodoxy can exist happily without fixing its doctrine in every detail for eternity and marking boundaries forever.

This Anglican approach is often described as a *via media* approach. This is not, as so many detractors describe it, a typical Anglican compromise or "fudge." Anglicanism, however, has always been suspicious of any suggestion of finalities of truth. It opted for a continuing seeking after truth. The Reformation, empowered by the Renaissance, had broken the stranglehold of Scholastic theology. In response Calvin produced a fully detailed system of theology through his *Institutes of the Christian Religion*. Anglicanism, on the other hand, opted for a new approach to doctrine using together the influence of the Scriptures, tradition, and reason. It was a clear distancing of itself from both Rome and the Continental Reformed tradition.

---

17. *Catechism of the Catholic Church*, 22.

Beating the Bounds

In contemporary postmodern Anglican theology there is also recognition by some scholars that even the church fathers should also be subjected to critical historical analysis. We have already seen already in this book how, both in the early church and in the contemporary Anglican struggles, power and politics have played a major part. This is a topic that could benefit from further analysis.

Love Has to Be the Key

> And now these three remain: faith, hope and love. But the greatest of these is love. (1 Cor 13:13)
>
> Hatred stirs up dissension, but love covers over all wrongs. (Prov 10:12)
>
> Above all, love each other deeply, because love covers over a multitude of sins. (1 Pet 4:8)

It is at this point that the necessity for the model of jazz improvisation becomes acute. The chord sequences have been laid out and the melody for the original tune has been played again and again. There have been various previous attempts at improvisation that were satisfying in their time and for the people of that time. Now, however, we are called and have to move to the front and take up the theme and make of it what we will as we believe God is inspiring us. It will have clear and strong links with what has gone before, of course, but the different contexts and different problems and, above all, different people will produce a very different improvisation.

There will be those who will want to hang on to what they believe is the original setting even though our knowledge of what really was the original setting is vague and probably is itself the result of another generation's improvisation.

There will be those who like their own improvisation best of all and see no reason to produce another and do not like the latest improvisation and what it seems to imply about their own. Neither will they like the way in which the new changes appear to be more daring than their own were.

In jazz such developments are obvious. The traditional jazz band takes a previously written simple melody and plays it one way, while a modern jazz group will have a very different approach, and each form has its band of dedicated admirers. What all have to confess, however, is that each group of jazz musicians is being true to itself and their beliefs about musical form and that the quality and skill of their musicianship cannot be denigrated just because we do not particularly like the style and form they produce.

In the church, as believers continue their God-given search for truth and meaning and seek to walk the path of holiness discovering how the will of the Lord and the life of the Spirit are to be expressed for their own generation, in their own context, there are similar tensions. We have already seen how ancient and modern theologians have agreed that unity must prevail over holiness and that, sometimes, it is better to accept the discomfort of a little heresy rather than allow the great pain of schism.

There is only one means of doing this and it requires obedience to the scriptural injunction to "in humility consider others better than yourselves."[18] That same passage cuts deeply into all our human pride and arrogance as we are called upon to imitate Christ in his humiliation, as he was prepared to go even to death for the sake of those he loved despite their total unloveliness. His love did not condone human sinfulness but neither did it judge it. He just loved, as the Apostle John said: "It was just before the Passover Feast. Jesus knew that the time had come for him to leave this world and go to the Father. Having loved his own who were in the world, he now showed them the full extent of his love."[19]

We are called to show the same non-judgmental love to those in our Christian family who are seeking to follow Jesus as Lord and with whom we differ on what that should mean in terms of theological understanding and practical day-to-day living. Of course we must be true to our own conscience and make known our different views but this must be done with respect and, above all, love: the same agape love that is a reflection of the very nature of the God we claim to serve, for 1 John 4:8 reminds us that "God is love." This is a love that has been defined by theologian Thomas Jay Oord as "an intentional response to promote well-being when responding to that which has generated ill-being." He goes on in his description,

> *Agape* repays evil with good, to use a phrase from Christian scripture. When we love our enemies and pray for those who persecute us, we express *agape*. In an effort to promote well-being, *agape* turns the other cheek. *Agape* acts to promote well-being in spite of the ill-being or evil (whether directed toward the lover or the larger society) that it confronts.[20]

---

18. Phil 2:3.
19. John 13:1.
20. Oord, "Love Racket," 934.

This sounds all well and good in theory but such a love is incredibly painful and costly. In the context of the current problems within the Anglican Communion it will require a humbling stepping down from the metaphorical high moral ground claimed by parties and individuals on all sides.

An illustration that is just as powerful as it is challenging is found in Margaret Silf's little booklet *Faith*. She speaks of a child playing with a bubble mixture and enjoying the beautiful colours of each bubble she makes. They appear so solid and well formed and we take delight in them, but the moment we try to grasp them and take them for ourselves they burst and their beauty is no more. Silf compares this phenomenon with the difference between our perceived certainties about the faith and the reality of the overarching mystery of God. The beautiful bubbles are the constructions we make as we rightly seek to discern more and more of God. We can delight in them and seek to live our lives by them, but the moment we attempt to make them into certainties to be imposed upon others who have discerned their own certainties we destroy the ultimate truth of the mystery of God.

"If we think we have 'got' it we have lost it.

If we think we have 'arrived', we have gone down a cul-de-sac." [21]

The only certainty we have is love: the love of God for us in Jesus Christ. We cannot even make a certainty of the mechanism of that, as the existence of the many and various theories of the atonement bear witness. How humbling such a position is and how beautiful it is to lovingly recognise the sincerity and integrity in those who, while sharing a clear faith in Christ, have come to very varied and different conclusions about many facets of the great mystery of God.

Bishop James Jones of Liverpool in the United Kingdom put it most eloquently to his diocesan synod in March 2012.

> When we are in Christ, we are in Christ with everybody else who is in Christ and in communion, whether we like it or not—or them or not, whether we agree with them or not. To be in Christ is an act of grace. It is a gift. I believe that whoever calls Jesus Christ Lord is in Christ. I know that for some this is an insufficient definition and down the centuries the Church has been driven by those who have sought to define it more

---

21. Silf, *Faith*, 21–22.

fully. But it is a New Testament maxim of Christian discipleship (1 Corinthian 12v3).[22]

This should be true, of course, for all relationships between members of the Christian church but particularly, in the context of this book, between all members of the Anglican Communion who, after all, share so much in common just by virtue of being Anglicans.

I am much taken with the way in which Martin Percy expresses it: ". . . politeness, integrity, restraint, diplomacy, patience, a willingness to listen and, above all, not to be ill-mannered—these are the things that enable the Anglican Communion to cohere." [23]

That this is not generally the case is probably due in some major part to the strong emphasis given in some quarters to the literal belief in an awesome and terrifying judgement followed by an unending, painful punishment in hell for those who fail to make the grade, whatever particular version of the grade might be held. If this is the vision then, whatever certainties are believed, combined with the absolute sense that there can be no other acceptable understanding of the truth, any respect for or willingness to listen to another point of view is almost beyond possibility.

This topic of universalism in its many forms has engendered new interest in recent days with the publications such as *Love Wins* by Rob Bell. The subject cannot be dealt with here but it would provide ample scope for further study in the context of relationships between believers. Suffice it to say that my own views on this and other subjects have shifted decisively during the writing of this book, as the following Cadenza section will describe.

I began this book with two quotations as a frontispiece. I feel the second quotation is suitable to sum up the radical change that writing this book has brought about for me. It is something I am extremely grateful for.

> *Orthodoxy or right belief is one of those subjects that need careful handling because it is often a place where bomb makers hide. Christian orthodoxy is claimed by two kinds of believers. The noisiest are those who see it as the acceptance and affirmation of propositions in creeds, texts, and doctrines. In effect, they are rationalists. For them, orthodoxy requires verbal assent to certain statements. At the extreme it is thought that, should Osama bin Laden on his deathbed accept Jesus Christ as his personal Lord and Saviour, he will go straight to heaven, while faithful and*

22. Jones, "Presidential Address," 3.
23. Percy, "On Sacrificing Purity," 36.

compassionate non-Christians will go to the other place no matter what. There is no doubt in my mind that a repentant terrorist can go to heaven, but the kind of orthodoxy that takes no account of the moral life but only of verbal assent is obscene. Judgment is a mystery and we leave it to God to judge between a hateful Christian and a Christlike atheist.[24]

---

24. Jones, *Common Prayer on Common Ground*, 19–20.

6

Cadenza

A Personal Statement

OFTEN, IN THE CLASSICAL period, a composer would instruct the orchestra to a sudden stop and allow a soloist to express him- or herself with a couple of minutes of difficult (or at least difficult-sounding) passage-work interspersed with fragments of melody derived from what had been previously heard. This music usually culminates in an extended trill, after which the orchestra re-enters, bringing the movement to a speedy conclusion, more often than not without any further participation from the soloist.

I have felt it best not to include this cadenza within the main body of the work in order not to distract from the structure and argument. It appears here, therefore, in order to allow me to share—with, I must say, some appropriate difficulty—the influence this work has had upon me.

As I indicated in the introduction, since my earliest days as a Christian I have been nurtured and developed as part of the evangelical wing of the Church of England. This has been the most powerful influence on my formation. I attended a theological college in England that boasted of the motto "Be right and persist!" It was drummed into me that, as an Anglican evangelical, I upheld what was seen as "The truth, the whole truth, and nothing but the truth." Any other view within the Anglican Communion was seen as at least deficient and more likely as heretical. It was my calling to uphold the gospel truth in the form that I had received it. Anything different would put me beyond the pale within the evangelical fraternity. This would include not just theological understanding but also matters of ritual, clerical dress, choice of liturgy. and certain ethical stances.

Beating the Bounds

It was, for example, assumed that an evangelical Anglican would be against abortion whatever the circumstance, and would regard homosexuality as a grave sin and demand abstinence and celibacy from any of those so "afflicted"! In England, when the European Common Market (which eventually became the European Union) was first mooted it was assumed by many that evangelicals would immediately see this as a fulfilment of prophecy of the resurrection of the old Roman Empire which would herald the coming of the great world leader whose number was 666! To vote against it at the referendum was a Christian duty.

After forty years of parish and schools ministry I believed that I had matured and gained wisdom and insight. It was, however, not until I emigrated from the United Kingdom to Australia and met with a very different form of evangelical Anglicanism that I came to see for myself the truth about the arrogance and lack of grace and love that is, sadly, the face of a significant section of Anglican evangelicalism in Australia.

It was also during this time that I found myself forming rich and lasting friendships with clergy of Catholic and more liberal persuasions who showed to me a love and grace and a demonstration of practical Christian discipleship that I did not find in many of my evangelical colleagues. When I was in deep spiritual and practical need it was these brothers and sisters in Christ who came alongside and supported me, whereas many of the evangelical clergy I think saw me as an embarrassment and a failure who had rather let the side down.

When in 2008 GAFCON attempted to spoil the Lambeth Conference and produced its Jerusalem Declaration, with its reiteration of the old evangelical certainties in a form and with a structure that appropriated to itself the authority and power, through its primates, to unchurch those who did not follow their line, I was stirred and wrote a simple paper that had a modest circulation in my own diocese of Adelaide and beyond. I was encouraged by the response and this led to the decision to take this study further in the form of this book.

These three years of writing have been transforming. I have become deeply aware of the richness of what is traditional Anglicanism in a way that I had never allowed myself to be before. I love its commitment to the regular reading of and commitment to the authority of Scripture through the lectionary—a practice sadly neglected by many evangelicals. While holding a true reverence of history and tradition, I have been stretched by the way the reverence is coupled with a real openness to the results of honest biblical and theological scholarship. I am also encouraged by its willingness to embrace the rich development of human knowledge in the sciences, in medicine and psychology, with all the responsibility that brings to ensure that the reading of Scripture and its application pays due regard to those developments and is not locked in a time warp of rigid conservatism that denies reality and condemns anything that seems to push against their self-imposed boundaries.

It will, of course, be for others to confirm or deny the truth of what I believe this study has done in my own life. It is my belief that the self-righteous, arrogant, and graceless conservative evangelical that was willing to judge and condemn others for being different is in the process of being transformed. This transformation is, I believe, creating a warmer, more accepting and tolerant individual who, knowing the grace, mercy, and love of God in Jesus Christ to one so unworthy and so unlovable, is more able now to recognise the grace, mercy, and love of God in the life and witness of those disciples of Jesus whose pilgrimage has led them in different ways and to different conclusions about what is, after all, the great mystery of God.

I am still an evangelical at heart but hesitate to use the label as frequently as I did for fear of upsetting those who have such deep pain and hurt because of the treatment they have received from those who gracelessly and arrogantly proclaim the title as though it is the only way Christian truth can be understood.

I am also aware that the stance taken in this book will not endear me to many of my erstwhile fellow worshippers and workers. Indeed, already there are those who have distanced themselves from me. I do not know all the reasons behind these decisions but I can only guess that, to some, I have become someone with whom to be in fellowship could bring the contagious taint of heresy.

On the other hand, there has been an outpouring of love and support from brothers and sisters in Christ of all persuasions with whom there has been a mutual recognition of integrity and fervent discipleship.

Most surprising, and perhaps most sad of all, has been the positive response to these thoughts from evangelical Christians who share their support of my thinking in muted tones for fear of being outed as heretical within their own conservative fellowships.

To all my fellow Christians I reach out my hand through these pages in the hope that what I have written might be as transforming and encouraging for them as it has been for me.

Bibliography

Adogame, Afe, Gerloff Roswith, and Klaus Hock. *Christianity in Africa and the African Diaspora: The Appropriaition of a Scattered Heritage.* Continuum Religious Studies. New York: Continuum, 2008.

Allen, Roland. *Missionary Methods: St. Paul's or Ours?.* Grand Rapids: Eerdmans, 1962.

American Anglican Council. "The Episcopal Church: Tearing the Fabric of Communion to Shreds." Online: http://www.americananglican.org/assets/Publications/Primates-Report-Final.pdf.

Anderson, Ray S. *An Emergent Theology for Emerging Churches.* Downers Grove, IL: InterVarsity, 2006.

———, editor. *Theological Foundations for Ministry: selected readings for a theology of the church in ministry.* Grand Rapids: Eerdmans, 1979.

Anglican Consultative Council. *The Virginia Report: The Report of the Inter-Anglican Theological and Doctrinal Commission.* London: Parternship House, 1997. Online: http://www.lambethconference.org/1998/documents/report-1.pdf.

———. *ACC Trinidad: The Third Meeting of the Anglican Consultative Council (March 23 to April 2, 1976).* London: ACC, 1976.

Anglican Network in Canada. "The Anglican Church of Canada: Tearing the Fabric to Shreds." Online: http://www.anglicannetwork.ca/pdf/anic_report_on_acoc_0209.pdf.

"The Anglican Way: Signposts on a Common Journey." Online: http://www.anglicancommunion.org/ministry/theological/signposts/english.cfm.

Anselm. *Cur Deus Homo.* Translated by S. N. Dean. Fort Worth, TX: RDMc Publishing, 2005.

Aranavsky, M. *Simfonichesktye Iskaniya (Symphonic Explorations).* Lenigrad: Sovetskty Kompozitor, 1979.

Armitage, David, editor. *British Political Thought in History, Literature and Theory, 1500–1800.* Cambridge: Cambridge University Press, 2006.

Aulén, Gustaf. *Christus Victor: An Historical Study of the Three Main Types of the Idea of Atonement.* Translated by A. G. Herbert. London: SPCK, 1931.

Avis, Paul. *The Anglican Understanding of the Church: An Introduction.* London: SPCK, 2000.

———. *Anglicanism and the Christian Church: Theological Resources in Historical Perspective.* Minneapolis: Fortress, 1989.

———. *Authority, Leadership, and Conflict in the Church.* London: Mowbray, 1992.

———, editor. *The Christian church: An Introduction to the Major Traditions.* London: SPCK, 2002.

———. *The Church in the Theology of the Reformers.* New Foundations Theological Library. Atlanta: John Knox, 1980.

———. *The Identity of Anglicanism: Essentials of Anglican Ecclesiology.* London: T. & T. Clark 2007.

Bibliography

———. "Keeping Faith with Anglicanism." In *The Future of Anglicanism*, edited by Robert Hannaford. Leominster: Fowler Wright, 1996.

Avis, Paul, and Stephen Pickard. *The Instruments of Communion*. Draft paper for the Inter-Anglican Standing Commission on Unity, Faith and Order. 2011.

Balthasar, Hans Urs von. *Truth Is Symphonic: Aspects of Christian Pluralism*. Translated by Graham Harrison. San Francisco: Ignatius, 1987.

Barr, James. *Beyond Fundamentalism*. Philadelphia: Westminster, 1984.

Batterson, M. *Primal: A Quest for the Lost Soul of Christianity*. Colorado Springs, CO: Moltnomah, 2009.

Bauer, Walter. *Orthodoxy and Heresy in Earliest Christianity*. Philadelphia: Fortress, 1971.

Bayne, Stephen S. *An Anglican Turning Point: Documents and Interpretations*, Austin, TX: Church Historical Society, 1964.

Begbie, Jeremy. "The Sense of an Ending." Lecture, UC Berkley, 2003.

Belcher, J. *Deep Church: A Third Way beyond Emerging and Traditional*. Downers Grove, IL: IVP Books, 2009.

Bell, Rob. *Love Wins: A Book about Heaven, Hell, and the Fate of Every Person Who Ever Lived*. New York: HarperCollins, 2010.

Billheimer, Paul, and Edwin Messerschmidt. *Destined for the Throne*. 4th ed. Bloomington, MN: Bethany House, 1996.

Church of England. *The Book of Common Prayer* (1662). London: n.p.

Boyer, Peter J. "A Church Asunder." *The New Yorker*, April 17, 2006.

Bradshaw, T. *The Olive Branch: An Evangelical Anglican Doctrine of the Church*. Carlisle: Paternoster, 1992.

Bridger, F. "Anglicanism: A Church in Crisis. Where to from Here?" Lecture. St. Matthew's Church, Adelaide, South Australia, 2007.

Brouwer, Steve, Paul Gifford, and Susan D. Rose. *Exporting the American Gospel: Global Christian Fundamentalism*. New York: Routledge, 1996.

Brown, Raymond Edward. *Biblical Exegesis and Church Doctrine*. Eugene, OR: Wipf and Stock, 2002.

Bultmann, Rudolf. *Theology of the New Testament*. Translated by Kendrick Grobel. Vol. 2. London: SCM, 1955.

Butler, David. *Dying to Be One: English Ecumenism—History, Theology and the Future*. London: SCM, 1996.

Buxton, Graham. *Dancing in the Dark: The Privilege of Participating in the Ministry of Christ*. Carlisle: Paternoster, 2001.

Carlyle, Thomas. *Oliver Cromwell: Letters and Speeches with Elucidations*. New York: William H. Colyer, 1846.

Cassidy, Michael. *The Prophetic Word in the Crisis Context*. Olivier Beguin Memorial Lecture. Canberra: Bible Society in Australia, 1986.

Catechism of the Catholic Church. London: Burns and Oates, 1994.

Chapman, Mark D. *The Anglican Covenant: Unity and Diversity in the Anglican Communion*. New York: Mowbray, 2008.

———, editor. *The Hope of Things to Come: Anglicanism and the Future*. London: Mowbray, 2010.

"Christianity's New Center – Africa." Prophecy News Watch. Online: http://www.prophecynewswatch.com/2010/January08/0885.html

Christie-Murray, David. *A History of Heresy*. London: New English Library, 1976.

Bibliography

Clapp, Rodney. *Border Crossings: Christian Trespasses on Popular Culture and Public Affairs.* Grand Rapids: Brazos, 2000.

Clatworthy, Jonathan, and David Bruce Taylor, editors. *The Windsor Report: A Liberal Response*, Winchester, UK: O Books, 2005.

Cocksworth, C. *Holding Together: Gospel, Church,and Spirit: The Essentials of Christian Identity.* Norwich, UK: Canterbury Press, 2008.

Coleridge, Samuel Taylor. *Aids to Reflection.* Edited by John Beer. Princeton, NJ: Princeton University Press, 1993.

Common Worship: Services and prayers for the Church of England. London: Church House Publishing, 2000.

Conger, George. "Behind the Scenes at the Primates' Meeting: Part 2." *Church of England Newspaper*, March 4 2005, p. 5.

———. "Global South Anglicans Warn Liberal Christians Must Repent." *Church of England Newspaper*, April 30, 2010, p. 2.

Cullman, Oscar. *Einheit durch Vielfalt: Grundlegung und Beitrag zur Diskussion* über *die Möglichkeiten ihrer Verwicklung.* Tübingen: Mohr, 1986.

Cunningham, David S. *These Three Are One: The Practice of Trinitarian Theology.* Challenges in Contemporary Theology. Malden, MA: Blackwell, 1998.

Cyril of Jerusalem. "Catechetical Lectures, XVIII." Translated by E. H. Gifford. *Nicene and Post-Nicene Fathers*, 2nd ser., vol. 7. Peabody, MA: Hendrickson, 1994.

"The Dallas Statement from the Anglican Life and Witness Conference." September 20–24, 1997. Online: http://www.theroadtoemmaus.org/RdLb/32Ang/Epis/DallasStmt.htm.

Dearborn, Kerry L. "Recovering a Trinitarian and Sacramental Ecclesiology." In *Evangelical Ecclesiology: Reality or Illusion?*, edited by John G. Stackhouse Jr., 39–73. Grand Rapids: Baker Academic., 2003.

Dickens, A. G. *Reformation Studies.* Historical Studies 9. London: Hambledon, 1982.

Doctrine Commission of the Church of England. *Christian Believing: The Nature of the Christian Faith and Its Expression in Holy Scripture and Creed.* London: SPCK, 1976.

Doe, Norman. *An Anglican Covenant: Theological and Legal Considerations for a Global Debate.* Norwich, UK: Canterbury Press, 2008.

Douglas, Ian T., and Paul F. Zahl. *Understanding the Windsor Report: Two Leaders in the American Church Speak Across the Divide.* New York: Church Publishing, 2005.

Driver, Jeffrey. "Anglicans and Covenant." Paper for the Anglican Diocese of Adelaide. Adelaide, South Australia, 2010.

———. "Towards an Anglican Future in a 'Polity of Persuasion.'" Paper for the Anglican Diocese of Adelaide. Adelaide, South Australia, 2010.

Driver, J. D. "Anglicanism beyond Windsor: Communion and Episcopacy with Particular Reference to the Anglican Church of Australia." PhD thesis, Charles Sturt University, Canberra, Australia, 2008.

Duin, J. "Bolivian Ordains Anglican Clerics." *Washington Times*, November 13, 2005, p. 12.

Dulles, Avery Robert. *Models of the Church.* Garden City, NY: Image Books, 1987.

Duncan, Anthony. *The Elements of Celtic Christianity.* Shaftesbury, Dorset: Element Books, 1992.

Duncan, R. "Mainstream Meeting Memo/Speech Notes." Online: http://www.cesld.org/pdf/F-Mainstream112003.pdf.

Bibliography

Dunn, James D. G. *Unity and Diversity in the New Testament.* London: SCM, 1977.
"The Eames Monotoring Group Report." August 1997. Online: http://www.lambethconference.org/1998/documents/report-10.pdf.
Edwards, David Lawrence, and John Stott. *Evangelical Essentials: A Liberal Evangelical Dialogue.* Downers Grove, IL: InterVarsity, 1988.
Ellis, Carl F. *Free At Last?: The Gospel in the African-American Experience.* 2nd ed. Downers Grove, IL: InterVarsity, 1996.
Elsdon, Peter. Review of *The Cambridge Companion to Jazz*, edited by Mervyn Cooke and David Horn. *Frankfürter Zeitschrift für Musikwissenschaft* 6 (2003) 159–75.
Evans, G. R. "Anglican Conciliar Theory: Provincial Autonomy and the Present Crisis." *One in Christ* 25/1 (1989) 34–52.
FCA. "Goals of the Fellowship of Confessing Anglicans." Online: http://fca.net/resources/goals_of_the_fellowship_of_confessing_anglicans/.
———. "Welcome." http://fca.net/welcome/.
Frame, Thomas R. *A House Divided?: The Quest for Unity within Anglicanism.* Brinswick East, Victoria, Australia: Acorn Press, 2010.
———. *On Being Anglican: Consensus in Diversity.* Goulburn, New South Wales, Australia: Hypercet, 2006.
Fraser, Antonia. *Cromwell: Our Chief of Men.* London: Phoenix, 2002.
Fritze, Ronald H., and Williams, B. Robison, editors. *Historical Dictionary of Stuart England, 1603–1689.* Westport, CT: Greenwood, 1996.
Frost, Michael, and Alan Hirsch. *The Shape of Things to Come.* Peabody, MA: Henderson, 2003.
Furstner, Michael. "Primer: Jazz Improvisation Course." Online: http://www.jazzclass.aust.com/im1.htm.
GAFCON. "The Jerusalem Declaration." 2008. Online: http://gafcon.org/news/gafcon_final_statement/.
———. "Oxford Statement of the Primates' Council." November 2010. Online: http://www.gafcon.org/news/oxford_statement_from_the_gafcon_fca_primates_council/.
———. "Statement on the Global Anglican Future and the Jerusalem Declaration." Online: http://www.gafcon.org/images/uploads/gafcon_way_truth_life.pdf.
Galilei, Galileo. *Galileo on the World Systems: A New Abridged Translation and Guide.* Translated by Maurice A. Finocchiaro. Berkeley, CA, University of California Press, 1997.
Galli, Mark. "The Problem with Christus Victor." *Christianity Today*, Soulwork, April 7, 2011. Online: http://www.christianitytoday.com/ct/2011/aprilweb-only/christusvicarious.html.
Gensichen, Hans-Werner. *We Condemn: How Luther and 16th-Century Lutheranism Condemned False Doctrine.* Translated by Herbert J. A. Bouman. St. Louis: Concordia, 1967.
Giles, Kevin. *What on Earth Is the Church?: A Biblical and Theological Inquiry.* London: SPCK, 1995.
Gilles, John. *The Works of ... The Revd. George Whitefield.* 1:126. London, 1777.
Gillingham, R. "Praxis and the Content of Theology in Gustavo Gutiérrez's Theological Methodology: A Comparative Critique." *Quodlibet Journal* 7/2 (2005). http://www.quodlibet.net/articles/gillingham-gutierrez.shtml.
Goetz, Ronald. "The Suffering God: The Rise of a New Orthodoxy." *Christian Century*, April 16, 1986, 385.

Goldingay, John. *Authority and Ministry,* Nottingham, UK: Grove, 1976.
Gore, C. *The Incarnation of the Son of God.* Bampton Lectures, 1891. London: J. Murray, 1891.
Greenslade, S. L. *Schism in the Early Church.* 2nd ed. London: SCM, 1953.
Groves, P. N. "A Model for Partnership." PhD thesis, University of Birmingham, 2009.
Guder, Darrel L., editor. *Missional Church: A Vision for the Sending of the Church in North America.* The Gospel and Our Culture Series. Grand Rapids: Eerdmans, 1998.
Gutiérrez, G. *Liberation Theology: A Documentary History.* Edited and translated by Alfred T. Hennelly. Maryknoll, NY: Orbis, 1990.
Hale, Stephen, and Andrew Curnow, editors. *Facing the Future: Bishops Imagine a Different Church.* Brunswick East, Victoria, Australia: Acorn, 2009.
Hall, Francis J. *Dogmatic Theology.* Vol. 2. New York: Amercian Church Publications, 1974.
Hardy, D. "A Magnificent Complexity." In *Essentials of Christian Community: Essays for Daniel W. Hardy,* edited by David F. Ford and Dennis L. Stamps, 332–34. Edinburgh: T. & T. Clark, 1996.
Hardy, D. W. "Anglicanism in the Twenty-First Century: Scriptural, Local and Global." Paper presented to the American Academy of Religion Anglican Studies Group, 2004.
Harrison, Robert. *The Writings of Robert Harrison and Robert Brown,* edited by Albert Peel and Leland H. Carlson. London: Allen and Unwin, 1953.
Harris, Tim. *Revolution: The Great Crisis of the British Monarchy, 1685–1720.* New York: Allen Lane, 2006.
Harrison, William H. Prudence and Custom: Revisiting Hooker on Authority." *Anglican Theological Review* 84/4 (Fall 2002) 897–913.
Hassett, Marinada Katherine. *Anglican Communion in Crisis: How Episcopal Dissidents and Their African Allies Are Reshaping Anglicanism.* Princeton, NJ: Princeton University Press, 2007.
Hebert, A. G. *Fundamentalism and the Church of God.* London: SCM, 1957.
Heller, Michael. "Deciphering the Mind of God." *First Things,* On the Square, March 19, 2008. Online: http://www.firstthings.com/onthesquare/2008/03/deciphering-the-mind-of-god.
Hick, John. *The Myth of God Incarnate.* 2nd ed. London: SCM, 1993.
Hiebert, Paul. G. *Anthropological Insights for Missionaries.* Grand Rapids: Baker, 1985.
———. *Anthropological Reflections on Missiological Issues.* Grand Rapids: Baker, 1984.
Hindmarsh, Bruce. "Is Evangelical Ecclesiology an Oxymoron?" In *Evangelical Ecclesiology: Reality or Illusion?,* edited by John G. Stackhouse Jr., 15–37. Grand Rapids: Baker, 2003.
Hjalmarson, L. "A New Way of Thinking about Church." MCM Conference, 2003. Online: http://nextreformation.com/wp-admin/resources/MCM-2003.pdf.
Hoad, Neville Wallace. *African Intimacies: Race, Homosexuality, and Globalization.* Minneapolis: University of Minnesota Press, 2007.
Hooker, Richard. *Of the Laws of Ecclesiastical Polity* [1593–97]. London: E. P. Dutton, 1954.
Hughes, Philip Edgcumbe. *The True Image: The Origin and Destiny of Man in Christ.* Grand Rapids, Eerdmans, 1989.

Bibliography

Hurtado, Larry W. *Lord Jesus Christ: Devotion to Jesus in Earliest Christianity*. Grand Rapids: Eerdmanns, 2003.

Ison, W. G. "Cultural Compromise—A Transitional State." M.Th. thesis, Tabor College, Adelaide, Australia, 2008.

Jensen, Peter. *Doctrine 1, Moore Theological College Correspondence Course*. Sydney: Moore Theological College, 1996.

———. Presidential Address to Sydney Diocesan Synod. Sydney, Australia, October 26, 2001.

Jewel, John. *Apology of the Church of England* (1562). Part 111. Charlottesville, NC: Folger Books, 1963.

Jinkins, Michael. *The Church Faces Death: Ecclesiology in a Post-Modern Context*. Oxford: Oxford University Press, 1999.

———. "The 'Gift' of the Church: Ecclesia Crucis, Peccatrix Maxima, and the Missio Dei." In *Evangelical Ecclesiology:Reality or Illusion?*, edited by John G. Stackhouse Jr., 179–209. Grand Rapids: Baker Academic, 2003.

Jones, Alan W. *Common Prayer on Common Ground: A Vision of Anglican Orthodoxy*. New York: Moorhouse, 2006.

Jones, James. "Presidential Address by Bishop James Jones." Delivered at the Liverpool Diocesan Synod, March 2010. Online: http://www.liverpool.anglican.org/index.php?p=1126.

Kaoma, Kapya. *Globalising the Culture Wars: U.S. Conservatives, African Churches, & Homophobia*. Somerville, MA: Political Research Associates, 2009. Online: http://www.publiceye.org/publications/globalizing-the-culture-wars/pdf/africa-full-report.pdf.

Käsemann, Ernst. "The Canon of the New Testament." In *Essays on New Testament Themes*, translated by W. J. Montague, 103–4. Studies in Biblical Theology 41. London: SCM, 1964.

———. "Unity and Multiplicity in the New Testament Doctrine of the Church." In *New Testament Questions of Today*, 252–59. London: SCM, 1969.

Kaye, Bruce Norman. *A Church Without Walls: Being an Anglican in Australia*. Victoria, Australia: Dove, 1995.

———. "The Covenant Is Not a Good Idea for Anglicans." Online: http://worldanglicanismforum.blogspot.com/2009/09/why-covenant-is-bad-idea-for-anglicans.html.

———. *Reinventing Anglicanism: A Vision of Confidence, Community and Engagement in Anglican Christianity*. Adelaide, Australia: Openbook, 2003.

Kelly, J. N. D. *Early Christian Creeds*. London: A. & C. Black, 1950.

Kermode, Frank. *The Sense of an Ending: Studies in the Theory of Fiction*. New ed. Oxford: Oxford University Press, 2000.

Knox, John. *The Early Church and the Coming Great Church*. London: Epworth, 1957.

Köstenberger, Aandreas J., and Michael J. Kruger. *The Heresy of Orthodoxy: How Contemporary Culture's Fascination with Diversity Has Reshaped Our Understanding of Early Christianity*. Nottingham, UK: Apollos, 2010.

"The Kuala Lumpur Statement on Human Sexuality - 2nd Encounter in the South, 10 to 15 Feb 97." Global South Anglican Online, February 15, 1997. Online: http://www.globalsouthanglican.org/index.php/comments/the_kuala_lumpur_statement_on_human_sexuality_2nd_encounter_in_the_south_10/.

Künneth, Walter. *The Theology of the Resurrection*. St. Louis: Concordia, 1965.

Lambeth Commission on Communion. *The Windsor Report 2004*. Online: http://www.anglicancommunion.org/windsor2004/section_c/index.cfm.
Lambeth Conference Resolutions Archive. Anglican Communion Office, 2008. Online: http://www.lambethconference.org/resolutions/index.cfm.
Lambeth Indaba: Capturing Conversations and Reflections from the Lambeth Conference 2008, http://www.lambethconference.org/resolutions/downloads/Reflections_Document_(final).pdf.
Lawson, Hilary. *Closure: A Story of Everything*. London: Routledge, 2001.
Link-Wieczorek, U. "Divine Reconciliation and Human Restitution in a Broken World: Revisiting Anselm's Satisfaction Theory." In *After Violence: Religion, Trauma and Reconciliation*, edited by Andrea Bieler et al., 219–38. Leipzig: Evangelische Verlagsanstalt, 2011.
Ludemann, Gerd. *Heretics: The Other Side of Early Christianity*. Translated by John Bowden. London: SCM, 1996.
Lugo, Luis, Brian J. Grim, and Elizabeth Podrebara. "Global Anglicanism at a Crossroads." Pew Forum, June 19, 2008. Online: http://pewforum.org/Christian/Global-Anglicanism-at-a-Crossroads.aspx.
MacArthur, John. *The Truth War: Fighting for Certainty in an Age of Deception*. Nashville: T. Nelson, 2007.
MacDougall, Scott. "The Covenant Conundrum: How Affirming an Eschatological Ecclesiology Could Help the Anglican Communion." *Anglican Theological Review* 94/1 (Winter 2012) 5–26.
Machle, Edward J. "How Is a Heresy False?" In *Studies in Religion: Sciences Religieuses* 1 (1971) 228.
Makgoba, T. "Essence of Indaba." In *Worship and Indaba Group Resources* by Rowan Williams and Winston Halapua. Canterbury, UK: Lambeth Conference, 2008.
Marshall, Michael. *Church at the Crossroads: Lambeth 1988*. San Francisco: Harper & Row, 1988.
Mascall, E. L. *Christ, the Christian and the Church: A Study of the Incarnation and Its Consequences*. London: Longmans, Green, 1946.
Maurice, Frederick Denison. *The Kingdom of Christ*. Edited by Alexander Roper Vidler. New ed. based on the 2nd ed. of 1842. Vol. 1. London: SCM, 1958.
McAdoo, Henry R. *The Spirit of Anglicanism: A Survey of Anglican Theological Method in the Seventeenth Century*. Hale Lectures of Seabury-Western Theological Seminary. New York: Scribner, 1965.
McBrien, R. P. *The Church: The Evolution of Catholicism,* New York: Harper Collins, 2008.
McGillion, Chris. *The Chosen Ones: The Politics of Salvation in the Anglican Church*. Crows Nest, New South Wales: Allen & Unwin, 2005.
McGrath, Alister E. *Heresy: A History of Defending the Truth*. New York: HarperOne, 2009.
———. *Reformation Thought: An Introduction*. 3rd ed. Oxford: Blackwell, 2001.
McLaren, Brian D. *The Church on the Other Side: Doing Ministry in the Postmodern Matrix*. Grand Rapids: Zondervan, 2006.
———. *A Generous Orthodoxy*. Grand Rapids: Zondervan, 2004.
———. *The Secret Message of Jesus: Uncovering the Truth That Could Change the World*. Nashville: T. Nelson, 2006.

Bibliography

McMullin, Ernan. "The Church's Ban on Copernicanism." In *The Church and Galileo*, edited by Ernan McMullin, 150–90. Notre Dame, IN: University of Notre Dame Press, 2005.

Milton, John. *Areopagitica*. London: MacMillian, 1915.

Moltmann, Jurgen. *The Open Church: Invitation to a Messiannic Lifestyle*. Translated by M. Douglas Meeks. London: SCM, 1978.

———. *Theology of Hope: On the Ground and the Implications of a Christian Eschatology*. London: SCM, 2002.

Moody, K. S. "A New Kind of Christian Is a New Kind of Atheist: Truth and A/theistic Orthodoxy in the Emerging Church Milieu." Paper presented at the Society for Continental Philosophy and Theology's fourth biennial conference, "Postmodernism, Truth and Religious Pluralism," Gordon College, Wenham, MA, 2008.

Morgan, R. "St. John's Gospel, the Incarnation and Christian Orthodoxy." In *Essentials of Christian Community: Essays for Daniel W. Hardy*, edited by David F. Ford and Dennis L. Stamps, 146–62. Edinburgh: T. & T. Clark, 1996.

Muller, Richard A. *Post-Reformation Reformed Dogmatics: The Rise and Development of Reformed Orthodoxy, ca. 1520 to ca. 1725*. Vol. 2. Grand Rapids: Baker, 2003.

Mullin, Robert Bruce. "What's Going On in the Anglican Communion?" Online: http://www.beliefnet.com/Faiths/Christianity/2006/07/Whats-Going-On-In-The-Anglican-Communion.aspx?p=1.

Mutua, Makau. "Kenya: Can the Gema Community Rescue Uhuru?" Daily Nation, On the Web, July 3, 2010. Online: http://allafrica.com/stories/201007050064.html.

Myers, Margaret. "Qualitative Research and the Generalizability Question: Standing Firm with Proteus." *The Qualitative Report* 4/3–4 (March 2000). Online: http://www.nova.edu/ssss/QR/QR4-3/myers.html.

National Committee on Responsive Philanthropy. *Moving a Public Policy Agenda: The Strategic Philanthropy of Conservative Foundations*. Washington, DC: NCRP, 1997.

Naughton, Jim. "Following the Money." *The Washington Window* special report. Online: http://www.canticlecommunications.com/Data/Sites/1/docs/following_the_money.pdf.

———. "Who speaks for Africa?" Episcopal Café. Online: http://www.episcopalcafe.com/lead/anglican_communion/who_speaks_for_africa.html.

———. "Windsor Report calls for expressions of regret." Episcopal Diocese of Washington. Online: http://www.edow.org/news/window/nov2004/windsor.html.

Ndungane, Njongonkulu. "A plea for Patience." *Church Times*, December 2, 2005. Online: http://www.churchtimes.co.uk/articles/2005/2-december/news/a-plea-for-patience.

Nehring, Arlene K. "Yet More Light and Truth." Eden United Church of Christ, Hayward, CA, June 8, 2003. Online: http://www.ucc.org/god-is-still-speaking/pdfs/Yet-more-light-and-truth.pdf.

Norman, E. "Authority in the Anglican Communion." Ecclesiastical Law Society Lecture delivered at the 1998 Lambeth Conference. Society of Archbishop Justus. Online: http://justus.anglican.org/resources/misc/norman98.html.

Oden, Thomac C. *The Rebirth of Orthodoxy*. San Francisco: HarperSanFrancisco, 2002.

O'Donovan, Joan Lockwood. "Subsidiarity and Political Authority in Theological Pesrpective." In *Bonds of Imperfection: Christian Politics, Past and Present*, by

Bibliography

Oliver O'Donovan and Joan Lockwood O'Donovan, 225–45. Grand Rapids: Eerdmans, 2004.

O'Leary, Daniel. "Defining Moments." *The Tablet*, January 24, 2009, p. 12.

Oord, T. J. "The Love Racket: Defining Love and Agape for the Love-and-Science Research Program." *Zygon* 40/4 (December 2005). Online: http://www.calvin.edu/~jks4/city/Oord~Defining%20Love.pdf.

"Ordination of Female Priests and Consecration of Female Bishops." Religious Tolerance. Online: http://www.religioustolerance.org/femclrg3.htm.

Outler, Albert C., and Richard P. Heizenrater, editors. *John Wesley's Sermons: An Anthology*. Nashville: Abingdon, 1991.

Oxbrow, Mark. "Anglicans and Reconciling Mission: An Assessment of Two Anglican International Gatherings." *International Bulletin of Missionary Research* 33/1 (2009) 8–10.

Packer, J. I. *A Quest for Godliness: The Puritan Vision of the Christian Life*, Wheaton, IL: Crossway, 1990.

Pelikan, Jaroslav. *The Christian Tradition: A History of the Development of Doctrine*. Vol. 4. Chicago: University of Chicago Press, 1983.

Pelikan, Jaroslav, and Helmut Lehmann, editors. *Luther's Works*. St. Louis: Fortress, 1955–1986.

Percy, M. "On Sacrificing Purity." In *Theological Liberalism: Creative and Critical*, edited by Ian Markham and J'annine Jobling, 114–23. London: SPCK, 2000.

Pickard, S. "Theology as a Power." In *Agendas for Australian Anglicanism: Essays in Honour of Bruce Kaye*, edited by Tom Frame and Geoffrey R. Treloar, 85–122. Adelaide: ATF Press, 2006.

Pierce, Ronald W., and Merrill Groothuis, editors. *Discovering Biblical Equality: Complementarity without Hierarchy*. Downers Grove, IL: InterVarsity, 2004.

Piggin, Stuart. *Firestorm of the Lord: The History and Prospects for Revival in the Church and the World*. Carlisle, Cumbria: Paternoster, 2000.

Pinnock, Clark. "The Destruction of the Finally Impenitent." Online: http://www.satsonline.org/userfiles/The%20Destruction%20of%20the%20Finally%20Impenitent.pdf.

Polkinghorne, John C., and Nicholas Beale. *Questions of Truth: Fifty-One Responses to Questions about God, Science, and Belief*. Louisville: Westminster John Knox, 2009.

Porter, Muriel. *Sydney Anglicans and the Threat to World Anglicanism: The Syndey Experiment*. Ashgate Contemporary Ecclesiology Series. Farnham, Surrey, UK: Ashgate, 2011.

Radner, Ephraim, and Philip Turner. *The Fate of Communion: The Agony of Anglicanism and the Future of a Global Church*. Grand Rapids: Eerdmans, 2006.

Ramsay, Michael. *The Anglican Spirit*. London: Church Publishers, 1991.

———. *The Gospel and the Catholic Church*. London: Longmans, 1936.

The Report of The Lambeth Conference 1978. London: Chuch Information Office, 1978.

Ruggieri, Giuseppe, and Miklós Tomka, editors. *The Church in Fragments: Towards What Kind of Unity?* Concilium 1997/3. London: SCM, 1997.

Sachs, William L. *The Transformation of Anglicanism: From State Church to Global Communion*. Cambridge: Cambridge University Press, 1993.

Bibliography

Sadgrove, Joanna, et al. "Constructing the Boundaries of Anglican Orthodoxy: An Analysis of the Global Anglican Future Conference (GAFCON)." *Religion* 40/3 (July 2010) 193–206.

Samuel, Vinay. "Why Did GAFCON Happen? – the Long View." Presentation to the Reform Conference, October 14, 2008. Online: http://www.anglican-mainstream.net/2008/10/19/where-is-anglicanism-heading-after-gafcon-and-lambeth-vinay-samuel/.

Santayana, George. *Reason in Common Sense*. New York: Dover, 1980.

Scariato, Albert. "A Question of Relationship." *Washington Window*, April 2005.

Schaeffer, Francis A. *Escape from Reason: A Penetrating Analysis of Trends in Modern Thought*. Downers Grove, IL: InterVarsity, 1968.

Schleiermacher, Friedrich. *The Christian Faith*. Edited by H. R. Mackintosh and J. S. Stewart. ET of 2nd German ed. Edinburgh: T .& T. Clark, 1928.

Schweizer, Eduard. *Church Order in the New Testament*. Studies in Biblical Theology 32. London: SCM, 1961.

Sharratt, Michael. *Galileo: Decisive Innovator*. Blackwell Science Biographies. Cambridge, MA: Cambridge University Press, 1994.

Shenk, W. R., et al. "A Special Relationship?" *International Bulletin of Missionary Research* 5/4 (1981) 168–72.

Sherrod, K. "First female bishops find warm welcome at Lambeth Conference." Note 1705, Anglican Communion News Service, 1998.

Silf, Margaret. *Faith*. London: Darton, Longman and Todd, 2011.

Simpson, James Beasley, and Edward M. Story. *The Long Shadows of Lambeth X: A Critical, Eye-Witness Account of the Tenth Decennial Conference of 462 Bishops of the Anglican Communion*. New York: McGraw-Hill, 1969.

Skidmore, David. "Women's ordination no longer a burning issue for most Anglicans." Episcopal News Service, July 1, 1998. Online: http://www.ecusa.anglican.org/3577_93381_ENG_HTM.htm.

Smedes, Lewis B.. "Like the Wideness of the Sea?" Online: http://abouthomosexuality.com/lewissmedes.pdf.

Snyder, Howard A. *Liberating the Church: The Ecology of Church and Kingdom*. Downers Grove, IL: InterVarsity, 1983.

Sperry, William Learoyd. *Religion in America*. Cambridge, MA: Cambridge University Press, 1945.

"A Statement by the Primates of the Anglican Communion Meeting in Lambeth Palace." Anglican Communion News Service, October 16, 2003. Online: http://www.anglicancommunion.org/acns/news.cfm/2003/10/16/ACNS3633.

Steiner, George. *After Babel: Aspects of Language and Translation*. 3rd ed. Oxford: Oxford University Press, 1998.

Sykes, Stephen, editor. *Authority in the Anglican Communion: Essays Presented to Bishop John Howe*. Toronto: Anglican Book Centre, 1987.

———. "The Genius of Anglicanism." In *The English Religious Tradition and the Genius of Anglicanism*, edited by Geoffrey Rowell, 239–40. Abingdon: Nashville, 1992.

———. *The Identity of Christianity: Theologians and Essence of Christianity from Schleiermacher to Barth*. Philadelphia: Fortress, 1984.

———. *The Integrity of Anglicanism*. London: Darton, Longman and Todd, 1978.

Bibliography

———. "'Orthodoxy' and 'Liberalism.'" In *Essentials of Christian Community: Essays for Daniel W. Hardy*, edited by David F. Ford and Dennis L. Stamps, 76–90. Edinburgh: T. & T. Clark, 1996.
———. *Unashamed Anglicanism*. London: Darton, Longman and Todd, 1995.
"Symphonic Form." Vukutu, August 3, 2010. Online: http://www.vukutu.com/blog/2010/08/symphonic-form/.
Tanner, Kathryn. *Theories of Culture: A New Agenda for Theology*. Minneapolis: Fortress, 1997.
Taylor, John Vernon. *The Go-Between God: The Holy Spirit and the Christian Mission*. London: SCM, 1972.
Thielicke, Helmut. *How Modern Should Theology Be?* Translated by H. George Anderson. Philadelphia: Fortress, 1969.
Inter-Anglican Theological and Doctrinal Commission. *Communion, Conflict and Hope: The Kuala Lumpur Report of the Third Inter-Anglican Theological and Doctrinal Commission*. London: Anglican Communion Office, 2008.
Thompson, Michael B. *When Should We Divide?: Schism and Discipline in the New Testament*. Grove Biblical Series B33. Cambridge, UK: Grove, 2004.
Thurman, Howard, and Ronald Eyre. "An Interview with Howard Thurman and Ronald Eyre." *Theology Today* 38/2 (1981) 208–13.
Tickle, Phyllis. *The Great Emergence: How Christianity Is Changing and Why*. Grand Rapids: Baker, 2008.
Toedt, D. C. "NT Wright's Lambeth Lecture about Scriptural Authority Reveals His Exaggerated View of Humanity's Importance." The Questioning Christian. Online: http://www.questioningchristian.com/2008/07/nt-wrights-lamb.html.
Tolliday, Phillip. "Global Witness: But of What Sort?" Paper presented at the Arbeitsgemeinschaft Ökumenische Forschung. Hamburg: Otto Lembeck, 2010.
Toon, Peter. *The Development of Doctrine in the Church*. Grand Rapids: Eerdmans, 1979.
Torrance, T. F. *Incarnation: The Person and Life of Christ*. Edited by Robert T. Walker. Milton Keynes, UK: Paternoster, 2008.
Travis, Stephen. *I Believe in the Second Coming of Jesus*. Grand Rapids: Eerdmans, 1982.
The Truth Shall Make You Free: The Lambeth Conference 1988: The Reports, Resolutions & Pastoral Letters from the Bishops. London: Church House, 1988.
Turner, H. E. W. *The Pattern of Christian Truth: A Study in the Relations between Orthodoxy and Heresy in the Early Church*. Bampton Lectures 1954. Oxford: Mowbray, 1954.
Vincent of Lerins. *The Commonitory Vincent of Lerins, for the Antiquity and Universality of the Catholic Faith against the Profane Novelties of All Heresies*. Translated by C. A. Heurtley. Online: http://www.ccel.org/ccel/schaff/npnf211.iii.html.
Volf, Miroslav. *After Our Likeness: The Church as the Image of the Trinity*. Grand Rapids: Eerdmans, 1998.
———. *Exclusion and Embrace: A Theological Exploration of Identity, Otherness and Reconciliation*. Nashville: Abingdon, 1996.
Völker, W. "Rechtglaubigkeit und Ketzerei im altesten Christentum." *Journal of Early Christian Studies*, Winter 2006, 399–405.
Vorster, Jakobus M. "Perspectives on the Core Characteristics of Religious Fundamentalism Today." *Journal for the Study of Religions and Ideology* 7/21 (Winter 2008) 44–65.

Bibliography

Wand, J. W. C. *The High Church Schism: Four Lectures on the Nonjurors*. London: Faith Press, 1951.

Ward, Kevin. *A History of Global Anglicanism*. Cambridge: Cambridge University Press, 2006.

Webber, Christopher. "A Brief History of the Lambeth Conference: Unity and Diversity." The Episcopal Majority, January 28, 2008. Online: http://episcopalmajority.blogspot.com/2008/01/brief-history-of-lambeth-conference.html.

Webber, Robert. *The Younger Evangelicals: Facing the Challenges of the New World*. Grand Rapids: Baker, 2002.

Wenham, J. *The Goodness of God*. Downers Grove, IL: InterVarsity, 1974.

Werner, Craig. *A Change Is Gonna Come: Music, Race & the Soul of America*. Ann Arbor: University of Michigan Press, 1998.

Westerhoff, John H. *Tomorrow's Church: A Community of Change*. Waco, TX: Word, 1976.

Whalon, Pierre W. "Peering Past Lambeth." Anglicans Online, June 22, 2008. Online: http://www.anglicansonline.org/resources/essays/whalon/PeeringPastLambeth.html.

———. "Towards a Distinctive Anglican Doctrine of the Church." Unpublished Paper. Paris: 2007.

White, B. R. *English Separatist Tradition: From the Marian Martyrs to the Pilgrim Fathers*. London: Oxford University Press, 1971.

White, James Boyd. *When Words Lose Their Meaning: Constitutions and Reconstitutions of Language, Character, and Community*. Chicago: University of Chicago Press, 1984.

White, Wesley. "Jazz and the Mode of Hopeful Transgression." Lecture presented to the Scottish Universities Theological Forum, May 2006. Online: http://www.opensourcetheology.net/node/929.

Williams, Rowan. *Anglican Identities*. London: Darton, Longman and Todd, 2004.

———. "Archbishop of Canterbury: Better Bishops for the Sake of a Better Church." April 23, 2008. Online: http://www.lambethconference.org/lc2008/news/news.cfm/2008/4/23/Archbishop-of-Canterbury-Better-Bishops-for-the-sake-of-a-better-Church.

———. "Archbishop of Canterbury's Advent Letter to Anglican Primates." 2011. Online: http://www.archbishopofcanterbury.org/articles.php/2268/archbishops-advent-letter-to-anglican-primates.

———. "Archbishop of Canterbury's Presidential Address (20 July)." Lambeth Conference 2008. Online: http://www.aco.org/vault/Lambeth%20opening%20address.pdf.

———. *Arius: Heresy and Tradition*. Cambridge: SCM, 2001.

———. *Silence and Honey Cakes: The Wisdom of the Desert*. Oxford: Lion, 2003.

Williams, R. I. "Sydney Anglicans." Online: http://www.sydneyanglicans.net/forums/viewthread/3394/.

Witham, Ted. *The Church at Risk: New Ways of Understanding Tradition*. Melbourne: Joint Board of Christian Education, 1995.

Worgul, George S. *From Magic to Metaphor: A Validation of Christian Sacraments*. Lanham, MD: University Press of America, 1985.

Wright, J. Robert. "The Authority of Lambeth Conferences, 1867–1988." In *Lambeth Conferences Past and Present*, by Guy Fitch Lytle. Cincinnati: Forward Movement, 1989.
Wright, J. Robert, and G. R. Evans, editors. *The Anglican Tradition: A Handbook of Sources*. London: SPCK, 1991.
Wright, N. T. "After GAFCON." Online: http://www.ntwrightpage.com/Wright_After_GAFCON.htm.
———. "The Bible and Tomorrow's World." Lambeth Conference, July 30, 1998. Online: http://www.fulcrum-anglican.org.uk/334.
———. "Further Thoughts on GAFCON and Related Matters." July 6, 2008. Online: http://www.fulcrum-anglican.org.uk/page.cfm?ID=324.
Zizioulas, Jean. *The One and the Many: Studies on God, Man, the Church, and the World Today*. Contemporary Christian Thought Series 6. Alhambra, CA: Sebastian, 2010.
Życiński, Józef. *God and Evolution: Fundamental Questions of Christian Evolutionism*. Translated by Kenneth W Kemp and Zuzanna Maslanka. Washington, DC: Catholic University of America Press, 2006.

Subject/Name Index

A

abortion, 40, 106
abstinence, 109, 112, 118
adiaphora, 48, 67–68, 169, 189
adultery, 74, 106–107
affection, 59, 99, 102, 129, 138, 184–185, 190
affirmation, 39, 57, 88, 129, 158, 167
Africa, 54, 56, 58, 81, 115–117, 124–125, 179
    negative effects of colonialism, 135–137
    suggestion of outside monetary influence in African Churches, 141–142
    questions about authenticity of African Christian voice, 143–146
    weighting of African numbers in worldwide church, 123–126
    motivation of African bishops, 134–137
Ahmanson, Howard and Roberta, 137–138, 141
Akinola, Peter, 122, 133
    influence on Newry Primates' meeting, 140–145,
Ambrose, 10
Anabaptists, 63
Anachronism a danger for international Anglicanism, 184
    view of Church by those outside of it, 34
anathema, 15, 83, 183
    evangelicals anathematize those who views are different, xxix
    modernist views on eschatology anathema to postmodernists, 183
    Global South anathematizes 'apostate' Episcopal Church in USA and Canada, 64
Anderson, David, 141
Anderson, Rufus, 46
Anderson, Ray, 72–73, 78–79
Andrewes, Lancelot, 52
Anglican Communion, 51–54, 64–66, 96–152, 175–181, 183–193
    The Instruments of Communion, 99
Anglicanism, 37–38, 47–48, 51–52, 65–66, 89–90, 95–96, 98–100, 121–125, 130–133, 143–146, 148–153, 156–162, 164–170, 172–173, 175–176, 178–180, 192–193
Anglican Consultative Council, 107, 132–133
annihilation, 14
Anselm, 10–11, 13
anthropology, 22, 148
Apollinarianism, 27
Apologia pro Vita Sua, 24
apologists, 141–142, 148
apostasy, 19, 64, 83
apostles, 1–2, 6, 19, 28, 44, 73, 129, 146–147, 155, 163
    apostolic, xxv, 5–6, 28, 48, 73, 98–99, 113, 132, 160–162, 167
Aquinas, 156
Archbishop of Canterbury, xxiii, xxv, 47, 108, 114, 116, 119–121, 129, 132, 137, 139, 142, 144, 154, 185, 190, 192

239

Subject/Name Index

Archbishop of Canterbury–continued
    First Instrument of Communion, 98–101
    Decline of the role as focus for unity, 125
Arianism, 18, 27, 29–30 (see Christology)
atonement, various theories of, 9–13, 82
Aulén, Gustav, 11 (see *Christus Victor*)
authority, 56–59, 61–62, 66, 70, 73, 87, 100–103, 118–119, 124, 130–133, 136, 163, 167, 171, 176, 180,
    Nonjurors view of authority, xxiii–xxiv,
    Heresy as an attack on authority, 17–18
    Postmodernism's suspicion of authority, 20
    derivation of Pauline authority, 28
    simple reduction of matters of doctrine to authority, 31
    extrinsic and *instrinsic* authority, 37–38
    Emerging Church asks, 'Where now is authority?', 53–54,
    Authority in the Anglican Communion, 145–152
    The place of the 39 Articles, 158–162,
autonomy, 7, 115, 187, 190–191
    autonomous, 46, 98–99, 138,

B

Balthasar, Hans Urs von, xvi
Bampton Lectures, xv, 5, 26
baptism, 6, 55, 63, 104–105, 115, 118, 130, 160, 162–163, 167–168, 171–172, 184, 189
Barebones Parliament, 184
Barr, James, 70–71
Batterson, Mark, 76
Bauer, Walter, 3–5, 7, 16–17, 19–20, 28–29, 32
    Turner's views on Bauer's thesis, 5–8
Baxter, Richard, 67
Bayne, Stephen, 107, 149–150, 185
Beale, Nicholas, xvi
Begbie, Jeremy, 182–183
Belcher, Jim, 83–84
Benedict, 53
Benedictine, 125, 173
Betz, Hans Dieter, 91–92
Bible, xxix, 3, 30, 34–37, 50, 59, 61, 76–77, 82, 85, 111, 117, 128, 131, 135–136, 177, 183, 186
    biblical, xxix, 3, 7, 10, 14–15, 25, 29–30, 39, 44, 61, 70, 122, 127, 133, 152, 160, 162, 166, 169, 177, 186, 191
    biblically, 14, 43
    biblicism, 39, 93
    Arius a biblicist, 29
    Possibility of rewriting the scriptures, 88
bishops, 58, 68, 74, 122, 124, 126–127, 133–134, 138–141, 142–144, 161–163, 179, 184, 188
    nonjuror bishops, xxiii–xxv
    influence of Roman Bishop in the early church definition of heresy, 29
    Donatist bishops, 54–56
    GAFCON declaring the ministry of certain bishops invalid, xxv, 63–64,
    role of bishops in provinces and dioceses, 97–100
    bishops at the Lambeth Conferences, 102–120
    reality of female bishops and the conservative response, 116–118
    prelates, 103, 131
Bonhoeffer, Dietrich, 8
Boyer, Peter, 143
Bradshaw, Timothy, 162–164
Brinklow, Henry, 68
Brouwer, Steve, 135
Brown, Raymond, 25
Browne, Robert, 64–65

Subject/Name Index

Brunner, Emil, 8
Bucer, Martin, 63
Buchanan, Duncan, 117
Bullinger, Heinrich, 69
Bultmann, Rudolf, 5, 19, 21, 32
Buxton, Graham, 35–36, 80–81

C

cacophony, xvi–xvii, 92, 149
Caecilian, 54
Calvin, John, 9, 11, 35, 50, 63, 69, 157
   Calvinist, 35, 71
Canada, 64, 77, 112, 116–117, 120, 143, 185
canon, 6, 19, 23, 28, 52, 90, 138, 147
   canonical, 84, 103, 139, 113, 121
   canonizing of scripture, 148
Canute, 112
catechism, 63, 147
   Catechetical, 31
Catholic, xxiii, 7, 55, 62, 67, 69, 78, 84, 98, 106, 112–113, 131, 135, 147, 153, 159–160, 165–166, 172, 185, 188
   terms 'catholic' and protestant' not antithetical, 24–25
   'catholic' orthodoxy not fixed, 29–31
   Cyril of Jerusalem's definition of 'catholic', 31
   catholicity, 2, 31, 99
Celtic, 47
Chalcedon, 171
Christendom, 29, 60, 70, 98, 161
Christie-Murray, David, 4, 61–62
Christologies, 22–23, 28
   Arian Christology, 18, 27, 29–30
   Christus Victor, 10–12, 15
clergy, xxiii, xxviii, xxx, 55, 68, 106–107, 111, 114, 132, 136–137, 140, 142–143, 160, 165, 168–170, 189
coercion, 152
   cosmos not 'coerced' into eschatological state, xv

   Christ's authority not coercive, 66, 152
   Hooker's view less coercive than continental reformation, 95
   Driver's view of Anglican Covenant as 'persuasive rather than coercive', 191
Coggan, Donald, 185
Colenso, John William, 103–104, 115
Coleridge, Samuel Taylor, 176
Colin, Coward, 140
Commonitory by St. Vincent of Lérins, 31
Commonwealth, 161
compromise, 14, 54, 143, 148
conciliar, 29, 133
condemnation, 65, 83, 109, 122
   condemned, xxv, 24, 28, 49, 62, 106, 110, 112, 118
confession, 6, 20, 28, 163, 167, 185
   confessionalism, xxvi–xxvii, 32, 79, 127, 149, 169, 184
   confessional structures often locked into another age, 70
   confessional differences are evidence of the gifts of the Holy Spirit, 91
   The Jerusalem Declaration is GAFCON's confession, 212
Conger, George, 140, 145
congregation, 64, 97, 114, 122, 132, 140, 143, 167
   early Separatists, 64–65
   dealing with sinners in the congregation, 59
   declining number of men in Anglican congregations, 112
Congregationalist, 64
conscience, xxiv, 65, 68, 72, 111, 114, 117, 126, 165
   conscientious objectors, 75
consecrate, 71, 114, 116, 144, 184
   Donatist view on validity of consecrations, 54–55, 58,
   problems over consecration of Gene Robinson, xxv, 47, 64, 102, 120, 122, 125, 133, 138–139, 188

241

Subject/Name Index

consensus, 29, 61–62, 66, 86, 88, 91, 98, 102, 122, 147, 161, 170, 192
conservatism, 24, 83, 137
Constantine, 4, 75
Constantinople, 18, 61, 173
Constantius, 18
constitution,
    of TEC, 46, 97
    difficulty of binding future generations to present constitutions, 50
    GAFCON constitution and new Primates' Conference, 57
contextual, 159
contextualised, 81, 84
contextualization, 81
contraception, 107–108, 110, 179
controversy, 8, 30, 38, 65, 103, 116, 120–121, 138, 147, 151, 191
convention, 98
    symphonic conventions, vxii
    2nd century church conventions not fixed, 30
    TEC General Convention, 102, 107, 120, 138
conversation, xxviii, xxvi, 83, 173, 129, 190
conviction, xxiv, xxiii, 48, 50, 63, 75, 81, 120, 154, 173, 187
Copernicanism, 9, 62
Council of Trent, 68
covenant, 64, 74, 121, 127, 133, 162–163, 166, 187, 191
    church as a covenant community, 42, 64
    The Virginia Report foreshadows Covenant, 186–187
    The Windsor Report proposes an Anglican Covenant, 189–190
    Anglican Covenant, 88, 190–197
Cranmer, Thomas, 68, 89, 168, 170
creation, xvi–xvii, xxix, 9–10, 12–13, 30, 66, 107, 177, 187
creativity, 37, 76, 17–21, 177
    Tanner's view on '*Diversity and Creativity*', 86–87
credenda, 6
credendi, 169
creeds, xvi, xvii, 6, 14, 19–20, 35, 43, 47, 50, 52, 60–61, 70–71, 76, 94, 159, 165, 167, 169, 173, 176, 184
Cromwell, Oliver, 184 (see Footnote 3)
Cullman, Oscar, 91
Cyril of Jerusalem, 31

D

Dearborn, Kerry, 90
democracy, 136–137, 140
    democrats, 24
    demographic, 124, 137, 179
denomination, xxiii, xxvi, xxx, 2, 35, 70, 80, 91, 123, 125, 135–137, 155, 164, 179–180
development, xvi, xxvii, 5, 9, 15, 18–19, 38, 45, 53, 61, 78, 130, 136, 138, 142, 144, 170, 177, 180
    Newman's doctrine of development, 24–25
    Toon on the development of doctrine, 70–71
    development of Anglican Primates' authority, 133–134,
deviance, xxv, 4, 22, 26, 33, 47, 88, 123, 193
diaconate, (*diakonia*), 113
diocesan, 97, 114, 116–120, 139, 161
diocese, xxviii, 48, 58, 65, 100, 114, 116–118, 120, 132, 137, 138–139, 142, 161, 184, 192
    place in Anglican Church organisation, 97–98,
Diocletian, 54
dissent, 102, 117, 120, 122
    dissenters, xxiv
    dissidents, 57–58
    dissenting, 69
disunity, 91, 165
diversities, 20
diversity, xxvi, 5, 28, 37, 43, 52, 73, 78, 80, 86, 102, 112, 119, 126, 167, 170, 177
    in the early church, 19–23
    positive contribution of diversity and conflict, 88–92

Subject/Name Index

division, xxii, xxvi–xxvii, 53, 71–72, 88, 114, 119–120, 126, 128, 163, 179, 184, 189
divorcees, 71, 73–74
Docetism, 22
doctrine, xxii–xxv, 2–5, 8–10, 19–23, 25–26, 32–34, 48, 57, 59–62, 70–71, 81–84, 103, 105–106, 112, 119, 132, 147–148, 153–155, 158, 164, 167–169, 172–173, 176–178, 180, 185
dogma, 8–9, 14, 47, 60–61, 71
    dogmatic, 21–22, 24, 34, 36, 56, 60–61, 86, 131
dominance, 4–5
Donatism, 27, 53–56, 58, 60, 95
donors, 137, 140, 142
Driver, Jeffrey, 191
Dromantine, 140–141
Duncan, Robert, 47, 125, 139, 142
Dwyer, Mark, 52
dynamism, xvi, 8, 53, 61, 95

E

Eames, Robert, 116–117, 141–142, 186, 189
Ebionism, 22
ecclesiastical, xxvii, xxx, 5, 19, 23, 53, 57, 63, 77, 91, 101, 121–122, 133, 144, 150–151, 160, 162, 169, 193
    ekklesia, 138, 140
ecclesiology, xix, xxiii, xxvi, xxix, 3, 22, 27, 44, 52, 63, 65–66, 72, 78–79, 84, 90, 101, 150–159, 161–168, 171–172, 175, 177–178, 180, 183, 192–193
    emergence of *koinonia* ecclesiology, 166
ecumenism, 20, 23, 39, 54, 60, 78, 148, 150, 157, 164, 166, 172, 176, 186
ECUSA, xxv, 142–143
Ehrman, Bart D., 28
Elizabeth 1st, Queen, 66
    Elizabethan Settlement, 164

emergence, 39, 53, 166, 193
    of global non-western Anglicanism, 123
emerging church, 38, 52–53, 62, 69, 72, 78, 83,
England, 103, 116, 140, 145, 148, 150, 159–161, 165, 170–171, 180, 189, 192
    nonjurors in 17th century England, xxii–xxiii
    Church of England, 47, 49, 51, 56, 63–68, 74–75, 97
    outposts of Empire, 97
    decline in the Church of England, 124
    Canterbury no longer the main focus, 125
Episcopacy, 71, 97, 105, 108, 113–117, 122, 160, 162–3, 184
episcopal, xxvii, 4–5, 74, 97, 106, 112, 114, 117, 120–121, 131, 151, 160, 172
Episcopalian, xxiv, 97, 124, 141
erastian, 161
error, 2, 7, 9, 58, 78, 88, 112, 135, 151–152, 159–160, 169, 171
eschatology, 1, 7, 49, 73, 181
    eschaton, 183
eternal, xxv, xvi, 13, 14, 49, 77, 181
ethically,
ethics, 26, 34, 59, 74, 93, 132, 136, 154, 179
Eucharist, 6, 48, 58, 69, 78, 95, 110, 115, 156, 160, 167, 171–172, 175, 184
Eutychianism, 27
evangelical, xxvi–xxvii, xxviii–xxix, 12, 14, 16–17, 39, 48, 65–66, 70–71, 74, 76, 79, 84–85, 90, 123, 134–135, 138, 140, 146, 162–164, 172, 179
evolution, 6, 25, 123
exclusion, 13, 42, 80, 85
excommunication, 31, 48, 63, 95, 185
exegesis, xxix, 6
ex opere operantis, 55
ex opere operato, 56
exposition, 1, 5, 153, 158, 178

243

Subject/Name Index

F

faith, xxv–xxvii, xxix, 3–5, 9, 12, 14–16, 18–19, 21, 23–24, 26–30, 35–36, 39, 42, 44–45, 47, 50, 52, 54, 56–57, 66, 68, 70–71, 78, 82, 85, 89–90, 92, 94, 98, 100, 103–106, 112, 123–124, 132, 141, 152–154, 159, 162–164, 167, 169–170, 173–174, 178, 187–189, 192–193
faiths, 27, 186
Felix of Aptunga, 54
fellowship, xxvii, 2, 47, 51, 65, 74–75, 88–89, 98, 126, 162, 166
femininity, 113
feminist, 35, 46
formula, 3, 6, 27, 47, 88, 105, 119, 125
freedom, xv–xvi, xxii, xxviii–xxix, 10, 17, 24, 35–36, 43, 46, 50, 64, 68, 72, 84, 87, 93–94, 104, 150, 152, 168–170, 180
Frith, John, 68
Frost, Michael, 42–43
Fryer, Godfrey, xxix
fundamentalist, xxvi–xxvii, 38, 39–41, 50, 93, 131, 146

G

GAFCON, xxi–xxii, xxv, xxvii, 32–34, 38, 40, 48, 50, 57–58, 61, 63–64, 72, 77, 83–84, 101, 115, 123, 125–126, 129, 131, 134, 137, 141, 144–145, 154, 176, 179–180, 183, 193
Galileo, Galilei, 9–10, 62
Galli, Mark, 11–12
gender, xxviii, 42, 66, 75, 102, 107, 110, 118, 122, 129, 131, 136
Gensichen, Hans-Werner, 65
Gillingham, Richard, 174
globalisation, 98, 135–136, 142
Gnosticism, 19
godly, 2, 31, 65, 122, 170, 177
Goetz, Ronald, 9

Goldingay, John, 37–38
gospel, xxv, xxvii, xxix, 20, 23, 36, 46, 51, 56, 65, 72, 79, 83–84, 90, 131–132, 135, 147, 155, 159, 163–164, 172, 179, 186, 192
governance, 154, 168
government, xxiii, 64, 108, 136, 138, 193
Greenslade, Sidney, 2, 54, 57–58, 86–87
Grindrod Report, 117 (Footnote 56)
Griswold, Frank, xxiv, 140
Groves, Phillip, 166, 184–191
guidance, 7, 48, 68, 95, 119, 132, 152
Gunn, Scott, 140

H

Hardy, Daniel, 3, 23, 32, 156, 175–177
Harnack, Adolf von, 5, 30, 71
Hassett, Marinada Katherine, xxiv, 115
Heller, Michael, xv–xvi
heresiarchs, 30
heresy, xxiii–xxv, 1–2, 4, 7–9, 17–20, 24–27, 28–30, 32–36, 54–58, 60–62, 66, 95, 102, 136, 152, 170
heterodoxy, xxii, xxv–xxvi, 36
Hiebert, Paul, 40–42, 45–47, 50, 93–94, 177
hierarchy, 38, 185
Hindmarsh, Bruce, xxvi–xxvii
Hirsch, Alan, 42–43
Hjalmarson, Len, 79
holiness, 49, 51, 55–57, 86, 94
Holocaust, 12
homilies, xxiii
homoousion, 61
homosexuality, xxiv–xxv, 70, 75, 78, 113, 115, 118, 136, 138–139, 143
homophobia, 136
Hooker, Richard, xxx, 27, 66, 95, 148, 151, 157–158, 160–161, 163
Hughes, Philip, 14
Hurtado, Larry, 18
Hussites, 49

Subject/Name Index

I

incarnate, 8
incarnation, xxii, 8, 11, 21–23, 45, 60, 163, 174
   incarnational, 98, 163
inclusion, 45, 54, 80, 112–113, 132, 153
   inclusive, xv, xxvii, 80, 156
indaba, 125–126
indefectible, 152
inerrancy, xxix, 38–39
infallible, 7, 92, 148, 152, 159, 169, 180
Inquisition, 9, 39, 62
institution, 37, 49, 56, 84, 89, 105–106
institutional, 38, 52, 126, 147, 149, 180, 192–193
integrity, xxiii–xxiv, 20, 25, 64, 148, 176, 180, 185
intercommunion, 106
intercourse, 108–109
interdenominational, 166
interdependence, 37, 90, 115, 119, 187–188
internecine, 13, 65
interpretation, xxviii, 15, 20, 25, 35, 38, 47, 49–51, 58–59, 69–70, 76, 82, 87, 94–95, 105, 127–128, 131, 146, 168–169, 176
interpretative, 146, 176
Ireland, 116, 161
Irenaeus, 10
Islamic, 56

J

Jagelman, ian, xxviii
Jamieson, Penny, 116–117
Jensen, Peter, 76–78, 139
Jerusalem, xxi, xxv, xxvii, 3, 20, 31, 48, 57, 72–73, 81, 129, 131, 154
Jinkins, Michael, xxvi, 3, 44, 49, 92
Jones, James, xxvi, 74–75, 123
Judaism, 155, 159
juridical, 18, 119, 187, 191, 193
jurisdiction, xxvii, 97, 117, 121, 131–132, 152, 157

justice, 10–11, 13, 15, 59, 69, 134–135, 137–138
justifiable, 34, 66
justification, 41

K

Kaoma, Kapya, 135–136, 142
Käsemann, Ernst, 19–21, 32
Kaye, Bruce, 37–38, 51, 66, 89–90, 133, 192–193
Kelly, J. N. D., 6
Kermode, Frank, 182
kingdom, xxiii, 57, 67, 80, 84, 102, 150
Kneller Hall, xvii
koinonia, 42, 166–167, 171
Köstenberger, Andreas, 16, 19, 28

L

Lambeth Conferences, xxv, 64, 67, 81, 102–121, 123, 125–135, 138, 141, 144, 146, 149–151, 161–162, 167, 171, 177, 179, 184–185, 189–190
   history of Lambeth Conference also the history of the emerging church, 53
   attitude of Separatists and GAFCON and Lambeth Conference 2008, 64 (see Footnote 80)
   Lambeth Conference defines what it means by Anglican Communion, 98
Lawson, Hilary15–16
leader, 14, 98, 123, 125, 145
   questions of integrity raised concerning actions of some GAFCON leaders, 139–142, 144–146
Lehmann, Helmut, 9
liberalism, xxii, xxix, 9, 24–25, 74, 83
liberation, 8, 11, 135–136, 174
Link-Wieczorek, Ulrike, 13
Liverpool, 74–75

245

Subject/Name Index

Lloyd Jones, Martin, xxvi, 123
Longley, Charles, 103, 151
Luther, Martin, 9, 35, 50, 62–63, 66, 69, 82, 95
   Lutheranism, 35, 65, 67, 71

M

Mac-Iyalla, David, 140
Macquarrie, John, 185
Maffeis, Angelo, 91
magisterium, 131, 147, 179–180
marginalise, 117, 133, 175
marriage, 60, 71, 73–74, 106–111, 118–119, 129, 130
martyrs, 39, 165
McAdoo, Henry, 157
McGillion, Chris, 49, 66, 72, 78
McGrath, Alister, 8, 15–21, 26–28, 45, 55, 57, 94
McLaren, Brian, 35, 80–83, 173–174, 176
Melanchthon, 67–68
Methodist, 71, 146
Millennium goals, 136 (see Footnote 104)
ministry, xxiv, xxvi, xxviii, 20, 37–38, 45, 48, 54–56, 58, 60, 63, 73, 90, 95, 97, 107, 111, 113, 116–117, 121, 126, 134, 145–147, 156, 160, 165, 167–169, 179, 188, 193
Minns, Martyn, 141, 144–145
mission, xxvii–xxix, 39, 43, 46, 72–73, 79, 83–84, 90, 99, 104, 111, 116–117, 119, 121, 127, 133–135, 142, 147, 156, 166, 175, 180, 183, 187–188
missionary, xxvii, 14, 46, 53, 97, 134, 164, 178
Moltmann, Jürgen, 8, 41–42, 89, 95
Moody, Katharine Sarah, 80–81
Morgan, Robert, 21–23
Moses, 69, 155
Mutua, Makau, 145–146
mutuality, 13, 24, 91, 110–111, 151, 168

Mwesigye, Aaron, 142
mystery, 15, 21, 26, 54, 82, 156, 175–176

N

Natal, 104, 115
Naughton, Jim, 123, 137–141, 144–145
Ndungane, Njongonkulu, 142
Nehring, Arlene, 35, 81
Nestorianism, 27
Newman, John Henry, 5, 24–25, 30, 71, 164
Nicaea, 10, 18, 30
   Nicene, 6, 61, 105, 173
Nicodemus, 50
Niebuhr, Reinhold, 8
Nigeria, 108, 124, 139–140, 142–145
Nonjurors, xxii–xxiv

O

O'Leary, Daniel, 84–85
Olupona, Jacob, 125
Olympia, 107
opposition, xvi, xxiv, 7, 30, 46, 48, 105, 108–109, 136
ordination, xxii, 58, 71, 73, 111–114, 116–118, 122, 184–185
organisations, xxvii, 4, 41, 43, 63, 81, 84, 86–87, 89, 115, 135, 137–138, 144
Origen, 3, 5, 10
Orr, James, 71
orthodoxy, xv–xvii, xxi–xxii, xxiv, 1–10, 14––32, 34, 37, 44–45, 48, 50, 53–54, 57–62, 70–71, 74, 76, 82, 93–94, 102, 123, 132, 143, 152–155, 159, 169, 171–174, 176, 178–181
orthopraxy, 44, 50, 102, 143, 174–175, 178
Oxbrow, Mark, 133

P

pacifism, 75
Packer, James, 77, 80
Pannenberg, Wolfhart, 8
papacy, 18, 62–63, 184
   papist, 66
   pontifical, 10
paradigm, 16, 21, 35, 44, 70, 87, 93, 133, 161–162, 183
partnership, 74, 120, 136, 166, 184–185, 187, 189–191
pastor, 14, 34, 46, 105
   pastoral, 97, 100, 105, 111, 113–115, 118–119, 121–122, 128, 132, 145, 171
Patripassianism, 8–9, 32
Pelikan, Jaroslav Jan, 49
perichoresis, 90–91, 95
persuasion, 47, 133–134
philosophy, 2, 9, 31, 157, 174
Pickard, Stephen, 97, 99, 101, 133, 167–168
Piggin, Stuart, xxviii
Pinnock, Clark, 14
Platonic, 4, 62
Pliny, 6
pluralism, xvi, 3, 24, 46
pneumatology, xxvi, 153–154
Polanyi, Michael, 99
polity, 39, 97, 131, 155, 160, 163, 172, 192
   polities, 23, 128, 130
Polkinghorne, John, xvi
polygamy, 104–105, 111, 115, 130, 171, 179
Ponet, John, 68
Popoola, Akintunde, 142, 145
postmodernism, xxix–xxx, 15, 17, 20–21, 34–36, 70, 79–81, 86–87, 93, 133, 151, 183
praxis, 146, 174
prayer, xxii, 111, 113, 118, 128–129, 168, 180, 186
preachers, xv, xxviii, 57
   preaching, 56, 84, 160, 189
precedent, 48, 69, 73–74, 81, 147, 173, 180, 193
preference, 40, 73, 136

prejudices, 58
presbyter, 119
Presbyterian, 67
priest, xvii, xxi, xxv, xxviii, 55–57, 71, 81, 102, 113, 116–118, 120, 137, 145–146, 160, 185
   priesthood, 62, 112–113, 116–117, 160, 177, 184–185, 189
primacy, 100, 163
primates, 57, 97, 101, 114, 119–120, 122, 124–125, 131–133, 138–142, 145, 154, 180
principles, xxiv, xxvii, 38–39, 24–26, 46, 56, 69, 76, 92, 105, 107, 109, 114–117, 121–123, 169, 177, 188–189, 191
prophetic, xvi, 37, 83, 85, 134
   prophecies, 1, 155, 184, 183, 187
   prophetically, 102, 152, 191
propositional, 20, 39, 41, 95, 158, 169
Protestant, xxiii, 9, 11, 24, 30, 38, 52–53, 69, 71, 78, 135, 148, 152, 161, 168
provinces, xxii, xxv, xxvii, 48, 97–99, 100–101, 105, 107, 110, 112–114, 116–117, 119–121, 129–130, 132, 137–139, 159, 165, 167, 170–171, 178, 180, 184–185, 188–189, 192–193
   provincial, xxv, 91, 107, 110, 115, 120, 127, 142, 187, 193
Puritanism, 65
purity, 32, 49, 55, 57, 93

Q

Quadrilateral, 105, 149, 184
Quaker, 125
quinquennium, 192

R

radicalism, 17, 51, 76, 81, 116, 174
Radner, Ephraim, 20, 32, 48, 52
Ramsay, Michael, 172
Rayner, Keith, 78

Subject/Name Index

reconciliation, 12–13, 57, 67, 80, 82, 114, 121
reformation, 34–35, 50, 76, 159, 180
    reformed, 2, 35, 65, 68, 163–164
    reformers, 11, 31, 52, 62–63, 66, 68, 76, 95, 145
relationships, 13, 18, 22–23, 30, 37, 42–43, 51, 58, 60, 70, 75–76, 81, 89, 90–91, 94, 99, 104, 106, 110, 113–114, 118, 120, 126, 129, 138, 157, 162,166–167, 175, 179,185–187, 189–191, 192
repentance, 2, 14, 64, 118, 122, 128
resolutions, 98, 100, 102–104, 110, 112, 117–119, 126, 128, 135, 151, 179, 182–183, 185, 191
responsibility, xxviii, 25, 48, 87, 97, 100, 111, 119, 123, 132, 189–190
resurrection, xxi, 11, 39, 44, 60, 163
revelation, xvi–xvii, 8, 22–23, 25–26, 28, 35, 38, 50, 69, 73, 77–78, 145–146
revision, xxii, 5, 15, 170
revisionist, xxvii, 48, 183
Ridley, Nicholas, 65, 68, 190
Righteous(ness), xxv, 10–12, 42, 49, 57, 134
Robinson, Gene, xxv, 47, 64 (Footnote 80), 102, 120, 122, 125, 133, 138–139, 188
Robinson, John, 34–35, 78
Roman Catholicism, 25, 66
Runcie, Robert, 116

S

Sabellianism, 27
Sachs, William, 149
sacraments, 54, 56–57, 63, 65–66, 97, 105, 107–108, 154, 160, 162, 180, 184
    sacramental, 55–57, 90, 102, 163–165, 167, 172
sacred, xv, 3, 9, 25, 31, 40, 54, 187
saints, 5, 54, 77, 155, 161
Sancroft, William, xxiii
sanctions, 88, 106–107, 180, 184

Satan, 10–11
Schaeffer, Francis, 177
schism, 49, 58, 81, 86, 102, 120, 127, 170
    schismatic, 54, 185
Schleiermacher, Friedrich, 26–27
scholar, 16, 17, 19, 28, 30, 93, 153, 170
    scholarship, 127, 136, 148–149, 155, 159, 170–171, 180
Schweizer, Eduard, 20, 63
science, 9, 31, 114, 153, 158–159, 178
scripture, 50, 59, 61–62, 66, 68, 76, 90, 94, 127–128, 147–148
    scriptural, xxv, 10, 48, 74, 113, 128, 149, 180
secession, 25, 144
secular, 25, 113, 137, 144, 152, 161, 190–191
    secularism, 41, 111
sensus plenior, 69
Seoka, Johannes, 142
Separatism, 63–65
sexuality, 66, 75, 102, 106–107, 109–110, 112–113, 115–116, 118–120, 123, 126, 128–129, 131, 133, 157
sinners, 13, 54, 58–59
sinful, 10, 20, 49, 54–55, 58, 60, 77, 82, 95
sinfulness, 2, 13, 154
Smedes, Lewis, 74, 78
soteriology, 22, 153–154, 180
spiritual, xxvii, 30–31, 46, 50, 56, 69, 79, 92, 100, 102, 109–110, 117, 122, 124, 150, 158, 164, 174, 187
spirituality, 29–30, 100, 134
Starkey, Thomas, 68
Stott, John, xxvi, 14, 123
submission, 40, 119, 149, 159, 164
subsidiarity, 188–189, 191
Sugden, Christopher, 141, 144–145
Sydney, xxviii, 48, 58, 65, 72, 76, 139
Sykes, Stephen, 3, 7, 23–25, 29, 32, 52, 77–78, 94, 148, 151, 158–162, 164, 169, 171, 178, 189
synods, 98, 103, 107, 144, 151
    synodical, 193

T

Tanner, Kathryn, 86–89, 151
Tertullian, 5, 15
The Tablet, 84
theologians, xv, xvi, xxvi, 3, 5, 7–9, 12, 13, 35, 46–48, 52, 60, 63, 74, 87, 89, 94, 151, 153, 155–156, 171–172, 174, 189
theology, xxii–xxiii, xxvii, xxix, 2–3, 6–7, 9, 12–18, 20–25, 29–30, 32–34, 41–42, 45–47, 50–51, 53, 60–62, 66–68, 70–73, 78, 81, 83, 86, 94–95, 100, 115, 124, 128, 130, 136–137, 143, 153–158, 162, 164, 167, 170, 172 174, 177–178, 185, 191
Thielicke, Helmut, 79
Thirty Nine Articles, xxix, 57, 63–64, 105–106
    not suitable as a test for orthodoxy, 159
    in need of reform, 159
Thurman, Howard, 61
Tickle, Phyllis, 38, 52–53, 62, 69, 94
tolerance, 118, 161, 165
    toleration, xxiii, 42, 68, 167, 181
Tolliday, Phillip, xxii, xxv, 115
Tomka, Miklós, 91
Toon, Peter, 70–72
tradition, xviii, xxii, xxviii–xxx, 3, 5, 7, 9, 11, 13, 19, 24, 39, 46–48, 51, 59–60, 66–67, 72–73, 77–81, 87, 91, 93, 96, 100, 112, 118–119, 127, 130, 134, 147, 160, 163–164, 167–168, 170–171, 173, 179, 187, 191–193
    traditionalists, 75–76
traditor, 54
traitor, 54
transformation, 1, 3, 5, 32, 118, 126, 133, 150, 168, 174
tribal, xxviii, 46, 145–146
    tribalism, 84
Trinitarian, 6, 89–90, 95, 160
truth, xxvi, xxix, 2, 6–7, 11, 21–22, 26–28, 33, 35, 41, 47, 49–50, 61, 68–69, 73–74, 76–77, 83, 85, 88, 90, 92, 108, 122, 146–148, 152, 162–163, 166, 168–171, 173–177, 180–181, 185
Turner, Philip, xv, 5–8, 17, 20, 29, 32, 48, 51–52

U

Uganda, 116, 139, 142
unity, xvi, xxvi, 20, 23, 41, 43, 47, 49, 52–53, 57, 62, 72–73, 81, 89, 91, 94–95, 102–103, 105, 112, 114–117, 119–122, 126, 129, 144, 148–151, 165–168, 182, 185–186, 188
universalism, 32
    universalist, 14

V

validity, 8, 54–59, 114, 160, 172
Venn, Henry, 46
Vincent of Lérins, 31
    Vincentian Canon, 22
violence, 12–13, 40, 69, 80, 118, 145, 158
Virginia, Report, 166, 186–190
Volf, Miroslav, 12–13, 90–91, 95
Vorster, Jacobus, 39–40, 93

W

Wales, 48, 116
Webber, Christopher, 38–39, 103, 105, 129–131
Wenham, John, 14
Wesley, John, xxvii
Westerhoff, John, 50, 85
westoxication, 40
Whalon, Pierre, 154–158, 164–165, 168–169, 171–172
Wiles, Maurice, 51
Wittenberg, 62
Woodhouse, John, 72

Subject/Name Index

worship, xxii–xxiii, xxix, 20, 23, 30, 41–42, 55, 67, 74, 84, 98, 103, 106, 111–112, 117, 127, 131, 154, 156, 165, 169–170, 175
Wright, J. Robert, 148–149

Z

Zimbabwe, 135
Zizioulas, John, 95
Zwingli, Ulrich, 69
Życiński, Józef, xv

www.ingramcontent.com/pod-product-compliance
Lightning Source LLC
Chambersburg PA
CBHW070338230426
43663CB00011B/2370